6/99

GYPSIES AND OTHER ITINERANT GROUPS

Gypsies and Other Itinerant Groups

A Socio-Historical Approach

Leo Lucassen

Wim Willems

Annemarie Cottaar

Centre for the History of Migrants
University of Amsterdam
The Netherlands

First published in Great Britain 1998 by
MACMILLAN PRESS LTD
Houndmills, Basingstoke, Hampshire RG21 6XS and London
Companies and representatives throughout the world

A catalogue record for this book is available from the British Library.

ISBN 0–333–68241–6

First published in the United States of America 1998 by
ST. MARTIN'S PRESS, INC.,
Scholarly and Reference Division,
175 Fifth Avenue, New York, N.Y. 10010

ISBN 0–312–21258–5

Library of Congress Cataloging-in-Publication Data
Lucassen, Leo, 1959–
Gypsies and other itinerant groups : a socio-historical approach /
Leo Lucassen, Wim Willems, Annemarie Cottaar.
p. cm.
Includes bibliographical references and index.
ISBN 0–312–21258–5 (cloth)
1. Gypsies—Europe—History. 2. Travelers—Europe—History.
3. Europe—Ethnic relations. I. Willems, Wim, 1951– .
II. Cottaar, Annemarie. III. Title.
DX145.L86 1998
305.891'49704—dc21   97–38692
                                                                                        CIP

This book is printed on paper suitable for recycling and made from fully managed and sustained forest sources.

10   9   8   7   6   5   4   3   2   1
07   06   05   04   03   02   01   00   99   98

Printed and bound in Great Britain by
Antony Rowe Ltd, Chippenham, Wiltshire

Contents

Preface

More than ten years ago Dik van Arkel, at the time still Professor of Social History at Leiden University, brought together a group of students working in the field of historical racism studies. Its members were focusing on subjects such as the causes of the negative attitude towards *unclean* Burakumin in Japan, the stereotyping of colonial migrants from the Netherlands Indies in the 1950s, the position of Black Americans in the contemporary ghettos in the large cities, the differences between left- and right-wing anti-Semitism in nineteenth-century France, and the relation between race, class and status in the social structure of Kaapstad from the seventeenth century onwards. All these themes were explored in an attempt to reveal the structure beneath the diverging manifestations of prejudices and social exclusion and thus to develop a general theory about the origin of racism.

As members of this society we observed that historical research into the nature of antisemitism and the discrimination against Black Americans had been expanding since the 1950s, but that our understanding of the deep-seated prejudices and the persistent social exclusion of Gypsies and other itinerant groups was still limited. Only recently has the world become aware of the fact that hundreds of thousands of them met the same horrendous fate as Jews and other Nazi victims between 1933 and 1945. Why have (social) historians been so blind to what has happened to wandering groups who made a living with ambulant occupations? That has been the leading question in our research during the last ten years. Besides that we have tried to fill the gap in knowledge about the history of these groups, especially by writing monographs about the life of so-called Gypsies and caravan-dwellers not only in the Netherlands, but also in other Western European countries.

Most of our findings have been published in Dutch. Only recently some books have appeared in German and English. We therefore thought that it was about time for a collection of our main articles in one volume, thus giving a state of the art from a socio-historical point of view. We have tried to present a range of diverging contributions to the historical study of Gypsies and other itinerant groups. For more than five centuries people have written about these groups as the ultimate aliens, who were supposedly a threat to society. We think that a new perspective can help a re-valuation of their position in European societies in the course of time and gain a better understanding of their fate during the twentieth century. If this volume stimulates the study of Gypsies and other itinerant groups from a social-historical perspective, our aim is achieved.

Centre for the History of Migrants
University of Amsterdam

1 Introduction
Leo Lucassen, Wim Willems and Annemarie Cottaar

A HISTORY IN FOOTNOTES

The student of European history who searches for Gypsies will find them only in footnotes. Today we still know little about how they worked and lived in the past. The same holds true for itinerant groups in general. That during the Second World War hundreds of thousands of them met the same horrendous fate as Jews and other Nazi victims has only been recognized with reluctance. Gypsies appear to appeal to the imagination simply as social outcasts and scapegoats, or, in a flattering but far from illuminating light, as romantic outsiders. The world is patently intrigued by them, yet at the same time regards them with anxiety as 'undesirable aliens'. For historical knowledge about these groups we have therefore to rely mainly on (often popular) books by social scientists, writers and enthusiastic amateurs interested in the folklore of Gypsies.[1]

It may come as no surprise that due to this situation a more thorough insight into the functions of Gypsies and other itinerant groups within the larger society through time is still wanting. One of the aims of this book is to remedy this and shed more light on the historical development of showpeople who go from fair to fair: musicians, conjures, jugglers, acrobats and others who perform their activities in the streets of big cities, collectors of scrap metal, and so on. These kinds of occupation have existed for a long time and are practised by all kinds of people, of whom the best known are those who travel in groups. They differ from others because they combine these occupations with an itinerant way of life, made visible by their choice to live in tents or caravans which enable them to move around *with* their families. In many countries these travelling people have been given names such as 'Gypsies', 'tinkers', 'bohemians', 'travellers' or 'caravan-dwellers'. They performed a wide range of functions, which had in common the spreading of goods and services that mostly could not be offered, or not at such a low price, by the sedentary professional class.

1

Because of their travelling lifestyle they were more vulnerable to negative treatment by groups who distrusted them. For example, authorities often thought Gypsies practised their occupations in order to beg and steal, while sedentary competitors now and then accused them of unfair competition. In both cases itinerant groups were unable to defend themselves properly. They lacked the organizational strength of the guilds and the privileges of most sedentary occupations. Moreover, from the Middle Ages onwards they were confronted with largely restrictive legislation and negative public opinion.

Before we go into their history in more detail, we want to indicate that in the past many terms have been used to label people who travel with their family. The variation between countries and in different periods of time is considerable. The term Gypsy, to mention the most widely used, was in many cases not reserved for those who considered themselves as an ethnic group; others who travelled with their family were also labelled as such. In this book we therefore use a more general definition of Gypsies, i.e. those who lead an itinerant way of life and who are stigmatized as Gypsy or who have been given similar labels – in Great Britain: travellers, among others; in France: *nomades, ambulants, bohémiens, romanichals*; in Germany: *Landfahrer* and *Jenischen*; in Sweden: *tattare*; and in the Netherlands: *woonwagenbewoners*. This is not to deny a 'Gypsy' or 'traveller' ethnicity nor to suggest that people have passively undergone this labelling, but simply takes as the point of departure the definitions used by authorities in the past.

In our opinion studies so far have yielded a rather peculiar harvest. Our knowledge has been severely restricted not only because of historical negligence, but also because of two closely connected paradigms, one which views Gypsies and other itinerant groups as criminal, marginal and poor, and another which focuses almost exclusively on their alleged common ethnic identity and origin. In this book we will question these assumptions and offer an alternative perspective with a greater explanatory power where the position of travelling groups is concerned. However, let us first of all make clear in what respects the existing historical knowledge is inadequate, starting with the inclination to view itinerant groups predominantly as down and out riff-raff.

THE RIFF-RAFF IMAGE

As a point of departure we take the observation of the English historian Tawney who in 1967 wrote that the history of vagrants has inevitably been written by its enemies.[2] With this statement he primarily referred to contemporaneous sources, in most cases those authorities whose task it was to repress vagrancy, but his observation can easily be extended to many historians who took these sources at face value and who were not critical enough of their biased and one-sided nature. Although three decades later the situation may have changed for the better on certain points, the picture of Gypsies and other itinerant groups – who have been lumped together with 'vagrants' in most historical analyses – is to a large extent a distorted one. Most works which entirely or partly deal with these categories have still not abandoned the context of criminality, marginality and poverty.

The *criminological* perspective has a long tradition. As demonstrated in Chapter 8, in past centuries the lower strata of society have been studied primarily as a criminal group, resulting in a pathological image of crime among *les classes dangereuses*, characterized by lawlessness, degeneration and moral corruption. In particular the alleged innate criminal behaviour of the wandering poor aroused interest. Before the Second World War this resulted, especially in Germany, in numerous studies on the so-called antisocials and Gypsies. During the postwar era in the social sciences the habit of explaining the pariah position in society as the result of individual flaws caused by racial degeneration was gradually criticized and slowly the attention shifted to the repressive and stigmatizing attitude of the dominant society. To put it more simply: the culprits became victims. In the past few years this new approach has been elaborated by scholars of the *ancien régime* who question the attitude of the state, explicitly using the theoretical insights of Elias and Foucault with regard to the civilization offensive from the sixteenth century onwards.[3] These studies mark an important step forwards to a more differentiating view, because the attitude of states towards groups called vagrants is studied in a comparative way. This has led to a less stereotypical image of wandering groups. Notwithstanding this critical sociological turn, the pathological explanation has proved to be tenacious and (often large) fragments still afflict these recent studies. A good example is the standard answer to the question of why Gypsies are so heavily persecuted through time. Most scholars stick to the idea that the antagonistic attitude towards itinerant groups is a direct consequence of their unorthodox lifestyle and the norms and values they uphold, which would automatically bring them into collision with established society time and again. Seen in this light, the persecutions are the condemnable, but in many cases also the comprehensible, consequence of the fundamental incompatibility of nomadic and sedentary lifestyles.[4]

A second important angle in studies on travelling groups is *marginality*. Instead of the economic status, the social position is highlighted. The founding father of this perspective is the well-known Polish historian Bronislaw Geremek, who wrote several works on marginal groups, especially on beggars and vagrants.[5] Although relics of the traditional criminality approach can still be found, leading to an ambiguous and inconsistent explanation, the emphasis on the stigmatizing role of church and state, on the other hand, marks an important breakthrough in the hitherto traditional historical studies in this field and formed a stimulus for many (mainly French) historians.[6]

As with the previous approaches, the framework chosen by studies on *poverty* already determines the outcome of the analysis. Ambulatory professions, seasonal labour and migration have often been considered as signs of social decline. The opinion dominated that only when there were no possibilities for making a living left did people start to wander and become vagrants. Furthermore scholars working in this tradition assume that the people concerned in the final analysis were beggars in disguise, being a nuisance to the people living in the country because of their intimidating and criminal behaviour.[7] A more balanced view is presented by recent studies on poverty in the *ancien régime*,[8] which make a clearer distinction between the definition of vagrancy by contemporary authorities and the people behind this label. Others have argued that the repression of vagrants was closely linked to the policy of disciplining workers and controlling the labour market.[9]

To summarize, since Tawney's insightful remark we can say that, notwithstanding the greater awareness of the selectivity and the biased sources and the interest in the influence of stigmatizing policies, the social history of the groups which have been labelled as Gypsies, vagrants and the like is still very much clouded. Due to the influence of the three dominating perspectives mentioned above, historians have developed a blind spot to the social and economic function of itinerant groups, which explains the virtual absence of historical case studies which go further than analysing the repressive policy towards them. As a matter of fact, historians have left this task to a large extent to social scientists,[10] who have produced a wealth of studies on contemporaneous itinerant groups. Some of these give a fairly differentiated and valuable analysis of their current social and economic role,[11] but when it comes to the historical background these social scientists present a very bleak picture. Thus the history of these groups is reduced to a litany of repression and persecution, which – as we have seen – is understandable considering the one-sided image produced by their historical colleagues. They, for their part, have been too content with the dominating ethnographic approach from the end of the eighteenth century onwards, developed by ethnographers, anthropologists and people outside the academic tradition interested in the folklore of Gypsies, like the well-known English-American Gypsy Lore Society (founded in 1888).[12]

THE DIASPORA IMAGE

This brings us to the second paradigm: the almost unshakeable conviction that in the end all Gypsies have the same origin and that up to the present day they can be considered as one people, scattered throughout the world, not unlike the Jewish diaspora.[13] Although many Gypsy studies experts are aware that the term Gypsy was constructed by the dominant society and is used to indicate certain nomadic groups, most still hold the opinion that it refers to a people (or 'race') originating from India. Fascinated by their alleged exotic origin, these latter scholars have concentrated primarily on describing the language, mores, customs and external aspects of Gypsies. The influence of this paradigm is best illustrated by the most recent reference work, written by an English representative of the Gypsy-lorists,[14] Angus Fraser. His book, *The Gypsies*, published in the distinguished 'The Peoples of Europe' series of Blackwell in 1992 and since reprinted several times, has attracted a lot of attention and was well received. Although Fraser displays a vast knowledge of the existing literature and avoids many pitfalls of authors before him, his point of departure is very much in the tradition of the much admired founders of the Gypsy Lore Society. Mainly leaning on linguistic research he upholds the view that Gypsies have to be considered a people with Indian roots, who would have succeeded in keeping their ethnicity intact since they fled their country of origin. As we argue in this book, and in earlier work as well,[15] this interpretation is not unproblematic and is in many respects based on speculation mixed with a fair proportion of teleological and wishful thinking. Fraser, and others with him, refuses to integrate competing evidence in his analysis and only uses what fits in with his preconceived idea of one Gypsy people. The possibility that through a process of labelling other itinerant groups have become known as Gypsies as well and in the end have internalized this image, or the fact that many Gypsies intermingled with others from the end of the Middle Ages onwards, make only minor inroads in his ideas. Moreover, he too easily discards the possibility that the 'people' concept is a fairly recent phenomenon, triggered off by nineteenth-century nationalistic ideology and not in the least promoted by the Gypsy Lore Society itself, in which footsteps he clearly follows.

THE INADEQUACY OF TRADITIONAL ANSWERS

We hope to make clear that more than a century of research by historians, linguists, ethnographers and other social scientists has been impressive in its volume, but less so in providing us with convincing answers to the two questions which form the leitmotiv in this book:

(a) In which ways have Gypsies and other itinerant groups been looked upon and treated by society?
(b) What was the social and economic position of Gypsies and other itinerant groups through time and how has this been influenced by government policy?

Contrary to studies that start from the assumption that it is mainly a matter of self-definition who should be considered as Gypsies, we postulate the idea that in their case stigmatization has influenced group formation – and along with it ethnic consciousness – to a large extent. Two aspects of stigmatization are distinguished for analytical purposes: the dissemination of negative ideas about a specific group (stigma) by an authoritative body, and the attachment of this stigma to specific groups (labelling).

By doing so we learn – as the chapters in this book show – that the manner in which Gypsies have been and still are defined at the level of the state and its officials demonstrates a clear connection with changing notions of the process of categorization in science. The labelling of Gypsies as 'deviants' appears to have been subject to revision, which also holds true for the accompanying argumentation. Although until the middle of the eighteenth century authoritative texts reproduced the definition used by governments in the implementation of their policies, after H.M.G. Grellmann's work of 1783[16] a shift in that process came about. Since the publication of his historical survey, the ethnic element of 'the Gypsy people' has acquired a master status which entails a codification of the alleged and ascribed characteristics. Judicial authorities in particular subsequently adopted his view and used it to legitimize their stigmatizing policy. There can be no mistaking this development when one traces the criminological tradition within Gypsy studies, culminating in its criminal-biological variant during the Nazi era.

Thus since the end of the eighteenth century academics and amateur scientists have played a vanguard role in the process of defining Gypsies. Grellmann has seen to it that the notion of a Gypsy people has become dominant and other group categories such as pilgrims, spies, criminal vagabonds, heathens and the mixed category of social outsiders have faded into the background. The 'people' concept fitted so well with the founding myths of nineteenth-century nationalism that it remained alive and kicking, notwithstanding mounting signs of integration (sedentarism, intermarriage, social mobility). The most important explanation for such steadfastness is the tradition of imagery, or the dictates of authoritative texts, as Edward Said likewise illustrated.[17] Prior to Grellmann a historical canon of publications on Gypsies already existed. Authors had primarily followed in each other's footsteps. This tradition of ongoing reproduction of the same sources did not undergo any demonstrable disruption with the appearance of Grellmann's study. His ethnographic portrait of the Gypsies was first and foremost a compilation of existing texts and not based on his own observations, and up to this day the countless authors on Gypsies use Grellmann's book – implicitly or explicitly – as a reference point. In this way it was practically inevitable that they would reach the conclusion that there were hardly any 'true Gypsies' left. Practically no one made an effort to discuss the existing image of Gypsies or test the tenability of generalizations about their history and

expressions of their culture. Even when authors discovered positive or functional aspects of the Gypsy way of life, this only occasionally led to a more subtle appraisal of their lifestyle. What we
see is that an exceptional category of 'true Gypsies' was created,
picturing the entire group as parasites, primitives, criminals, thieves
or persecuted victims.

Besides that, there is insufficient information from 'Gypsy circles' available concerning their self-definition to acquire a reliable
picture of the history of their group formation. Nor does the literature
permit us to determine whether current fragmentation mirrors a
pattern that is centuries old. Up until now it does not seem likely
that Gypsy and other travelling groups themselves have exercised
much influence on the labelling process and we can assume that
they will seldom have recognized themselves in recurrent images
of Gypsies as parasites, criminals and romantic outcasts.

ALTERNATIVE APPROACHES

This book, however, is not merely a critical analysis of the way
Gypsies and other itinerant groups have been looked upon by historians, social scientists and policy-makers. Although it is important to stress that we should be careful in portraying these groups
as criminals, marginals and beggars, it is equally important not to
end up at the other extreme. We have to realize that the people
who are hidden behind these labels were not only, or mainly, (passive)
victims of repression and persecution.[18] Above all we should resist
the lure of the Gypsy-lorists and scholars working in their tradition, who have been quite successful in spreading the image of
Gypsies as a remarkable and century old ethnic group, whose behaviour can to a large extent be explained by their cultural characteristics. Instead, we need a change in perspective and the time
has come to realize that they are no *Fremdkörper* or highly exotic
people, but are inextricably interwoven with the development of
European societies from the Middle Ages onwards. In the following we therefore suggest alternative approaches and argue in favour of an integration of the new results in this field into the fabric
of social-historical sciences.

To reach this goal we have elaborated two alternative approaches.
The first is dealt with in Chapters 4–7 and can be summarized as
the stigmatization perspective. In essence it argues that the – often

marginal – position of Gypsies and other itinerants has first of all to be seen in the light of the way they have been treated by dominant groups in society, especially (judicial) authorities, and the sometimes indirect negative effects of their wandering lifestyle. Although one has to take the interaction between travellers and authorities (and the rest of the population) into account as well, for a better understanding it is highly instructive to analyse the attitude and behaviour of authorities separately and to realize that the deviant and sometimes criminal behaviour is much more the consequence of stigmatizing policies than the cause of it.[19]

The point is that the policies of governments, towards a distinctly categorized group, are based on a set of negative value judgements, a stigma. To comprehend this process it is important to investigate the way in which an individual is branded or labelled as a member of such a group. Above all with groups whose members are not always recognizable as such at a single glance, the government, in order to carry out a consistent policy, finds itself obliged with regularity to spell out who, to its way of thinking, belongs to the group in question. In an analysis of the possible stigmatizing effect of government policy, the following five factors should be differentiated:

(a) *Categorizing*: the creation of a (group) category with a name.

(b) The emergence of a *negative image* which colours perceptions of that category.

(c) The formation of a negative group characterization, a *stigma*.

(d) *Labelling*: making explicit who belongs to the negatively characterized group.

(e) *Stigmatizing*: application, as policy, of the stigma, thus the invocation of negative value judgements, as supporting arguments during the making of policy decisions.

The second alternative is presented in the last section of the book, on the *socio-economic functioning* of travelling groups. Here we suggest that it can be very revealing to abandon the dominant perspective and look upon them as individuals and families who – like other people – try to make a living and much more often than is commonly assumed succeed in reaching a modest state of welfare and sometimes are even outright successful. This implies that in our research we have to take seriously their economic functioning in the labour market and – more specifically – link their economic activities to our knowledge about labour migration in general. As our work, as well as that of other historians,[20] demonstrates, this is far from an easy task due to the scarcity of sources. If followed persistently, this path offers remarkable outcomes and shows that the reality was much more heterogeneous than is often assumed. Therefore, we disagree with the view that these people were in general social outcasts, rejected by the rest of society. Although the analysis of stereotyping and repressive policy might bring us to such a point of view, the new insights into their economic roles irresistibly leads to a much more differentiated conclusion. As many itinerants evidently had a valued economic function, be it as knife-grinder, pedlar or whatever, there must have existed some form of understanding and trust between them and their (sedentary) customers. Furthermore we know of many examples in which they had fixed abodes for at least a part of the year and in which their presence in local communities was tolerated and not very problematic.

For both the economic and the social dimension it would be fruitful and in many respects essential to compare their role with other groups with corresponding characteristics, in order to detect and explain similarities and differences in behaviour and treatment. The most obvious candidates at the *economic* level are those ambulant professionals who travelled without their families, and whose experiences have so far, unjustly, been considered irrelevant for the history of itinerant groups. The same holds true for groups with similarities at other levels, for example in relation to *discrimination* (minorities like Jews) and *migration behaviour* (seasonal migrants).

WIDER RELEVANCE

Finally, this book is not only meant as a re-evaluation of the role of these groups in the past. The alternative approaches can also enrich our insight into more general developments and research questions. Following the sequence of this book we first of all point at *formation of minorities* and *social construction*. We hope to make clear that it is time to break loose from the Gypsy-lorist paradigm and to use more modern theoretical concepts which focus on the social construction of groups and devote serious attention to the influence of stigmatization on group formation.[21] Combining this framework with a thorough examination of historical sources – as demonstrated in Chapters 6, 7 and 10 – the past becomes much more complicated than is often assumed. Gypsies and travellers have always intermingled with other people, both sedentary and mobile, and moreover it is highly questionable whether the various groups did consider themselves as one people before this concept was introduced by scholars from the end of the eighteenth century onwards. We therefore think that it would be extremely important and interesting – also to the wider field of ethnic studies – to study the differences between the numerous travelling groups and not to view all Gypsies a priori as belonging to more or less the same ethnic category. Such analyses, as we hope to demonstrate in this book, will shed new light on the way people and groups regard themselves and on the influences by which such perceptions have changed through time.

Furthermore, the analysis of the attitude of both local and central authorities mirrors the essential characteristics of the *poor relief* system in Western Europe and, closely linked to this, it also puts the *exclusion of aliens* and the *regulation of migration* in another perspective. We will show that by restricting the poor relief from the fifteenth century onwards to the local poor and simultaneously refusing citizenship rights to poor immigrants, categories of 'vagrants' and 'Gypsies' were created. Although we still need much research, especially local studies which make clear how this policy was enforced, it is clear that the poor relief system had far-reaching effects on the stigmatization of travelling groups who (rightfully or not) were expected to descend into beggary. The final transition in the nineteenth century which linked poor relief to the place where one lived did not change a great deal for the groups in question. On the contrary, every municipality then ran the 'risk' of becoming liable for their support, which motivated authorities to prevent itinerants staying, let alone settling. Also in a wider context, what the history of the poor relief does make so relevant and interesting is that the same mechanisms can be detected as the ones we stumble on in the nineteenth- and twentieth-century aliens policy. In fact, the restriction of poor relief by the cities in the sixteenth century formed a prelude for the later aliens policy at a national level. This development not only affected Gypsies and other itinerant groups, but migrants and aliens in general as well.

From this it is not a big leap to the process of *state formation*. As Noiriel and Moch, among others, have showed, the expansion of the state had a profound influence on the control of migration (internal as well as between states) and on the definition of citizenship.[22] By a combination of democratization, the expansion of the state from the nineteenth century onwards and nationalism, citizens were granted more rights and thus it became increasingly important to define who belonged to the state and who did not. Simultaneously with the making and controlling of boundaries, migration was looked upon more unfavourably and discouraged if policy-makers considered it expedient. For travelling groups, especially those who had to cross national boundaries for their work, this aggravated their way of living even more. They were confronted with difficulties at borders – not only those between states, but also between smaller territorial units. Perhaps more important in their new quality as aliens, they became more visible for authorities and thus an object of the general aliens policy as well. The specialization of the aliens police that gathered momentum in Western Europe after the First World War therefore increased the stigmatization.

In this respect, we think that the policies towards Gypsies and itinerant groups can also shed new light on the process of the *professionalization of the police* in the course of the nineteenth century, which formed an integral part of the state-formation process. The modern state, characterized by direct rule, has an interest in controlling migration and for general purposes (conscription, taxes, etc.) wants to know where its citizens are. Moreover, the growing fear of the criminality of the underclasses, especially when on the move, contributed to the wish to establish a permanent system of supervision. The foremost control apparatus to perform this task was the police. This can be explained not only in a quantitative way by an increase in the number of policemen, but also in the specialization of the police in types of crime or 'dangerous' groups: anarchists, antisocials, aliens, Gypsies, etc. This professionalization and specialization created a certain autonomous space for police forces and at the same time stimulated the labelling of potential criminals, who had to be watched carefully and if possible arrested. The criminalizing effects have been felt by many groups, but in our case the examples of the vagrants and Gypsies, especially in Germany, are the most instructive. The power of definition and its consequences were far reaching and facilitated by new techniques used for the tracing and identifying of people. This process of labelling, the fixing of stigmatizing labels as vagrant or Gypsy to individuals by registering and supervision, is typical of the modern state. Whereas in the *ancien régime* the labelling was quite primitive, modern techniques combined with a proactive policy (registration, fingerprints, photographs) made it a lot more difficult for people to escape stigmatization.

Finally we hope to contribute to the field of *migration studies*, which so far has seldom considered the travelling lifestyle of family groups as part of – at least normal – migration behaviour. However, if we consider Gypsies and other itinerants as clans of self-sufficient economic beings who down through the centuries have acquired a certain identity under the influence of circumstances which remain to be studied in more detail, it becomes possible to analyse their socio-economic mobility and their emergence as minorities in various countries with a much greater degree of differentiation. Therefore, a better understanding of their migration patterns will help to uncover the function of this type of migrant labourer and broaden our insight into the position of similar wandering craftsmen, pedlars and musicians who travelled without their families.[23]

STRUCTURE OF THE BOOK

In order to address the themes mentioned in this introduction in a systematic way, we have divided the book into three major parts. In the first part we present two chapters devoted mainly to a critical analysis of the current popular and scholarly ideas about Gypsies and other itinerants. In the second part the stigmatization concept is applied to the history of these groups in Western Europe from the Middle Ages onwards, showing that their often marginal position cannot be explained without taking the repressive policies into account which heavily contributed to the construction of an ethnically defined minority. The third part is meant to show that an alternative socio-economic (bottom-up) approach can lead to different outcomes and offer a much more refined image of travelling groups in the past. In this respect it serves as a necessary counterbalance not only to the riff-raff image, but also to the top-down perspective employed in the second part.

Part I
Images and Representations

2 Ethnicity as a Death-Trap: the History of Gypsy Studies[1]

Wim Willems

A HISTORICAL *SONDERWEG*

For a long time we have wondered why the findings of research into Gypsy groups have so rarely been the subject of scholarly debate in the field of historical studies on migration, settlement and ethnicity. Why do new insights on Gypsies and other itinerant groups so seldom reach the academic curriculum or become part of public understanding? There seems to be a *communis opinio* about who they are and where they come from, while at the same time little substantial knowledge about their past exists as such. It is even possible to put forward the proposition that the traditionally negative view of Gypsies may drag on without end because of the splendid isolation in which Gypsy studies have come to be placed. Another factor is that by focusing exclusively on the group level instead of on interactions with the surrounding society and on comparisons with other groups in the same socio-economic position, our historical knowledge of the functioning of Gypsies has remained one-sided.

In a recent article the linguist Anthony P. Grant came to the generally accepted but very pretentious conclusion: 'As Grellmann pointed out over two centuries ago, the history of the Romá is to be found in their language.'[2] It is a pity that this point of departure is still accepted, for we think that the consequence of this approach has been that our entrance into the history of Gypsy groups in Europe has been seriously blocked, for more than 200 years already. The study of language as an indicator of the origins of a people has led to many speculations. Because of their strong determination to designate a country of origin, scholars have not paused to reflect sufficiently on a number of questions which from a historical point of view are equally interesting, for example the reasons for the departure of so-called Gypsy groups from central and northwest India or elsewhere in the world, or their socio-economic

17

functioning and cultural background in the respective countries into which they migrated. We also do not know what kind of relations these people, who lived everywhere in disparate circumstances, maintained with each other over time. It is impossible to comprehend how linguistics will ever be able to give conclusive answers to all such questions which directly concern the historical reconstruction of the Gypsies' ups and downs. Besides that, the criterion of language is utterly inadequate to clarify why people were (or still are) defined as Gypsies.

Ethnologists and folklorists have also blocked our way into the history of Gypsy groups, by focusing solely on their ethnic identity. As a result their fortunes were isolated from the national histories of the countries where they lived. In the academic field they received a kind of *Sonderbehandlung,* as the Nazis called it. They were – and still are – looked upon as one people, dispersed over the world. It is true that in the 1970s social scientists like Acton and Salo had already pointed out that we encounter a variety of ethnic groups behind the label 'Gypsy' and they even warned against a rigid ethnocentric point of view.[3] Following in the footsteps of the linguists and authors who focused on the origin of the migrants who left India, most scholars in the field of Gypsy studies have, however, continued to look for common features, which they then interpret in terms of ethnic or cultural background.

What we also observe is that the overall idea exists that Gypsies in Europe have only met rejection and discrimination, and have been persecuted and victimized up to the present day. It remains, however, an open question whether the 'Gypsy category' actually was the source of much specific trouble and was felt to be unusually oppressive.[4] There are no empirical studies available to settle the matter and the publications which do exist are characterized by an almost exclusive reliance on official judicial sources. As a result the one-dimensional picture has come into being that historically Gypsies have only known persecution and marginalization. In contemporary socio-historical research at any rate they only make the scene in a context of poverty, mendacity, vagabondage, marginality and criminality.[5] No one seems to doubt that in their case it was aimless vagrants whose criminal or asocial behaviour impelled the authorities to take cruel suppressive measures. Publications dealing exclusively with Gypsies do not arrive at an essentially different interpretation, except that in these we encounter the practically obligatory observation that governments or chroniclers were afflicted with the prejudices of their time. Nevertheless authors put their trust in these texts and refer to the lack of tolerance since the sixteenth century because the Gypsies, as (camouflaged) beggars and criminals, are purported to have been a nuisance to the population. Through this selection of sources information that points to the integration of Gypsies is consistently ignored or played down – the musical tradition which in several countries they were able to build up, the prosperity which some groups of horse traders achieved, their occasionally being absorbed as a matter of due course into the ranks of sedentary society and their marriages with indigenous peoples which explain the 'mixed population' in many countries. These are all indications of social integration, and for the success of such an interactive process, concessions are necessary from both sides, newcomers and long-standing inhabitants, which implies that Gypsy societies were less closed than is often assumed.

The most important cause for the failure of the historical picture to admit change is that most writers about Gypsies accept the premise that they constitute one people with a number of fixed characteristics.[6] It is said that it is because of the specific nature of the Gypsy people that they always end up having difficulties and meet with rejection from others in the societies where they live. As a result of this point of view few researchers have an eye for the socio-economic and ethnic-cultural variety which is incorporated into the history of these groups. This fact is of primary importance, for authoritative scholarly texts in particular have played such a prominent role in the process of defining Gypsies and in the formation of ideas about their group character, certainly since the last quarter of the eighteenth century. Until then writers followed for the most part in the footsteps of the government and considered Gypsies as one of many categories of vagrants. For a long time they were thus more followers than leaders. A change in this situation occurred when a number of German authors 'proved' with great powers of persuasion that Gypsies are the descendants of an Indian caste of pariahs, with all the unfavourable traits which would belong to such ancestors. From then on governments and judicial authorities could legitimize their stigmatizing policy by invoking scientific arguments.

THE PAPER GYPSIES OF HEINRICH GRELLMANN

The book in which the thesis of one Gypsy people was elaborated for the first time was published in 1783 by the German historian Heinrich Moritz Gottlieb Grellmann (1753–1804).[7] It became quite a success in Germany as well as in England, France and the Netherlands. The influence of the book was and still is enormous. Reading the bibliography of Black on Gypsies (from 1913), with more than 4,000 titles, the eye of the reader is regularly confronted with the phrase 'based on (or derived from) Grellmann'. Almost every historical work on Gypsies in Europe takes Grellmann into account as a serious source, a unique ethnographical sketch, never outdated if we are to believe contemporary German and Austrian studies. Other illustrations of his influence are to be found in encyclopaedias. The whole scope of the work and the structure are still (partly) copied by contemporary writers on Gypsies. Grellmann set the tone for the following two centuries.

In the latest popular general overview, *The Gypsies* (1992), Angus Fraser concludes that Grellmann at the end of the eighteenth century restored the ethnic identity of Gypsies by revealing their origins through the means of examining their language.[8] There are, however, also indications that it was far more a matter of his constructing a Gypsy identity which, as such, had not previously existed. What took place was not the historical retrieval of knowledge which had been lost, but the synthesis of different approaches and the creation of unity in ways of thinking about diverse population groups. Grellmann's generalizing conclusions were based on a collection of sources about dissimilar groups which, to his mind, had a number of traits in common. They were said to have differed from others in their surroundings by virtue of their (previous) itinerant way of life, their being 'foreigners' or of oriental descent and, wherever in the world they resided, their being devoid of religion – in short an image of mutually related, alien heathens who lived parasitic, highly mobile lives. They might be called by different names in different places, but Grellmann gathered them all under the label of 'Gypsies'. By so doing he made them into one people, endowed with a common ethnographic profile.

Grellmann derived his most important information from a series of articles about the lives and works of Gypsies in Hungary and Transylvania written by a Hungarian minister, Samuel Augustini ab Hortis.[9] We do not know whether this minister had his own observations to thank for his expertise. In any event his pronouncements were extrapolated by Grellmann to apply to all groups known to him from the literature which matched his idea of Gypsy characteristics. Thus there emerged the portrait of an ethnic group which he subsequently, by comparing lists of words from a parental language, *Romani*, provided with a surprising new land of origin, namely India. To what extent all the people whom he called 'Gypsies' had a command of *Romani* he had no idea. He was also in the dark about the reasons why they left their original homeland at the start of the fifteenth century. Yet he did not hesitate, making use of travellers' accounts, to point out parallels with the way of life of outcasts in Indian society. By carrying on in this way he provided all Gypsy groups with a common descent. He also constructed a national history by compiling every scrap of information about them which he could find in chronicles, cosmographies, theological tracts, legal documents and other such sources. So he believed he had penetrated to the essence of the Gypsy people.

Whoever holds up critically to the light the sources which Grellmann selected, as well as his work methods, detects, however, a deficiency of reliable empirical information, an approach which, in the last analysis, shows little originality, and a set of dubious presuppositions as well.[10] Thus the early history of Gypsy studies discloses that retroactively an authority was conferred on texts in which during the fifteenth to the eighteenth centuries gypsy-like groups were mentioned, an authority which these writings might perhaps never have enjoyed had not Grellmann and several of his predecessors compiled them and put them in order. In addition no consensus existed in the periods preceding him about the way in which Gypsies were defined. On one occasion they comprised one category in the midst of many kinds of vagrants; on another they were the degraded descendants of fifteenth-century pilgrims or the criminal allies of indigenous villains and imposters who, for opportunistic reasons, called themselves Gypsies. Some chronicles report their exceptional wealth, other tracts emphasize only their behaviour as social deviants. Epithets such as 'alien heathens', 'spies for the Ottoman enemy' or even 'pseudo-Jews' continued to be heard. In authoritative texts of the seventeenth century, in keeping with the perspective of the state, they were portrayed as a mixed population of (half) criminals, beggars and other 'lawless wastrels'. This definition in social terms came to an end with the appearance of Grellmann's book which introduced a categorization of Gypsies as

a *distinct people*. This approach caught on, with Grellmann's contemporaries and with later writers. A number of factors contributed to its success.

First of all there were current, timely motives for taking a scientific look at the origins of Gypsies; the subject hung, as it were, in
the air. Grellmann was still a history student in those days and was
possibly inspired to write an essay on the subject by a Swedish
Academy essay competition during the 1770s. The reason that his
paper grew and grew was the result of the coincidence that two of
his teachers, August Schlözer and Christian Büttner, put their historical and linguistic sources at his disposal which made a more
extensive analysis possible. While he was busy news reached him
about the notorious Hungarian accusation in 1782 that Gypsies had
practised cannibalism. The media covered the drawn-out yet dramatic trial which ensued in all its gory detail. Grellmann's book
thus profited from a public appetite for knowing more about these
'heathen and uncivilized foreigners' who were fomenting the wildest fantasies. We should also not forget that most people at this
time already had some notion of Gypsies who had for centuries
been a favourite literary theme and part of an iconographic tradition. The literate public knew them as beautiful young women and
terrifying witches, as magicians and agents from a magic realm, as
highwaymen and exotic misfits. As figures in literature they created
a sensation and in the plastic arts they tickled the imagination.
Grellmann's book made people aware that these mythical representatives from some in-between world also existed in reality. The
scientifically presented group portrait evidently dovetailed well into
the prevailing picture. Herein fascination with and dread of Gypsies
fought for supremacy and the assertion can be defended that this
same ambivalence of feeling has continued down into the present.

What Grellmann's success with his book about these exotic groups
of outsiders within one's own borders accomplished was that he
welded together a number of scientific traditions. In addition to
interest in the mysterious anti-world shadowland of vagabonds,
beggars, criminals and other nonconformist denizens, a disposition
to concentrate on the historical roots of one's own state dominated
academic debate at the time. Enlightened historiographers in Germany combed chronicles and sources of other sorts which seemed
likely to enable them to compile a reconstruction of their own,
common past. In addition ethnographic interest increased in peoples
about whom contemporary travellers who undertook expeditions

in different capacities to the far corners of the world published reports. Physical anthropology – the study of skulls and physiognomy – contributed its anatomical findings and Johann Gottfried von Herder introduced the concept of 'a people' as the expression of a *Nationalgeist*. This gave impetus to a grail-like search for the elemental foundations of the national past.[11] But the methods of arrangement and classification led inevitably to a hierarchy of peoples, values and ways of living within which the Gypsies were allocated a lowly position. Grellmann's assumption that Gypsy groups, wherever in the world they happened to be, all belonged to one people with an essentially immutable national spirit was wholly consistent with the principles formulated by von Herder.[12] That was equally true for the thought that language is an expression of all the people, which also explains why the link he made – following others – between the Gypsy language and Hindi prompted the conclusion that Gypsies came from India.

One people, one language, a homeland that was left behind long ago – the way in which Grellmann supplied a common ethnic base to Gypsy groups living scattered from each other by characterizing them extensively as a group with a static culture and way of life is familiar to us from popular West European conceptions about Jews in the diaspora. Indeed various authors before him had actually worked out the hypothesis that Gypsies were a group that had split off from the Jews.[13] In a certain sense Grellmann joined ranks with this tradition by modelling his ideas about Gypsies on the accepted image of Jews. About both, one had the idea that a separate people was involved which lived as a state within the state, with their own morals and customs, a language of their own, an endogamous marriage pattern and an oriental appearance. On grounds of this origin they were said not to be assimilable, for in essence they always remained themselves and only appeared to adapt to their surroundings. This analogy underpinned Grellmann's notions about Gypsies as a distinct people. Only their language pointed the way to a different ethnic origin. Nonetheless the parallels continued to surface in various publications during the two centuries after him and in the Nazi era they were emphasized even more than ever.[14]

One last aspect which deserves mention in connection with the success of the first major work about Gypsies is that it matched with the political climate of the time. On a number of occasions Grellmann reported that he had been inspired by the guidelines for the civilizing of Gypsies (and other 'deviant groups') which the

Habsburg monarchs Maria Theresa and Joseph II had promulgated; accordingly he emerges as a policy researcher *avant la lettre*. He made no evaluation of the directives but acted like a loyal follower intent on providing scientific justification for what he praised as an enlightened government approach. Critics and other contemporaries praised him for his efforts and the university rewarded him with a professor's chair.

In this context there is an ambivalence which can be pointed out in Grellmann's thinking, the traces of which remain detectable all the way into the twentieth century. At the core of the Enlightenment is the thought that people are improvable which condones government policy directed towards this end. In such a perspective culture is presumed more potent than nature. Incompatible with this position was the Herderian idea of a people, a notion which was founded on the essence of a *Nationalgeist*, thus on a principle of exclusivity. What is essentially innate is by its very nature unchangeable. According to Grellmann, Gypsies, as Orientals, clung very tightly to their own norms and values which explained why they had been able to preserve their essence as a people for so many centuries. Yet he still thought it necessary that they be ruled with an iron hand so that they would obey the orders of Joseph II. This ideologically tinted belief in change contends for primacy in his book with his rational scepticism concerning the success of the undertaking. Such being of two minds is characteristic of general European thinking about Gypsies.

THE NINETEENTH-CENTURY CHANGE IN CATEGORIZING

Consulting written sources exclusively, Grellmann had constructed an ethnic homogeneity and a coherent picture of the history of the Gypsies. After him various writers moved among the people themselves and reported at length about their personal encounters and experiences. The question is whether, for example, the influential (literary) author George Borrow (1803–81),[15] and in his wake the English and Austro-Hungarian folklorists, who contributed hundreds of articles to the *Journal of the Gypsy Lore Society*, increased the subtlety of the image of Gypsies through their observations. Did they leave the paper Gypsies behind them and come forward with trustworthy ethnographic articles?

First of all the leading men of the Gypsy Lore Society (founded in 1888)[16] were responsible for a major shift in the categorizing. It appeared difficult for them to rhyme the reality which they discovered with the image handed down through the literature. Nevertheless, they did not challenge earlier authoritative texts, but began to differentiate among Gypsies and were soon convinced that the true Gypsies, as they knew them from the ethnographic sketches which had been published since their appearance in Europe, hardly existed any longer. Only here and there one met a solitary example of the ancient race, as Borrow called them, and such individuals therefore were a valuable source of information. These were the ones on whom researchers depended, for a price, to initiate them into the secrets of their 'vanishing people'. The problem was that this method did not altogether correspond with the prevailing image of Gypsies as people who were unwilling to reveal anything about their language or customs to non-Gypsies. This complaint about an inclination to secrecy was one already voiced by Grellmann and his predecessors. The new thing about Borrow and those who came after him was that they prided themselves on having demolished the wall of suspicion. Thus on paper they created the romantic image of the *Romany Rye* who was a regular visitor to the tents and was accepted as an intimate, the Gypsies' friend, who, obviously, was privy to the rituals of their lives.

The obdurate reality which Gypsy researchers confront in the field time and again brings them to the conclusion that authentic Gypsy culture is on the brink of disappearing. This notion has in the meantime held them captive for a good century and a half and constitutes an important argument for their existence. For they feel called upon as archaeologists to collect the surviving relics of a centuries-old culture, to analyse but above all to preserve them, in the course of which they demonstrate a special interest in folklore: Gypsy motifs in art and literature, their songs and verses, magic rituals and religion, kinds of healing, apparel, music and dance. In addition the study of language variants has enjoyed continuing interest (with a burst of popularity during the last ten years) and articles appear with regularity in which the author makes known a previously lost text from the early Middle Ages in which reference is said to be made to the presence of Gypsies in, for example, Persia, Greece or Middle Europe. By now a small reference library full of books has been turned out about the origin of Gypsies and their first appearance in Europe. Whether all these inventories of words, musical forms and customs rightly belong in one collection is a question which only a few ask themselves. As a rule Gypsy specialists concentrate on striking likenesses and have far less keen an eye for differences. Even more so they believe that the way of life of those who, to their way of thinking, do not belong to the true 'Gypsy race' has already in the distant past sullied the reputation of the whole category of itinerants. This turnabout in thinking about Gypsies was initiated by George Borrow and his heirs of the Gypsy Lore Society.

MIXED BLOODS AS THE ROOT OF EVIL

In the 1930s German eugenists added a biological component to the ethnic and social (dis)qualifications of nineteenth-century Gypsy specialists. An analysis of the work of youth psychiatrist and criminal biologist Robert Ritter (1901–51)[17] concluded that he also took the idea of the true Gypsy as the prototypical nomad as a starting point. In his portrait of this practically mythological figure we recognize the traits which Grellmann had collected, but can discover an element as well stemming from the tradition in which 'natural' peoples are contrasted with 'cultured' ones. He compared them specifically with hunters and gatherers from prehistoric times who were said to be incapable of keeping pace with the forward march of civilization. The stagnation in their mental growth explains, as he sees it, their restive and parasitical behaviour; even their itinerancy he attributes to this prehistoric core. The socially unacceptable conduct of those with 'mixed blood' who came later was alleged to derive from their biological inheritance. Through relations across group lines, a gene for rootlessness made its way into the 'blood' of previously sedentary Germans. The biological legacy of the latter had in its turn seen to it that 'halfbloods' were more asocial and criminal than 'true Gypsies' because their potential for deviance was strengthened by their German cleverness and enterprising boldness. Relations between sedentary and non-sedentary peoples were, according to Ritter, invariably disadvantageous for both. The anxiety for contamination with inherited Gypsy characteristics was so strong that he wrote a single mixed match could stain the blood for many generations. Such notions of purity and a belief in the determinant force of the genetic underpinned all his research and, lest we forget, that of many of his European contemporaries.[18]

Ritter relied strongly on genealogical research, which brought to light that 90 per cent of the people who fell into his categories were partly of non-Gypsy descent. Most reports of Gypsy crimes, it was Ritter's conviction, unsupported by statistical evidence, involved this *Jenische Menschenschlag* that moved about like Gypsies. As early as 1934 Ritter had formed an idea of what Gypsy mixed-bloods – his preferred name for the category – were like. Throughout the coming years it would not undergo any change worth mentioning. From this product of a crossing of races, all the positive characteristics of the 'true Gypsy' seemed to be missing, while all those traits worthy of condemnation which people exhibited who were looked down on as socially inferior could be found. These people, he maintained – also in the eyes of 'true Gypsies' – were the roots of all evil.

To Ritter's way of looking at things, asociability was one of the most disadvantageous inherited characteristics of rovers. Only in the early 1940s would he declare the label to be applicable to a far larger category of people.[19] Then in fact it became a collective designation for everyone, excluding the sick and invalided, who cost the community time, money and energy. Closer reading of his publications also discloses that in a certain sense he was constantly concerned with the same – in practice poorly demarcated – categories of people, whether writing about Gypsies, *Jenischen*, half-castes or marginal riff-raff, except that he was constantly shifting his perspective. The point of departure of his research on asociability in the 1930s (which, indeed, was not confined to Germany) was that many people hardly had any economic value for the community. The spotlight was accordingly turned on families and communities of paupers, recipients of the dole and the neglected. The concept of asociability in the first decades of the twentieth century became increasingly an expression of a kind of moral criterion. People who earlier were referred to as dishonourable or who were known as notorious good-for-nothings in these years became tagged as asocial. Since this was a word from a foreign language, it was replaced under the Nazis by such terms as *gemeinschaftsfremd* and *gemeinschaftsunfähig*.[20] In this context Ritter cited a ministerial decree from 18 July 1940 with guidelines for evaluating hereditary health. Herein *gemeinschaftsfremd* pertained to all persons with an inclination towards one form or another of condemnable behaviour (including psychopaths, addicts and troublemakers) whose nature precluded any possibility of amelioration. Ritter attributed five attitudes towards society to these people which, one by one, he found fault with: they were weak, troublesome, destructive, recalcitrant and hostile.[21] How he applied these in the execution of his research, he fails to mention.

One of the most important categories under the label *Gemeinschaftsfremden* was that of hereditarily tainted criminals, so-called born wrongdoers.[22] They, too, according to Ritter, seldom came from a sedentary milieu. Usually they belonged to the ranks of the mentally less developed and the both economically and socially weaker members of society, which was also how he looked upon casual labourers. These people, it was his idea, had no steadfastness, but shifted about restively. The need to do research aimed specifically at this category, especially in wartime, was, according to Ritter, twofold. Society should be protected from dangerous characters and *Gemeinschaftsfremden*, and those fit to work and socially adjusted should be employed in places where their productivity was badly needed.[23] He did not assume, however, that the criminal type could be identified at a glance. He was of the opinion that contemporary research had rendered obsolete Lombroso's criminological-anthropological notions about atavism, the reversion of people to an (ancestral) state of primitiveness. He did not believe that someone's natural bent could be read from external features, proof that he had little confidence in physical anthropology. Only by analysing genealogically the hereditary circle of the criminal under scrutiny was it possible, Ritter found, to achieve results.[24] Although elsewhere he had remarked that how complex character traits were inherited was not yet known, in the genealogy of families he thought he could locate enough evidence to go on to stamp people with the mark of criminality.[25]

Official criteria for distinguishing the categories of Gypsies, half-castes and gypsy-like groups were only established late on during the Nazi regime. In practice, for purposes of classification, for their indicators of choice the police authorities had for a long time already latched onto external appearance, way of life, language and names, in combination with occupations. From the time of Heinrich Himmler's decree of 16 December 1938 they saw themselves obliged to use as their point of departure the racial diagnoses which Ritter's institutes had drafted on grounds of genealogical data and the social evaluation of a person's individual family history. Not only the police authorities but also the Gypsies in question – if at any rate the term in this connection is still fitting – were, according to Ritter, informed of the results of the diagnosis and could contest it by handing over genealogical documents with contradictory information. These racial diagnoses, known in German as *gutachtliche Äusserungen*, served as the basis for the selection of Gypsies and 'gypsy-like' individuals for Auschwitz,[26] but they have never been analysed because after the war they became scattered throughout Germany and to a large extent apparently lost. Remarkably, in February 1941 Ritter wrote that he had completed 10,000 of them, whereas it appears from the copies of racial diagnoses which we collected that on 8 July 1941 number 2,322 was written – the person in question was classified as ZM (+), that is to say a Gypsy with mixed blood of predominantly Gypsy descent. Under Ritter's responsibility racial diagnoses continued to be written out until January 1945, at which time number 24,411 was completed. In this instance diagnosis took into account a number of categories, although Ritter's publications leave us in the dark about what criteria were decisive. In any event the formal rubrication was as follows.[27]

(a) A Gypsy is someone who has three pure Gypsies among his grandparents.

(b) A Gypsy half-caste (+) (first grade) is anyone with fewer than three pure Gypsies among his grandparents.

(c) A Gypsy half-caste (−) (second grade) is anyone who has at least two Gypsy half-castes among his grandparents.

(d) Non-Gypsy: all other cases.

The dramatic irony of this process was that Ritter, with his genealogical research on people labelled 'Gypsies' by the government, demonstrated that their ethnic identity was non-existent, at least in the primordial form which Grellmann had constructed. Consequently he felt obliged to break the all-embracing category down into a number of vaguely defined subcategories dominated in the first instance by that of the mixed population. They constituted, both for Ritter and for the Nazis whose policy he prepared, a defamation of the racial purity of the German people, a view which engendered proposals for sterilization and, in a later phase, all but inevitably, deportation to Auschwitz.

THE DICTATES OF AUTHORITATIVE TEXTS

The manner in which down through the centuries Gypsies have been and still are defined at the governmental level demonstrates a clear connection with changing notions of the process of categorization in science. The labelling of Gypsies as 'deviants' appears to have been subject to revision, which also holds true for the accompanying argumentation. It is far from evident to what extent the scientific construction of the Gypsy identity mirrored the (historical) existence of the different groups discernible behind the name. Although until the middle of the eighteenth century authoritative texts promulgated the definition used by governments in the implementation of their policies, after Grellmann a shift in that process came about. Since the publication of his historical survey, the ethnic element of 'the Gypsy people' has acquired a master status which entails a codification of the opposite characteristics. Judicial authorities in particular subsequently adopted his view of things and used it to legitimize their stigmatizing policy. There can be no mistaking this development when one traces the criminological tradition within Gypsy studies culminating in its criminal-biological variant during the Nazi era. In the practice of law enforcement, however, it did often prove difficult to base the combating of vagrancy or the limitation of possibilities for earning a living by means of an itinerant vocation on an ethnic categorization.

Thus since Grellmann academics and amateur scholars have played a vanguard role in the process of defining Gypsies. He has seen to it that the notion of a Gypsy people has become dominant and other group categories such as pilgrims, spies, criminal vagabonds, heathens and the mixed category of social outsiders have faded into the background. The 'people' concept appears to have meshed together so well with the founding myths of nineteenth-century nationalism that it remained in use even after evidence of integration (sedentarism, intermarriage, social mobility) kept gradually accumulating. That was true for governments but also for many experts on Gypsies. This leads us to the question of why scholarship with the passage of time has undergone so little essential change in its vision of Gypsies' history and way of life.

The most important explanation for such steadfastness is the tradition of imagery, the 'dictates of authoritative texts' or the 'family tree of ideas', as Said likewise puts forward in his inspiring study.[28] He shows how in the European process of exercising hegemony and domination one's own culture is constantly defined in terms of its opposite. Thus the identity of Europe is, for example, presented as the mirror image of 'the Orient', a designation for the other half of the world. Similar analyses are perpetrated in Western literature concerning America, 'Indians' and black populations in Africa.[29] Each image of another, so it appears, is always a reflection of a facet of the image of self. Said, to be sure, is not so much interested in imagery for its own sake as in the power relations of which imagery is an expression. He points out that writers on the Middle East, whom he groups together under the institutionalized collective term of Orientalists, have, through their texts, wielded definitional power over the people whom they describe. As a consequence a static cultural picture has come into existence of 'the Orient', which to a large extent obfuscates the historical identities of the inhabitants of Eastern countries. Ideas which have been formulated about Orientals, Said contends, correspond only in some small part with reality, for many administrative civil servants, adventurers, philologists and writers who spent some time in an Eastern country and then took up a pen closed ranks as a rule behind a tradition of 'authoritative texts' within which a Western image of the Orient held sway. We encounter a similar chain of events where Gypsy studies are concerned.

Already prior to Grellmann a historical canon of publications on Gypsies existed. Authors had primarily followed in each other's footsteps. This tradition of ongoing reproduction of the same sources and sentences did not undergo any demonstrable disruption with the appearance of Grellmann's study. In the final analysis his book is first and foremost a compilation of existing texts, a summary of the current state of knowledge on the subject. By combining a number of scientific traditions he introduced a fundamental change in how 'Gypsies' were defined but without disclosing any new sources about them. His interpretation of their history he derived from authoritative writers who, in their brief passages on the subject, had often based themselves on the chronicles of a century or longer ago. His ethnographic portrait of 'the essence' or 'the character' of Gypsies was likewise culled from the text of others and not his own observations. He continued the pattern of his predecessors and after him little changed in the situation, for Borrow and countless other authors also depended upon earlier texts on the subject and weighed their own experiences against what had been written. In this way it was practically inevitable for them to reach the conclusion that 'true Gypsies' hardly survived any longer, except for – and in this sense they constrained reality to suit their purposes – those whom they knew best, because of all Gypsies these in their eyes were (morally) the most pure. That process of identifying exceptions was adopted by, for example, the poet Pushkin and Borrow, and also by Heinrich Himmler and Ritter with their 'racially pure' Gypsy families. The idea 'Gypsy' was thus preserved, while the actual Gypsies whom they came across continued to constitute a problem.

THE 'SPLENDID ISOLATION' OF GYPSY STUDIES

For anyone surveying the history of Gypsy studies, it is striking that practically all perspectives which have been developed still persist, each way of thinking with its own history and a strong claim to a right to exist. In the tradition of the Romantics, who have always emphasized that Gypsies are the most free of primitive peoples, the accepted line at present is that they live in resistance to the conformists' world. Evangelically inspired or other civilizing movements stress even today that Gypsies, as deprived outsiders living in pathetic conditions, require special attention. Folklorists carry on with their search for authentic traces of Gypsy culture with undiminished zeal, including linguists who have elevated *Romani*-philology to a special status. In judicial circles in the course of the twentieth century the criminological tradition in Gypsy studies has even expanded and become more intricately than ever entwined with government policy in a general sense, policy which even after the Second World War has remained strongly oriented to the promotion of assimilation within existing social structures. If in the past it was felt that Gypsies needed to be 'tamed', nowadays governments are intent on integrating them while assuring the preservation of their own (ethnic) identity as – at any rate in the West – policy jargon would put it. Although all these approaches may have their own motives for engagement with Gypsies, the image of the Gypsy has not lost any of its uniformity. Fascination with the Gypsies' life has endured, together with disapproval. In a certain sense they are romantic outcasts without equal.

The social isolation of Gypsies, together with the failure, until the 1970s, of special interest groups to tackle in an organized way existing prejudices or to occupy themselves with helping Gypsies to catch up, probably explain why historians never demonstrated much interest in their past. To the extent that there was interest it usually was complementary to the perspective of the governments then in power. Yet even historians who regarded their invariably biased sources critically do not for the most part appear to have been capable of adding subtler shades of meaning to the one-sided picture presented there, a number of recent studies excepted. Scrutiny of Gypsy persecution under the Nazi regime has, to be sure, increased sharply, especially in Germany since the beginning of the 1980s. Virtually all the writers involved, however, a not inconsiderable proportion of whom have been commissioned by organizations which promote Gypsies' interests, similarly accept as their point of departure that Gypsies comprise one people, a folk which since their assumed departure from their homeland in India in the early Middle Ages have barely mingled with others and therefore have been able to maintain a character all their own. This is despite the fact that there are countless indications and pieces of evidence establishing that the term 'Gypsy' was applied in a number of instances rather generally by sitting governments, and certainly not simply to denote the ancestors of today's *Sinti* and *Roma*. The entanglement of science and politics on this (post-war) terrain has thus generated a number of analyses critical of government policy but at the same time it has confirmed some stereotypical ideas about the folk character of *the* Gypsies.

Another academic discipline whose absence from Gypsy studies has been sorely missed is social and cultural anthropology which has become institutionalized within universities since the final quarter of the nineteenth century. Not until long after the Second World War was any empirical anthropological fieldwork undertaken. Only guesswork is possible about the reasons for this omission. Was it true here as well that at the university level people simply did not consider the morals and customs, cultural manifestations and way of life of the Gypsy groups, recognized as marginal, worthy of serious study? Or is access to Gypsy groups for scientific research more difficult than access to other ethnic (minority) groups? Only folklorists have seemed to attach any value to what the members of a – for them – disappearing primitive people have left behind. The conclusion is even justified that Gypsy studies are actually only intensively pursued in these circles. That is likely to be one of the reasons why the field revels in such splendid isolation. Gypsy folklore, with its upgraded amateurism and, since 1888, its own journal, has always dominated the field. It was an enclave of enthusiastic 'Gypsy friends' who, in their longing for specialization, stuck to their own, delimited work terrain. They moved among like-minded spirits who shared practically identical ideas about how to approach their subject. As a result connections with historical and social sciences were only established after the Second World War, and even then only on a modest scale. What hindered progress was a lack of reflection concerning historical sources. From whom, for example, must anthropology derive material for comparisons? There are hardly any reliable empirical studies available from either the eighteenth or nineteenth centuries and, what's more, most (partial) studies confined themselves to narrowly delineated groups in diverse countries about the extent of whose mutual ethno-historical ties nothing is known. The danger of unjustified generalizations still looms large as life.

According to Edward Said, Orientalism was only attacked and (in part) exposed for what it was once the decolonization of formerly oppressed peoples or nations had been achieved. Since for some Gypsy groups in Western European countries the process of emancipation has only commenced recently, hardly any revaluation of extant historical knowledge has yet taken place. It remains questionable, moreover, whether corrections are to be anticipated from this corner since the intelligentsia in Gypsy circles are not likely to profit very much by challenging the core concepts of Gypsy studies. For political and pragmatic reasons they will sooner close ranks in support of the idea of a *collective* Gypsy identity, including a language which belongs to them. Recognition as an ethnic minority culminates, to be sure, in more agreements pertaining to specific rights. It will in part depend upon the choices made by Gypsy leaders and representatives to what extent and in what way the definition of Gypsies from above and the stigma it entails will be set right with all the social and political ramifications of such correction. However, this tentatively launched process may prove to develop further; until now practitioners of Gypsy studies appear to be preaching simply to their own parishioners. The study of the history of workers' groups and of women may now constitute recognized academic specialities, and social scientific studies of (ethnic) minorities may already have been burgeoning for years, but still the number of Gypsy studies incorporated within standard curricula has so far remained small. Only if isolation is shattered and a fundamental debate about the premises of Gypsy studies takes place in prestigious periodicals and is addressed to a broad academic public can we expect, perhaps, to arrive at a deeper understanding of the history of Gypsies in the future.

3 The Church of Knowledge: Representation of Gypsies in Encyclopaedias[1]

Wim Willems and Leo Lucassen

A GENEALOGY OF IDEAS

In order to grasp the West European image of Gypsies during the last two hundred and fifty years, we have oral, iconographic and written sources at our disposal: surveys, sculpture, literature, magazines and newspapers which can tell us much about the norms, values and impressions of a society. These sources contain a wealth of information about people's ideas, their behaviour towards others and their internal relations. In this chapter we focus on one written source in particular: encyclopaedias.[2] We assume that they contain summaries of current information, and that they are written in more or less the same way. Because encyclopaedic information has always been seen as authoritative, we can use it to trace the prevailing opinions through time. The assumption is that encyclopaedias have played an important role in spreading a certain view of Gypsies, particularly among the upper classes. The fact that the people who decided on the policies concerning them came from those ranks justifies the choice of encyclopaedias as a main source.

Because of the derived character of the entries in encyclopaedias, a study of the representation of Gypsies should also be concerned with the sources which have been used by the editors.[3] After all, encyclopaedias function as a channel for the existing knowledge about Gypsies; they show what is considered the objective opinion of the moment. A critical examination of the sources is often left out by the editors. Consequently, both the prejudiced and non-prejudiced views belonging to a certain period can be deduced from the entries. The aim of this chapter is to set up a genealogy of ideas about Gypsies and to make a contribution to demythologize the stereotypes concerning them. We will show that certain stereotypic views tenaciously appear in encyclopaedias and scholarly works, while other views change at a certain point. We will try to provide an explanation for both phenomena. A number of recurring themes in the sources, such as physical appearance, national character, morals and customs, religion, occupations and art, have been chosen as guidelines for the discussion.

PHYSICAL APPEARANCE

The ideas about the physical appearance of Gypsies and the way these ideas have been put into words have hardly changed over the past two and a half centuries. In other words, a general feeling about the physical characteristics of the category 'Gypsies' exists, and what stands out is that the descriptions commonly used are fairly positive.[4] The physical appearance of Gypsies compels admiration; the features which can be distinguished are all exemplary. According to many authors, depravity is a distinctive characteristic of the Gypsies, but there is no hint of this in the encyclopaedia descriptions of Gypsy physiognomy. This is particularly remarkable when we consider that certain branches of anthropology (namely phrenology and physiognomy) always emphasized the connection between man's inner self and his physical appearance.[5] By means of scientific measurements and comparisons of skulls and faces, people thought to gain insight into the characters of nations and races. Anthropological sources were often used to support statements about the nature and the morals of Gypsies. Comparative linguistics was also used as a source, and this discipline, in its search towards the nature of language, was tempted into the kind of speculation which proved to be grist to the mill of later racists. In particular the work of Friedrich Max Müller (1823–1900), who for a long time thought that he had arrived at the essence of man by means of language classifications, encouraged the belief that something like an Aryan race existed, with Indian ancestors, interconnected by a common language. At the end of his life, he rejected this idea. He began to realize that the existence of Aryan languages does not necessarily imply that people who speak this language have the same (Aryan) ancestors. In this way, he saw to it that the Aryan myth was reconsidered. By that time, however, his ideas had already become widespread.[6]

The description of the physical appearance of Gypsies does not appear to be influenced by these ideas. The fascination with their exotic facial and physical characteristics created a portrait which in some of its details is reminiscent of the Grecian ideal of beauty. However, we do not come across such positive descriptions in the sixteenth or seventeenth centuries. In those times, Gypsies were often described as frightening and hideous. A good example is provided by Münster's *Cosmographia Universalis* (1550). In the eighteenth century, the Gypsies' physical appearance was interpreted more positively, as in the Viennese journal *Anzeigen aus der sämmtlichen Kaiserl. Königl. Erbländern* (1770–6), which, as we saw in the previous chapter, was used as a main source for an ethnographic portrait of Gypsies by Heinrich Grellmann. From this journal, the German founding father of Gypsy studies distilled a type of standard description, which has been adopted and in some points expanded upon by many later writers.

The encyclopaedias emulate their sources carefully, and this has resulted in the following image of Gypsies: mesocephalic skull (the normal 'European type'),[7] raven hair, dark complexion, a high forehead, coal-black, lively eyes, a somewhat bent nose, a fine mouth with snow-white teeth, slender and flexible, olive skin (also dark or yellowish brown). One or two people mention a bronze-like skin; others think that the glow of the Gypsies' skin originates from the East. The girls have a somewhat lighter skin colour, and are generally found to be very attractive. However, it is often noted that their beauty is doomed to fade quickly. The idea that their dark skin colour is the result of their Eastern heritage has not always dominated. For instance, Grellmann posits that the Gypsies' skin colour, like that of the Laplanders, has to do with their way of life. Supposedly they do not wash themselves, and they constantly sit in the smoke from their fires: '... längst würde er aufgehört haben, negerartig zu sein, wenn er aufgehört hätte, zigeunerisch zu leben', is his conclusion.[8] He did not connect skin colour with race, but with living conditions.

According to several nineteenth-century editors, the fact that Gypsies are well formed has also to do with their nomadic existence. The pure mountain air and the smell of herbs which they breathe supposedly give them the ability to survive all hardships and to reach, quite often, the ripe old age of 100. According to the same editors, there are no fat-bellied, hunchbacked, blind or lame Gypsies, and they are never ill.

NATIONAL CHARACTER

Judging by the ideal sculptured features of the Gypsies, one would never expect that their nature has been described in the most negative terms from the very beginning. They might be physically attractive, according to the views of the time, but they do not have the appropriate harmony of soul to match their physical appearance. The eighteenth- and nineteenth-century editors provide a good example of how science managed, by way of language studies, to trace the origins of both the Gypsies and the West Europeans to India, only to argue, in an incredible manner amounting to wishful thinking, that the Gypsies have a pernicious nature, while the 'Aryans' have a noble nature. Before Rüdiger (1782) and Grellmann pointed out this Indian heritage, others had also tried to establish a relationship between the national character of the Gypsies and their supposed origin. For instance, in some quite scholarly writings during the eighteenth century, it was thought that Egypt was their place of origin. People tried to make this hypothesis acceptable by pointing out similar (usually negative) characteristics of the Egyptians. In this way, Swinburne suggested that Gypsies originated from the worshippers of Isis, who distinguished themselves by fortune-telling, a nomadic existence and thievery.[9] Twiss saw a resemblance with Egyptian sorcerers, while Salmon, whose work has been translated into Dutch, lumped the Gypsies together with contemporary Egyptians.[10] Apparently, the latter were stereotyped for their mendacity, for their lazy nature and for being thieves.

In 1724, when the first Dutch encyclopaedia appeared, people were already convinced that Gypsies were thieves who proved to be a great nuisance to the indigenous populations, and for that reason their persecution has been justified by different governments. However, the editors went no further than to present bits of superficial information. Once one had been led towards India, as mentioned before, via language studies, a scientific rationalization came into being which functioned as a source of negative views of Gypsies for more than two centuries. We saw that Grellmann based his notion of the Gypsy's Indian heritage on two factors: the first comprised comparative language studies which, according to him, indicated a strong affinity between the Romani language of the Gypsies and the Hindustani languages. The second factor originated from the in those days very popular travellers' journals which informed Grellmann about the existence of the caste of the Pariahs, whose colour, build, character, morals and customs showed many similarities with the image he had of the Gypsies and their way of life.[11]

Besides the caste of the Pariahs, another group supposedly lived in India. These people were hard-working, agrarian Aryans who were noted for their steadfast character (all the middle-class capitalistic virtues of the nineteenth century are included in this image). They left India at a time when Sanskrit was still spoken there and settled in Western Europe, distinguishing themselves positively from the Indians who stayed behind.[12] The Gypsies, however, supposedly left India and retained their national character, which was to be found in its purest form among the caste of the Pariahs, except that the Gypsies changed from a sedentary to a nomadic way of life. It is generally conceded that this nomadic way of life gradually took root in the Gypsies.

This analogy between the national character of the Gypsies and that of the Indian Pariahs dominated Gypsy studies until the twentieth century. This development probably contributed to the fact that in various encyclopaedias the character of the Gypsies has been described in terms which are remarkably similar. A number of characteristics stand out in the impression promulgated by the encyclopaedias and their sources. Gypsies are supposed, for example, to show a predilection for a life without ties, to prefer the *dolce far niente* (the sweetness of doing nothing) and to be prepared to put up with the worst consequences of their own attitude. These characteristics, along with many others, are, according to a range of authors, not only inherent in Gypsies, but also in the Eastern and Slavic nations. Popp Serboianu wrote that they are sly by nature and like all the Orientals supposedly live from day to day, not interested in the future.[13] Thus, they are lazy and workshy. They will work only when forced by the utmost necessity. The workshy character of the Gypsies comprises one of the many constants in scholarly writings from the eighteenth century onwards. Once again, Grellmann is the great popularizer.[14] According to him, Gypsies detest work, particularly when it requires an effort. They would rather submit to hunger and misery than improve their lot by working. Kogalnitchan (1837) completely agreed with that point of view.[15] In his opinion, a Gypsy liked doing nothing at all and preferred stealing to working. More than a century after Grellmann's work, Wlislocki, who presented himself as the protector of Gypsy culture, failed to change this view.[16] Although this 'Gypsy expert' insisted on being without prejudices, because, unlike other observers, he had intensely involved himself in the Gypsy world, it is remarkable that many of his descriptions are taken word for word from earlier authors.[17]

The general opinion is that Gypsies do not lack cleverness, but because of their upbringing and low morality, this characteristic usually develops into slyness. And this, in particular, helps them in stealing and committing fraud. They are trained from a very early age, and they subsequently develop a great dexterity in these skills. According to many authors, they usually operate on a small scale. This limitation is often explained by a reference to their cowardice. We can already observe this supposed characteristic in Grellmann's work. This author claims that Gypsies are afraid to commit robberies at night. Kogalnitchan explains this by referring to the centuries of Gypsy serfdom in the Balkans: 'Muth und Tapferkeit sind niemals das Erbtheil eines zum Sklaven herabgewürdigten Menschen.'[18] That Gypsies limit themselves mainly to small burglaries is seldom appreciated as a positive point. It is always the negative characteristics (cowardice, inability to think) which prevent them from committing larger crimes.[19]

Because Gypsies (generally) are supposed to lack notions of morality, they would allow their instincts to rule them more easily, have no sense of honour, are greedy, wasteful, intemperate with food and drink, lecherous and frivolous. However, the opinions concerning their loose morals vary considerably. For some these are beyond questioning.[20] For instance, Twiss claimed that all Spanish female Gypsies practised prostitution. Borrow, however, some fifty years later, emphasized the chastity of the Spanish Gypsies.[21] Then again, a century later Popp Serboianu claimed that Gypsies have absolutely no sexual control; according to him, the Gypsies' love life solely constituted an indulgence in sensuality.[22] Block (1936) did not support this claim.[23] He argued that while Gypsy women may look sensual, this says nothing of their inner nature. Because they are a primitive people, the outward appearance and behaviour (dancing) of the women apparently do not excite Gypsy men in the way civilized men would be. It is only when modern anthropological research developed that the supposed licentiousness of the Gypsies was proved to be a fable.[24] Further it seems to be undisputed that Gypsies are rough and uncivilized, which has led to the following standard description in nineteenth-century encyclopaedias: 'Although they have lived among Christian people for centuries, they have not cast off their heathendom, and they have remained rude and uncivilized, attached to a nomadic existence, making do with sober and sometimes disgusting food in miserable huts.'[25]

A number of characteristics which are inferred from these sources are mendacity, disloyalty and cruelty towards animals. Moreover, the Gypsies supposedly lack courage and bravery, and they are faint-hearted.[26] This cruelty, which is also directed at people, has generated prolific writings. What particularly seems to have encouraged this view is that from the fifteenth century onward Gypsies were hired as executioners in Romania and Hungary. Borrow later adds a horrible story which enforces this particular image:[27] an old man is tortured by Gypsies, who rub fresh peppers into his eyes in order to find out where he has hidden his money. Even the French professor Bloch repeated this story in the 1950s without comment, even though he pleaded for more understanding for the group.[28]

The attributed thievish nature of the Gypsies, which only disappeared from the Dutch encyclopaedias after the Second World War (and even then not completely) raised fears of moral degeneration in late nineteenth-century thinking as well as in the first half of the twentieth century. Inspired by the work of the Dutch orthodox Christian statesman Abraham Kuyper *Om de Oude Wereldzee* (1907/8), the Christian encyclopaedias in particular emphasized that the heathenish and amoral behaviour of the Gypsies was dangerously contagious: 'Their influence on several nations in Europe manifested itself in the cultivation of banditry, in the encouragement of superstition and fortune-telling, and in a spirit of cunning and guile.'[29] Even though this passage indicates religious intolerance only, the idea of degeneration had far-reaching consequences for the concept of race, which was first worked out by physical anthropologists and later shamelessly exploited by the Nazis. In actual practice it became clear that authors obsessed by purity are at the same time fixated on the lack of it. That was definitely the case with anthropological and especially the eugenic research on the 'Gypsy race', as we showed in the previous chapter. In the course of the nineteenth century, people began to distinguish between the naturally 'pure Gypsies' and the mixed forms. In this respect, it is remarkable that before the breakthrough of the idea of race (in the second half of the nineteenth century) people were convinced that nothing would be more preferable than to mix Gypsies with Europeans. According to this line of thought, the nomadic character of the Gypsies would then automatically disappear. Taking away children from their parents must also have been seen in this light. Upbringing rather than race or heredity was looked upon as a determining factor.[30]

Anthropometrical research, which concerns the measurements and proportions of the human body, was one of the factors which particularly influenced the development of the concept of race. Pittard studied Gypsies in the Balkan countries and in Hungary because they were supposedly the purest race of European Gypsies. In his report in 1908/9, he noted that the Gypsies had mingled with all kinds of people. Supposedly, the Scandinavian and north Germanic Gypsies in particular originated partly from native drifters. In several countries Gypsies could be found among the 'normal' travelling folk. He therefore concluded that the Gypsies did not belong to the Hindu-type and that a mixed heritage (from the 'original population' in India) should be assumed. The dichotomy between 'original' and 'mixed', which is often related to nomadism and a sedentary life, prevailed until the 1940s. References to a mixed heritage and to the Aryan race did not disappear from the Dutch entries concerning Gypsies until 1953.

MORALS AND CUSTOMS

It is almost inevitable that the extended description of the Gypsy character, which is already marked by a complete lack of values, does not show the morals and customs of the Gypsies in a favourable light. Even after the Second World War, the encyclopaedias propagated ideas like 'once a thief, always a thief' and stated that those who live off society like parasites cannot, by definition, have enviable manners or cultural traditions. That the Gypsies are different is emphasized again and again, and the opinion which plays underneath is that they are a peculiar people. No stone is left unturned when it comes to proving that they are barbarians. According to the most contemporary views, they may have been unjustly persecuted and oppressed, but that does not take away the fact that they are deviants whose function, particularly in modern society, is unclear.

If we examine the way people perceived the social organization of the Gypsies through the centuries, we observe that eighteenth-century ideas on the subject were fairly romantic. Later, it is continually pointed out that they travel in bands of 200 to 300 people. Each tribe is headed by a chosen leader, called the *raj*. He is the highest judge and represents the tribe to the outside world. He decides the direction in which the tribe travels, and he allocates a travelling area to each extended family. The editors have always been fascinated by Gypsy titles. For instance, the *Volkenkundige* (Ethnographical) *Encyclopedie* of 1962 points out that more or less related groups have a queen, an idea which became popular in the nineteenth century. It is not until 1976 that the *Grote Winkler Prins* indicated that while the outside world refers to a king or queen, the Gypsies themselves reject these titles as incorrect. Jan Yoors, an artist who grew up in Antwerp, travelled with a Lowara Gypsy group for more than ten years from the age of twelve. In his books, written in the postwar period, he described the other side, based on his own experiences, and he too rejected those titles. He did concede that the Gypsy communities do present certain members as kings, but he also mentioned that these kings mainly function as lightning rods during conflicts with the *gaze* (non-Gypsies).

The dietary habits of Gypsies are also seldom left out. Most editors feel that they must first point out that Gypsy cooking is disgusting. They apparently enjoy vegetables like onions and garlic the most. Usually it is added that this habit is in accordance with Eastern customs. Although they usually live on bread and water (according to the 1912 *Winkler Prins*), they do not scorn fat meat, game or pork. One editor mentions that the hedgehog is a national dish for the Gypsies, while another notes that they even eat dogs, cats, rats and mice. Moreover even some twentieth-century works claim that Gypsies particularly like the meat of dead animals. Some, like Borrow, went even further and were convinced that Gypsies use their knowledge of medicine in order to deliberately cause cattle diseases and even poison animals; subsequently, they would visit the farmers in order to pick up the cadavers. Borrow admitted that this allegation was based largely on rumour, but in view of the Gypsies' nature, he thought there was a high probability that it was true.[31] Others claimed that Gypsies dig up dead animals in order to eat them later. For example, Schwicker was informed that Gypsies in Temesvar had to be kept away from a dead horse by soldiers, but 'die Zigeuner gruben es später dennoch heraus und verzehrten es'.[32] The American author and folklorist Leland pointed out that the Indian Pariahs hang on to the same custom.[33]

Often, a direct connection between eating cadavers and cannibalism is inferred. The most notorious accusation of Gypsy cannibalism dates from 1782, when 200 of them were suspected of it. After being tortured by the villagers, some of them confessed, and 49 Gypsies had already been executed (partially beheaded, partially

hung, then put on the rack and quartered) when an official inves-
tigations committee arrived, sent there by Kaiser Joseph II. The
committee soon discovered that the confessions must have been
false, because the supposed victims were still alive.[34] However, the
fascination with this type of excess remained so intense that it over-
shadowed any notion of disbelief. Although the accusation of cannibalism was first heard of around 1629 in Spain, little attention was
paid to the matter outside that country. Only after Borrow quoted
the Spanish source on cannibalism, Quinones (1632), do we find it
in other works.[35] For central and northwest Europe, the allegation
probably started at an earlier date. Most students in Gypsy studies
refer to the famous Hungarian trial in 1782. Grellmann, the first
author to mention this trial, even wrote that he had no knowledge
of older accusations.[36] The nineteenth and twentieth centuries have
witnessed sporadic accusations of cannibalism, but only a few authors
really believe them. In recent studies, as far as we know, only
Serboianu was convinced that Gypsies are indeed cannibals. Block,
who referred to the same trial, dismissed the allegations as a fable.[37]

Child-stealing is often mentioned in one and the same breath
with the allegation of cannibalism. The idea proves to be tenacious,
for even in *Oosthoek*'s 1940 encyclopaedia (Z-885) the following is
found: 'Accusations of child-stealing and even (mutual) cannibalism repeatedly lead to persecution in the 19th and 20th century;
however, these accusations were *seldom* substantiated' (emphasis
added). This standard phrase changes only in later editions, after
the Second World War, and then it becomes: 'The child-stealing
allegations continually proved to be mere insinuations.' It is remarkable that Grellmann, who usually opted for the most negative
interpretation, rejected the allegations of both child-stealing and
cannibalism. Influenced by the ideas of the Enlightenment, he considered these allegations as signs of superstition and irrational thinking.[38] The opinions of Borrow and Serboianu are directly opposed
to this.[39] The former claimed that Gypsies stole children in order
to sell them, and Serboianu thought that these children were muti-
lated in order to turn them into beggars. Block's view of the matter differed completely. According to this author, Gypsies stole white
children because of a 'Selbsterhaltungstrieb der Zigeuner als Rasse.'[40]
In this way, degeneration of the Gypsy race would be prevented.

The marital traditions of the Gypsies have also generated the
wildest speculations. To many, the abduction of the bride, the in-
cestuous conduct and unchristian marriage rituals which are attri-

buted to the Gypsies are a thorn in the side. It would definitely be interesting to find out when accusations of incest started to be projected on Gypsy societies and what arguments were used, for the imagination of many a scholar has been richly stimulated by this subject.

We will not go into the Indian origins of Romany, the generic term for all Gypsy dialects. This consideration is not important to the image of Gypsy. What we wish to consider summarily is a claim which is first made in the 1938 *Winkler Prins* encyclopaedia that, besides their colloquial language, the Gypsies had developed a sign language which they used while on the road in order to inform the groups following them about the best route, the behaviour of the police, the well-being of the inhabitants, and so on. As far as we know, Avé-Lallemant was the first to note the supposed influence of the Gypsy language on secret sign languages.[41] In his influential work about the German criminal, the Gypsies are equated to thieves without the slightest mitigating nuance. Because of this, the author thought that there was a connection between the German word for scoundrel *(Gauner)* and the word *Zigeuner* (Gypsy). The latter term is supposedly a collocation of *Zieh* (roam or wander) and *Gauner.*[42] In the second half of the century the secret sign language of the Gypsies became an increasingly popular theme, particularly in German criminology. Liebich went into great detail on the subject, and the authoritative criminologist Lombroso, who maintained a very negative view of the Gypsies in his works, also referred to their secret sign language.[43] Later, the work of these authors on the subject was worked out in great detail by Gross.[44] According to him, the Gypsies used the signs mainly to facilitate their criminal activities such as theft, murder and so on. This negative interpretation did not diminish until long after the Second World War.

RELIGION

From the eighteenth century up to today, encyclopaedias have insisted that Gypsies are not religious, at least not in the true sense of the word. They might appear to follow the way of Christ in Christian countries, and to be Mohammedans in Islamic countries, but according to the editors, they do this only for opportunistic reasons, such as gaining access to a particular country. In addition, it is noted that they never bother about religious concepts, religious education or customs,[45] except for – and no encyclopaedia fails to emphasize this – their alleged custom of having a newborn child baptized as often as possible in order to get a fair number of gifts from the various godparents. Taking into account the negative view of the Gypsies, it is not surprising that baptism for money and presents has always been interpreted as proof of begging and fraud. Besides the question of how widespread this custom actually was, a critical remark is especially justified here, particularly because this so-called custom is often mentioned in order to illustrate how undesirable Gypsies were in earlier times (as well as today). We can find a good example of such a negative interpretation in van Kappen's dissertation on the early history of Gypsies in the Netherlands.[46] The author is convinced that Gypsies had their children baptized mainly for the sake of the presents from the godparents. He bases his conclusion on the decisions of various synods of the Dutch Reformed Church at the beginning of the seventeenth century. These synods imposed injunctions which were not against baptizing Gypsy children, but against petitions for godfathers and godmothers. Van Kappen sees this as proof that multiple baptisms did occur and that society found this objectionable. At the same time, he shows that such injunctions did not prevent the rural population from giving the Gypsies money after a baptism ceremony.[47] If we also take into account that the injunctions against godparenthood were circumvented, one can conclude just as easily that the Gypsies were not as unwanted as was supposed earlier, particularly where the rural population was concerned.

Around the middle of the nineteenth century, opinions concerning the Gypsies' official beliefs changed in scholarly writings; they might have been religious in only a superficial way, but it could not be denied that they had religious feelings. Kogalnitchan was the first who presented us with this idea.[48] Later, the same idea was worked out in much greater detail by Liebich, Schwicker and Wlislocki (1891). Wlislocki in particular examined all kinds of creation myths, fairy tales, superstitions, magic and such. In the twentieth century this theme has been elaborated upon in various ways.[49] Around the turn of the century the realization that Gypsy communities have certain religious ideas and customs slowly starts to penetrate the encyclopaedias. Nevertheless, the Christian encyclopaedias are always quick to note that the fundamental principles of the Gypsies are inspired by heathendom and atheism. The *Oosthoek* mentions that Gypsy customs concerning their oldest woman are indicative of ancient religious ideas. The fact that some foods are forbidden (horse flesh in particular), that there are declarations of impurity (of their midwives, among others) and that certain trees and animals are worshipped point towards the same conclusion. According to the *Oosthoek,* the Gypsies' ancestor worship originates from fear of the dead. It is not until 1976 that the *Grote Winkler Prins* reports that this type of worship has a central function in the religious experience of the Gypsies. During this century, the emphasis has been more and more on the alleged superstitious beliefs of the Gypsies.

PROFESSIONS

In many studies about Gypsies – and the same holds true for en-cyclopaedias – two contradictory views can be found on their voca-tional activities: because of their specialized professions, Gypsies have always played a unique role in the labour market, for instance as tinkers or sieve-makers; and, conversely, Gypsies are extremely workshy and hardly ever work. Most authors do not seem to be aware of this contradiction. Nevertheless, logically one of the views must be untenable. After all, it is impossible to master a manual profession to the finest detail without long-term training and instruction.

In the eighteenth century, people already seemed to be convinced that Gypsies preferred jobs which required little effort,[50] and above all no permanent residence (see the 1940 *Oosthoek*). In view of the prevailing impression of the Gypsy character, this interpreta-tion is hardly surprising. In addition, attempts have been made to categorize Gypsies according to group or tribe, on the basis of descent and according to their way of life. For example, *Nieuwenhuis'* 1844 encyclopaedia divides the so-called Kroon-Ciganen into four groups: Rudari, mainly goldwashers; Ursari, who are well known as bearleaders; Lingurari, who make wooden utensils (especially spoons); and Laïessie, who roam around without practising a real profession. This last group in particular is described in a negative fashion. In addition, the author distinguishes the Batrassi, slaves of the Bojars, Romanian landed gentry. The Gypsies have supposedly become sedentary and are active in all kinds of professions. Many passages indicate with little subtlety that even these Gypsies cannot escape the blemish of their heritage.

The element of fraud is brought in consistently in discussions of the horse trade. *De Chalmot* even suggests that this was an important cause of the government's negative attitude towards Gypsies. The way people perceived the role of Gypsies in horse trading provides a good illustration of the premise stated in the beginning of this section. The illegalities which pervaded this market must have been taken as a matter of course probably because inflating prices or trickery must have been part of horse trading and every dealer, Gypsy and non-Gypsy, must have operated in that way. Otherwise one cannot explain why, through the centuries, people continued to buy horses from Gypsies. However, no one bothers about this contradiction in scholarly literature until after the Second World War. Such inconsistencies easily found their way into the negative interpretation of the Gypsy lifestyle. The explanation of fraud in the horse-trading business usually pointed towards the backwardness of the farmers who were tricked again and again. In addition, it was claimed that the psychological qualities of the Gypsy played a decisive role. He supposedly sensed how a potential buyer was to be approached.[51]

Many other professions worthy of closer examination are mentioned in the encyclopaedias, but for the sake of brevity, these must be passed over. What does need to be mentioned is that almost every encyclopaedia reports that Gypsies visited markets and fairs yearly in order to perform as acrobats, magicians, dancers and musicians (once again, occupations which require highly developed skills), while the older women foretold the future by reading cards and palms. Particularly this chiromancy, predicting the future by reading the lines of a human hand, has always appealed to the imagination. The encyclopaedia of *Witsen Geysbeek* (1861) even claims that the old Gypsy women were not afraid to resort to murder in order to make their predictions come true.

ART

The only appreciation which the Gypsies have really gained has been in the area of art. However, this appraisal is often presented in the form of an indestructible stereotype: the Gypsy's fiery temperament combined with his musical virtuosity, expressing his unbridled existence. Up to the twentieth century, the folkloristic side of the Gypsies' means of expression has been highlighted. For instance, we read that Gypsy dancers were held in high regard in Russia. Indeed, there are even examples of distinguished gentlemen who asked such gifted Gypsy girls to marry them. The improvisational talent of the Hungarian and Balkan Gypsies, mostly on the violin, in particular has generated many exhaustive descriptions. For instance, the *Algemene Muziek Encyclopedie* of 1963 (and 1984) relates the anecdote of Bihari, a Gypsy violinist, who was praised highly by Liszt in 1821 for his virtuosity. This violinist had a servant carry his violin in front of him on a satin pillow; the most beautiful moment of his life occurred when he moved Queen Elisabeth of Hungary to tears with his playing.

In the 1930s, when music encyclopaedias begin to focus on the characteristics of Gypsy music, it starts to be emphasized that the Gypsy, rather than being creative, often copies and reproduces, which although particularly noticeable in his music extends to other activities as well. The explanation goes as follows: Gypsies in central or northwest Europe have been displaying their arts and crafts at fairs since the fifteenth century, capturing the citizenry's interest in music, dance and magic. They partially took over the role of wandering acrobats and jugglers, and gave the ancient profession of the musician a new unprecedented exotic flavour by singing in a strange language with grace-notes, trills and timbres which are undeniably Asian. This view also argues that the musicians preferred to concentrate on and adapt to local melodies and rhythms for commercial reasons. That is why Gypsy music is seen more as a specific way of performing, a style of singing and playing that already exists among the local population, rather than as an indigenous music which belongs to the tradition brought along by the travelling musicians themselves. Indeed, this is the way they entered European history, as itinerant musicians, socially abused, but much admired as musical craftsmen (*Grote Winkler Prins*, 1979, Part XX). On the one hand then, there is a laudatory emphasis on the fact that all Gypsy music has an expressive vitality in common, and that Gypsies saw to it that the Spanish flamenco was handed down. On the other hand, it is claimed again and again, particularly during the past few decades, that they do not possess an original musical culture.

A similar development can be observed in ideas about the literary traditions of Gypsies. In 1906, *Vivat's* illustrated encyclopaedia managed only to report that there were poets among the Gypsies, and with that we have the first encyclopaedia to mention this aspect.

One of the first students in Gypsy studies who examined Gypsy fairy tales and songs was the Austrian linguist Miklosich (1875). After him, Schwicker praised the poetry and the narrative skills of Gypsies, deviating for the first time from his shining example, Liebich, who found their poetry 'dürftig und armselig'.[52] Wlislocki must also be named as a great animator and popularizer in this branch of studies.[53] This author, who was more blinded than enlightened by his observations (only partly through participation), left the beaten track at this point and collected many folk-tales, songs, poems and fairy tales from Gypsies.[54]

In 1923, the *Oosthoek* encyclopaedia, which apparently had learned little and was badly informed on contemporary literature, wrote that Gypsies did not have a literary tradition. In the second edition in 1932 an addition was made: '... except for fairy tales and stories which display little that is special'. And suddenly, in the fourth edition in 1953, the Gypsies are seen as musical, cheerful, lively people, with a talent for reciting arts, crafts and languages. Moreover, they have a treasury of Eastern fairy tales and songs which is of utmost importance. The role of Gypsies as storytellers with a repertoire of hundreds of legends and other folk-tales also comes into focus in the 1970s. The 1979 *Grote Winkler Prins* is even the first to devote a long section to the popular literature of Gypsies. However, the Gypsy's originality is denied again. There is talk of imitation and a mixture of motifs and subjects of foreign origins without Indian traces, which are adapted to become completely gypsy-like. Texts of the Gypsies retain, as it were, the sediment of the cultures which they have encountered during their travels. Essentially, this attempt at appreciation proves to be yet another negative interpretation, because little justice is done to the merits of Gypsy culture.

CONCLUSIONS

The question as to the source of the representation of Gypsies in (Dutch) encyclopaedias, which we raised in the introduction, can be answered very simply. The knowledge upon which this representation is based is taken straight from the scholarly works which existed at the time. Whatever is presented in these works is adopted without criticism from the original source. Grellmann's work in particular has had a pivotal function. This does not apply to the first two encyclopaedias, one by Luïscius (1724–34) and one by Hübner (1748), whose fairly short entries were based upon sixteenth- and seventeenth-century chronicles. After De Chalmot (1789), who based his entry of 16 columns entirely on Grellmann, the tone is set for a long time.

It was Grellmann who believed he had demonstrated that Gypsies were an untrustworthy, childish people, who could only reach a degree of higher civilization through careful guidance. The rationalizations which he presented in his work began to lead a life of their own as stereotypes, and were soon used to justify attacks by society which were launched on several fronts. Later works, in which Grellmann's prejudices were continued, produced practically the same images. Even those who wished the Gypsies well, who thought they could rid themselves of their prejudices by travelling and living with them like Wlislocki and Block, did not manage to escape the impressions which had been handed down. At times, people went even further and interpreted an initially positive impression in a negative way at the last moment. We can see this mechanism in operation very clearly in the representation of the musical talents of Gypsies. Although they are praised for the virtuosity of their performances, particularly in the nineteenth century, once musicology, and subsequently the encyclopaedias, took a critical look at their repertoire, it was soon 'demonstrated' that their music totally lacked originality, and that its nature was reproductive rather than creative. The same supposedly went for their oral tradition, whose imitative character was continually emphasized. Leaving aside the question of whether 'imitation' and 'originality' are valid concepts in this context, as they quickly lead to the argument of the chicken and the egg, it must be noted that other performing arts and folk-tales never have to answer to such requirements.

Encyclopaedias are generally distinguished from scholarly works by the outdated concepts and representations which continue to appear in them. Editors are slow in accepting recent studies, particularly those which deviate from the norm, such as the social-scientific research from about 1960 onwards which concentrates on the marginal and minority position of Gypsies.[55] An extreme example is found in the Christian (1929, 1961, 1977) and Catholic (1955, 1983) encyclopaedias in the Netherlands. These hold tenaciously to the work that the Dutch political leader Abraham Kuyper wrote around the turn of the century and in which he was exceptionally negative about Gypsies, Jews and 'the Asian danger'. The encyclopaedia *Thieme* from 1984 proves that outdated views are not limited to encyclopaedias with a religious character. *Thieme* presents a number of backward ideas about Gypsies which we do not find in the recent editions of encyclopaedias such as *Oosthoek*, *Spectrum* and the *Winkler Prins*. These encyclopaedias emphasize, at least from the 1960s onward, the Gypsies' position as a discriminated minority through the ages.

Part II
Stigmatization and
Government Policies

4 Eternal Vagrants? State Formation, Migration and Travelling Groups in Western Europe, 1350–1914[1]

Leo Lucassen

INTRODUCTION

In this chapter we will try to give an explanation why European societies, especially the authorities, pursued such a repressive policy towards travelling groups, whom they labelled as 'Gypsies' or 'vagrants' from the Middle Ages onwards, and how the stigmatization of these groups has been fixed. The assumption that the attitude of the authorities and the state towards migration in general and itinerant groups in particular is pivotal in explaining the co-existence of a strong and ongoing stigmatization of these groups as social misfits and their simultaneous functional economic role is not enough. State formation alone does not do the trick. In order to avoid a circular argument and in order to gain a clear insight into the interaction between the authorities and travelling groups, we also have to consider the function of migration for the labour market. The main reason for this is that the nucleus of the accusation is economic: the travellers were working under the cloak of begging and stealing or refusing to work. If we want to understand the stigmatization, we therefore have to link the ideas on travelling groups to the structural economic developments from the Middle Ages onwards.

CHANGING CONCEPTIONS OF VAGRANCY AND LABOUR MIGRATION, 1350–1550

According to Bronislaw Geremek, who wrote a number of fundamental and influential studies on the changing attitude in Europe towards the poor in general and 'vagrants' in particular, the stigmatization of travelling groups has its origin in the fourteenth century. Vagrancy had a negative connotation and referred to undesired wandering behaviour, and soon it was considered a crime in itself.[2] The negative stereotyping started in the 1340s and culminated at the beginning of the sixteenth century in popular books such as *Das Narrenschiff* (1494) and the *Liber Vagatorum* (about 1510) and publications on the secret language of rogues.[3] In these works vagabonds and beggars were depicted as professional thieves, robbers and cheats. This image strongly influenced public opinion and was supported by state and church alike. The result was that people without a fixed abode and labelled as beggars or vagabonds were increasingly stigmatized as lazy and crime-prone.

The explanation for this stigmatization offered in the literature is mainly economic, namely the change from a feudal to a market-oriented capitalist system – in other words, from bound to free labour. It is further stressed that due to the dramatic plagues in the fourteenth century that almost halved Western Europe's population, a serious labour shortage came about leading to rising wages and a short 'golden age' for workers. For many of them it could be profitable to leave their master and try to get another job with a higher wage. Employers, together with the authorities, tried to prevent this by enlisting as many workers as possible. People who preferred to make their living in another way, for example as self-employed itinerants, were increasingly viewed with suspicious eyes and stigmatized as vagabonds. One of the measures taken to bind labour to capital and fix wages was the Statute of Labourers issued in England in 1351 (a similar Act was passed two years later in France).[4]

The result of these structural ideological and economic changes was the emergence of a repressive policy towards people looked upon as vagrants and an attempt to control labour migration. Migration was only admitted within institutionalized frameworks: pilgrims, emigrants, *compagnonnage*, colonists, seasonal labourers and others. People who travelled without such an 'alibi' took the risk of being stigmatized as vagrants, *gens sans aveu* or masterless men and treated as such. This accounted especially for travelling groups, because being on the move with one's family without an apparent aim to settle again symbolized the pre-eminently unwanted lifestyle. The appearance of the first 'Egyptians' travelling in family groups in Western Europe (1419) fits well in this categorization. As they claimed to be pilgrims from Little Egypt, they were tolerated and sometimes supported. When doubts about their pilgrim status arose (and they were suspected of being spies for the Turks), they were soon stigmatized. Their supposed behaviour became a symbol of the lazy and criminal vagrant and a very repressive policy towards this category came about from 1500 onwards.

The extent to which the general vagrant policy could be executed depended on the power and organization of the states and on the interpretation at the local level of who was to be considered a vagrant. We do not agree with Vexliard and Geremek that this category consisted mainly of people without ties with 'normal' society and who had retreated from it.[5] This image, close to that of the present homeless, ignores their ongoing economic functioning (also after stigmatization) and further suggests that it was to a large extent an objective category. When we take a closer look at government policy, however, we see that the label was quite flexible and could be applied to all sorts of mobile people, including seasonal labourers and self-employed pedlars.[6] More or less the same holds true for the label 'Gypsy'.

THE RISE OF COMMERCIAL CAPITALISM AND THE SLOW SHIFT TO DIRECT RULE: 1550–1815

The 'long sixteenth century' was a period of economic expansion in Western Europe, which led to the concentration and commercialization of the agricultural and trading sectors. The labour shortage disappeared due to population growth and wages became relatively stable.[7] We would therefore expect that the stigmatization of labour migration, so prominent in the former period, would wane because it had lost its functionality. In general terms, this is indeed what seems to have happened. The expanding economies needed seasonal labour and peddling middlemen, and repressing them would not have been very wise from an economic point of view. As we know from the economic history of Western Europe there are important regional differences. The best examples that are in tune with our expectations are the sea provinces of the Dutch Republic, where a capital-intensive economy developed that depended on migrant labour from low capital regions in the eastern part of the Republic and in the western part of Germany.[8]

In England, where commercial capitalism spread its wings almost a century later than in the Dutch Republic, we see a marked difference, however. The commercialization and the emergence of capitalist farmers, who increasingly replaced the small peasants, led to considerable proletarianization. Moreover, the early development of the English state was characterized by a much higher degree of integration of local and central authorities than the loosely connected provinces of the federal Dutch Republic. The combination of these economic and political forces gave way to another outcome in England. The state felt threatened by the growing numbers of landless and sometimes masterless men, associated them with being uprooted and disorderly,[9] and tried to control their movements and bind them to capital, using a sandwich formula of vagrant and poor laws both aimed at curbing migration. The period 1560–1640 can therefore aptly be characterized as the 'peak of state activity against vagabonds'.[10]

A third type of relationship between economic and political developments is provided by France and Germany west of the Elbe. Here we see a combination of low capital and high coercion, to borrow Tilly's analytical tools. The countryside maintained its fragmented character, with the mass of the peasants (in contrast to the commercial farmers in the northwest) bound to their land. The population growth, however, led to smaller parcels of land, forcing many to combine their framework with activities that in many cases stimulated migration. One of the possibilities enabling the retention of (some) land and making a living was seasonal labour. Others, mostly young people without land, often became servants. To what extent this process of (partial) proletarianization produced a structural vagrancy problem, as Hufton and Lis and Soly argue,[11] is not clear, but what is more important, the extensive forms of local and circular migration[12] did worry the authorities at the local and regional level. Their fear was not altogether irrational. Poor vagrants could cause financial and security problems in this age of religious wars, of which the Thirty Years War is an outstanding example producing large groups of plundering and marauding mercenary soldiers. This does not mean, however, that migration was curbed.[13]

The preliminary conclusion of this still very rough typology would then be that, although the economic circumstances that produced the stigmatization of migrant labour in the fourteenth and fifteenth centuries changed fundamentally with the economic expansion from about 1450 onwards, the interplay between capital and coercion in the process of state formation makes it understandable why, with the Dutch Republic as an exception, migration kept worrying the authorities.

So far we have looked at the general attitude towards labour migration. Let us direct our attention now at the main topic of this chapter: travelling groups and the fear of vagrancy. At a first glance travelling groups do not fit the vagrancy pattern, because the changing negative attitude towards beggars and vagrants since the fifteenth century was a general Western European phenomenon. The main explanation for this is the major change in the organization of poor relief.[14] The initiative was taken by urban authorities who took over the coordination of poor relief from the various private and religious bodies. This not only led to a more rational and bureaucratic distribution of alms, but also to the exclusion of alien beggars, whose stay in cities was formally forbidden from the sixteenth century onwards. This by no means implies that their entrance could be stopped. It was difficult to distinguish them from indigenous beggars, whereas many citizens tolerated their stay and thus frustrated the official policy.[15] Furthermore this transition took place very gradually.[16]

Nevertheless, as time moved on, the attempts of the cities (and later also villages) to restrict poor relief to their own people made life more difficult for people who could not prove that they belonged in a certain place, and stimulated a kind of local aliens policy *avant la lettre*. One of the aims of the reorganization of poor relief was to establish better regulation and control of the labour reserves. As the demand for labour fluctuated strongly, it was important for employers to offer relief during bad times.[17] In Germany the main pillar of the exclusion policy of alien (alleged) poor was the *Heimat* principle. Every city or village was given the right to send back aliens to the place where they were supposed to have some sort of citizenship, mostly the place of their birth. In many cases travelling people could not assert their rights and thus a class of wandering and illegal (to use the modern term) people was created.[18]

It does not come as a surprise that quite soon after the reorganization of the poor relief acts and regulations aimed at repressing these vagrants commenced, whereby the category was much more broadly defined and equated with criminals. The intention, however, to ban poor aliens from the cities was not put into practice in general. Beggary persisted as a widespread phenomenon and the centralization of poor relief remained a utopia. The implementation of this legislation, which from the seventeenth century onwards was enacted at state level in Germany (and not by the

Reich), therefore proved to be quite difficult, not only because these weak states had to rely on local authorities and the cooperation of their citizens, but also because the distinction between the 'good' and the 'bad' was not as simple as the acts assumed. The group of itinerant people was very heterogeneous. To start with there were a number of migrants who had an alibi (in the sense of Geremek) against stigmatization, such as seasonal labourers, well-off pedlars and showmen and apprentices who served as a flexible working force.[19] Their mobility was more or less controlled and accepted. This was less the case for all kinds of itinerants who performed a variety of services, such as the catching of mice and rats, the mending of kettles, playing music and peddling. In general their socio-economic functions were also indispensable for the premodern society. Many authorities nevertheless considered itinerants' mobility a problem, because they were on the whole poorer and therefore suspected of begging and stealing. A third category consisted of people denounced, rightfully or not, as beggars and vagrants, who were often equated with the Egyptians. This category was regarded as the most dangerous and the legislation in Western Europe was mainly aimed at repressing their mobility. Being the *ultimate alien*, Gypsies were the symbol for the unwanted itinerant. Their way of living, travelling with their families, seemed to indicate a permanent wandering, and being seen as aliens they could not just be sent back to their places of birth, so the legislation simply forbade their stay in the country and aimed at expelling them. Although these 'Egyptians' were pictured in ethnic terms (having a dark complexion, wearing a distinct costume), the edicts made clear that it was primarily their way of life that formed the core of the accusation, very similar to the accusations levelled against vagrants. Soon their category was therefore enlarged to include all kinds of other travellers: vagrants and people with certain itinerant professions, especially entertainers and pedlars. The edicts also warned against so-called counterfeits, people disguised as Egyptians. It may not be altogether clear whether this new label ('counterfayte Egyptians') was created to hang on the native-born offspring of the original immigrants. As was the case in England, it is probable that this extension was also aimed at indigenous travellers who joined or imitated them.[20]

There are indications that, at least partly as a consequence of this stigmatization, Gypsies and others indeed became engaged in organized crime in the course of the seventeenth century.[21] This process is not only discernible for Gypsies, but also for some of the itinerant Jews who migrated in the seventeenth and eighteenth centuries from Poland to Western Europe, in the so-called *smousen*. Although the economic transformation in the sixteenth century did produce a growing mass of poor and wandering people and possibly led to more criminality, the stigmatization cannot be explained mainly by objective factors. Bandits and professional criminals, so prominent in the negative stereotyping, only formed a small part of what was called the vagrant class. The idea, essential to nineteenth-century rogue literature, that the social problems of the early modern period can be explained by pointing to the vagrants has been rejected by recent research.[22] The emergence of stigmatized categories (vagrants, Egyptians) and discriminatory regulations aimed at them, however, and the (organized) criminality to which they gave rise, produced a self-fulfilling prophecy. By the increasing convergence of these labels with criminality, people and authorities alike saw their ideas confirmed by selective perception and thus this process reinforced the stigmatization.

Poor relief may have been the general propelling force behind the exclusion of the alien poor and most of the travelling groups, but it does not explain the differences between the repressive policies pursued in Western Europe. The best way to make this clear is to take a closer look at the persecution of Gypsies in the seventeenth and eighteenth centuries. In all Western European states their lifestyle was increasingly criminalized by the authorities in the course of the sixteenth century. The edicts forbade their stay in the country and threatened them with torture and death in the end. In the course of the seventeenth century, and especially during the first decades of the eighteenth, a radicalization of the legislation towards Gypsies and other vagrants took place, making their mere presence a crime that could result in the death penalty. However, the enforcement of these acts – all issued by the central authorities – was quite a different story. If we look at the map of Western Europe, it becomes clear that the 'gypsy hunts', which made it possible to kill Gypsies without any reason or trial, took place in a rather restricted area.

First of all we see that in Germany the centre of these hunts lay in the southern area, stretching from the Palatine (immediately west of the French Lorraine where hunts were also organized) through Baden, Württemberg and Bavaria to Thüringen and Saxony.[23] The traditional explanation for this geographical concentration relies on the political fragmentation of the area into many tiny states and separate juridical entities and, further, into the inaccessible terrain, full of hills and woods. Both would make it an attractive area for bandits, vagrants and Gypsies. Although plausible, these arguments do not convince. First of all we have to keep in mind that vagrancy and banditry were general phenomena in an age when the state was unable to maintain its monopoly on violence and were not restricted to certain areas. More important, however, are the insights that can be derived from the body of literature on the recruitment of the poor for the galleys and the army in general. In both cases it is clear that, especially in the second half of the seventeenth century, the demand for soldiers and rowers in the galleys could not be met. This was not only the result of the warmongering by Louis XIV between 1672 and 1714, but also because of an absolute and relative increase in the men under arms in Europe in the course of the seventeenth century, especially in the second half.[24] The increased demand for soldiers put a stress on recruitment and the responsible agents therefore turned to the poor and vagrant classes. Redlich has shown that after 1675 a number of German states, whose authorities increasingly took recruitment into their own hands, forced people whom they considered as unwanted to enlist. States such as Prussia, Brandenburg and Saxony ordered their districts to supply them with enough recruits, to be gathered by means of hunts on vagrants.[25]

It comes as no surprise that the number of regulations in Germany ordering local authorities to ban and round up vagrants and Gypsies reached an all-time high in the period after 1675.[26] At the same time we see another situation in the South. Here the demand for soldiers was less, but was substituted by the demand for rowers in the galleys of Venice, Genoa and Marseilles. Service in the galleys was already an alternative to the death penalty during the sixteenth century. In the middle of this century, however, it became difficult for these states to find enough volunteers and – just as in the Turkish navy – they therefore turned to slaves who were captured during raids on the Balkans.[27] A small proportion of these rowers were bought from prisons in Northern states, such as the Austro-Hungarian Empire, Bavaria, Württemberg and Baden.[28] Again we see a remarkable correspondence between the demand for slaves and the raids on vagrants: in both cases concentrated in the second half of the seventeenth century and ending quite abruptly – due to a change in naval techniques – around 1730.[29]

When we combine the modes of recruitment in the North and the South of Germany the 'outlaw corridor' in the middle becomes of interest, and the traditional explanation may be extended with a whole new theory. In short the hypothesis is as follows: due to the demand for soldiers and rowers the increasing round-up of 'unwanted elements' in Germany led to a concentration of 'vagrants' in the corridor between the Palatine and Saxony, which was too far from the Prussian-Brandenburg recruitment area as well as from the Mediterranean (in the latter case the transport costs were higher than the price per slave). The states in the corridor were therefore confronted with a double problem: they could not get rid of vagrants and moreover faced an immigration of those who wanted to evade enlistment in other areas of Germany. In some cases these hunted groups combined forces and by their criminal actions these bandits threatened the lives and goods of the inhabitants. The reaction of the authorities was to issue regulations which became more severe every year and ended up in draconian measures outlawing Gypsies and other vagrants. As a result, in a number of cases – for the corridor some 100 are documented[30] – people were killed without a trial.

The policy towards vagrants and Gypsies in France also seems to fit very well into the military recruitment hypothesis. The repressive policy in France started to get more severe around the middle of the seventeenth century, but most important was the royal decree of 1682 against the 'bohemians' which stated that all Gypsies and vagrants had to be rounded up and sent to the galleys. For the enactment of this decree the central government in this age of 'brokerage', as Tilly called it, had to rely on intermediary groups such as the nobility. According to Vaux de Foletier, many of them, however, were not inclined to help in any way and some of them even protected the 'bohemians', the reason being that most Gypsies were *not* criminal and fulfilled services that were wanted by this group, especially dancing (by women) and the making of music and the like.[31] Maybe the lack of cooperation on the local level was one of the reasons why only five years later the central government decided to establish the first fully centralized police force in Western Europe, the *marechaussée*, whose most important task it was to execute the policy towards vagrants and Gypsies. In the last years of the seventeenth century the *marechaussée* was mainly arresting people they considered to be vagrants and Gypsies. In contrast to Germany and the eastern provinces of the Dutch Republic this did not lead to 'gypsy hunts' (except in Lorraine in 1723).[32] Notwithstanding the local and regional autonomy, in contrast to Germany with its hundreds of autonomous areas, France as a whole was much more centralized. This explains why the state, symbolized by the *marechaussée* force, was able to round up the vagrants in the entire country and, with the possible exception of the newly conquered region Alsace-Lorraine in the periphery – which was only integrated into the French state from about 1780 onwards – outlawing and killing did not take place. What happened after capture, however, is not entirely clear. Although France also sent more than a thousand people to its galleys in the period 1680–1715, few of them were categorized as *bohesme* (Gypsy). The number of rounded up Gypsies, together with other vagrants, grew fast, however, between 1716 and 1748.[33]

The Dutch Republic, finally, to a certain extent resembled Germany. Here was also a region, consisting of the eastern provinces Gelderland and Overijssel, characterized by the outlawing of vagrants and Gypsies, where so-called gypsy-hunts were organized in the first decades of the eighteenth century. According to Egmond this process has to be interpreted as a reaction of the local, and later regional, authorities to the growing criminality of certain organized groups of Gypsies and people who had joined them, including former mercenaries. Furthermore, Egmond argues that there are strong indications that many of them had recently come from France and the German states.[34]

The persecution may by no means have been as massive and all-encompassing as some believe – not in the least because of the limited coercive means – but it marked an important break with the former period in the sense that the power of authorities in such different states as France, the German principalities and the eastern provinces of the Dutch Republic proved capable of organizing such a general repression. Further, this repression reinforced the existing stigma, because Gypsies and criminality were more firmly connected than ever before. This break in policy also fits well with the change of state formation in Western Europe from brokerage to nationalization. A decisive shift took place from the traditional private to the public domain. The growing power of the state was embodied in the emergence of a police apparatus and effective criminal procedures. The persecution of crime was gradually taken over by state institutions and the rights of privileged groups (guilds, nobility, etc.) were curtailed.[35] It can be considered as the first step in the change from indirect to direct rule, and from a reactive to the proactive policy that was firmly established in the nineteenth century.

How did the gradual change to direct rule together with the growing coercive power of the state influence the general attitude towards vagrants and people considered as poor migrants in general during the long eighteenth century we are dealing with here? To start with we see a remarkable difference between Great Britain and the other states. In the British Isles the policy can be described as a system of control. The *central* state may not have been as strong as in France or in the absolutist principalities of Germany, but Great Britain was the only state that was capable of implementing acts and regulations at the local level. For us the Settlement Act of 1662 and the old Poor Law (1601–1834) are of particular interest. According to Snell the Poor Law created 'miniature welfare states' and thus helped to reduce vagrancy and slow down migration by a system of relatively generous relief and the mobilization of the local poor for temporary labour.[36]

In France and the German states no such arrangements existed and the state resorted to *repression* instead of *control*, notwithstanding efforts to create a system of workhouses (which stand in the shadow of the systematic English approach), prisons and *dépôts*.[37] As we have already seen, the best example of the repression model can be found in France with the establishment of the *marechaussée*. In the eighteenth century this force was expanded and became the foremost state instrument in the offensive against the mobile poor. Schwartz has argued that due to the authorities' specialization in vagrants and their success in repressing banditry, people living in the countryside began putting their trust in them during the last decades of the eighteenth century, and people's conception of the state gradually changed. The purely parasitical image, especially embodied in the French state, had to give way to a certain extent to the image of the state as protector of property and guardian of peace.[38] The *marechaussée* were not only concerned with crime but with all kinds of disorderly behaviour and (in their eyes) suspect forms of migration. Although many officials recognized the functionality of migrant labour, this did not alter the view of the *marechaussée*.[39]

In the period of the greatest repression in France, the *marechaussée* therefore aimed in the first place at vagrants and Gypsies, but it is not totally unsurprising that in some cases they also arrested pedlars and seasonal labourers.[40] As in England and Germany the term vagrant was interpreted very widely as all persons suspected of crimes and misdemeanours when there was insufficient evidence to secure conviction by trial.[41] Although this policing seems to have been quite effective, at least in France, and contributed to safety in the countryside, by indiscriminately lumping together bandits with all kinds of migrant people the stigmatization of the mobile poor in general and travelling groups in particular was reinforced, and not only by the association with organized crime, but also by the growing gulf between the sedentary population and so-called vagrants.

In the other continental states the enforcement of this repression was mainly the responsibility of local and regional authorities whose means were very limited. Only gradually did the state enter the scene and take over. Notwithstanding the general absolutist rhetoric, the attempts of Western European states to monopolize the use of violence and establish a state police force were embryonic and only gained impetus at the end of the eighteenth century. It would not be until after the Napoleonic wars that German states (as well as the Netherlands) would take over the French gendarmerie system.[42]

MODERN STATE FORMATION IN AN AGE OF INDUSTRIALISM AND URBANIZATION, 1815–1914

From the end of the eighteenth century onwards internal migration in Western Europe increased. Proletarianization continued and due to the ongoing commercialization of the agricultural sector and the jerky character of industrialization jobs became less secure, leading to a growing mobility. In agriculture year-contracts were replaced by irregular demand,[43] and in industry much work was still seasonal (construction), whereas factory work was often temporary as well. This unstable feature of the labour market caused many labourers to move constantly from one place to another.[44]

In view of the traditional ideas on migration and mobility it is not surprising that this situation led to growing concerns among the authorities. Migration may have been the rule, as it had been in pre-industrial Europe, but the norm still was sedentarism. The fear of a great mass of rootless and wandering paupers was widespread. At the same time the fast urbanization that attracted many people from the countryside gave rise to similar ideas. This is well illustrated by the work of Chevalier on Paris and Stedman-Jones on London.[45] In both cities the ruling classes saw the poor immigrants as pathological nomads, who did not want to work and would live by theft and begging alone. The image of these new barbarians did not differ much from that of vagrants and they were often not differentiated by the central authorities.

Apart from political disturbances, fear of the mobile poor, especially those who were labelled as vagrants, seems to have been one of the major reasons for the professionalization of the police in Western Europe. This was especially the case in Great Britain. In other parts of the realm the motives were similar.[46] In discussions of the professionalization of the police in 1840–50 the repression of vagrancy was stressed and crime was mainly associated with migrants.[47] According to Steedman the County and Borrow Police Act 1856 was directly caused by the wish to repress vagrancy.[48] The most important means for the police was the Vagrancy Act of 1824, characterized as 'the most pernicious piece of legislation against Gypsies and travellers in the nineteenth century'.[49] The definition of vagrant had become so wide and the discretionary power of the police so big that all obnoxious behaviour could be labelled as such.[50] In practice, however, it was aimed in the first place against migrants. Although this policy was in some cases neutralized by the protective effects of other acts,[51] it made life for migrant labourers and travelling groups quite hard and frustrated their economic functioning. Nevertheless there is no proof that these groups were disproportionally responsible for theft in the countryside.

In France the professionalization of the police was not only linked to vagrancy, but first of all to the insecure political situation and the fear of revolution and disturbances of the public order.[52] After 1850, however, criminality also became a dominant theme and as in Great Britain the causes were primarily sought among the poor: unskilled, unemployed paupers and vagabonds, whose personal defects were thought to be responsible for their criminal behaviour. The vagabond was depicted as the prototype of the criminal, because of his alleged refusal to work and to accumulate possessions.[53] According to Wright the vagabond question was dealt with in an atmosphere of paranoia about criminality in general and in 1885 a law was passed that made it possible to transport backsliders, among whom were many vagrants, to the colonies. In this respect it is noteworthy that England was already pursuing this policy a century earlier by sending criminals, which it considered as cancerous tumours in the national body, to the Americas first and after the

war of independence to Australia. This supports the argument used
in previous paragraphs that the English state formation was way
ahead of developments on the continent. In Germany the situation, at least before the unification, was more complicated and differed from state to state. In general, however, Tilly's characterization
of nineteenth-century police policy as proactive seems to be confirmed by what we know on the professionalization of the police.
This preventive activity is especially well illustrated by the emergence of police journals, containing all kinds of descriptions of people
wanted, missing or expelled.[54] For each person comprehensive information was given, in some cases including the labels given to
them (Jew, Gypsy, vagrant). The proactive element was that the
status of people was fixed, so that other authorities could act upon
it in the future. For the persons concerned it became more difficult to get rid of the label once it was attached to them. After the
Napoleonic wars these incidental warrants were slowly replaced by
police journals that appeared on a regular basis.

Much attention in these journals was paid to the *gemeinschädliche
Umhertreiber* (harmful tramps). Although most of them did not commit (serious) crimes, the police tried to establish constant supervision and control by spreading detailed information about them among
the local police forces. As Lüdtke has observed, the tenor of executive
police conduct was directly influenced by the increase in population and migratory movements.[55]

The dissolution of the guilds and the breaking up of the patriar-
chal relations in agriculture forced the state to take over control.
At the same time the national state began to define its citizens,
and the attention of the emerging gendarmerie forces on the
continent was primarily aimed at preventing alien vagrants from
entering the country and monitoring the indigenous migrant population.[56] This was not a straightforward process. For a long time
the state tried to delegate the control to the estates. The erosion
of the old order proved to be final, however, and once the state
took responsibility the process was irreversible.

The ongoing stigmatization in the nineteenth century cannot be
fully explained by pointing to the process of state formation and
economic change alone. Again we have to take poor relief into
consideration. From the end of the eighteenth century the state
became more involved in this locally organized system. One of the

consequences of the centralization that took place in all countries of Western Europe, but especially in the Netherlands and Germany, was that it became clear that the state was responsible for all its citizens and therefore also for its poor. In Prussia – and in other states as well – we see a similar development. This safety net was especially meant for people without a fixed place to stay, a category that only increased after 1820 because of the successful restrictive policy of municipalities with regard to the granting of citizenship to newcomers.

Because of this increasing involvement of the state in the distribution of poor relief, it was forced to define who was a Prussian citizen and who was not. As Brubaker argues, this was speeded up by the codification of the citizenship in 1842 and the economic liberalization (*Freizügigkeit*), which made the question of nationality suddenly acute.[57] Conflicts about responsibility for the poor were no longer fought out among municipalities, but between states. As Germany was divided into some 39 states before 1870 this could easily have led to a growing consciousness of foreigners.

In other countries the concern for the poor wandering foreigners, or people regarded as such (as was the case with 'Gypsies'), also played a pivotal role in the completion of aliens acts. Dutch representatives, for example, spent the lion's share of their debate on the (very liberal) Aliens Act of 1849 on the category of the 'destitute alien', personalized among others by the Gypsies. Together with the politically dangerous aliens they were the only ones whose entrance into the kingdom had to be prevented.

In the period until 1914, when there was no coherent aliens policy, it was mainly the 'destitute aliens', and from 1868 onward Gypsies, who were the objects of policy. In France travelling groups also served as a test case for the general legislation towards aliens. With the act on *nomades* of 1912 the French government for the first time made obligatory a separate identity card for people (indigenous as well as aliens) who travelled with their families and had no fixed abode. This *carnet anthropométrique* not only mentioned their civil state and profession, but also details about their physical appearance, fingerprints and two photographs. Although the act was not aimed at aliens in particular, it was this category that the promoters of the law had in mind. It took only five years before this card was made obligatory for all aliens.[58]

The consequences of growing state interference on the stigmatization of itinerants and travelling groups were far-reaching. This can well be illustrated by the growing concern about criminality in Western Europe. In the nineteenth century for the first time crime statistics were made, showing an alarming increase in crime rates. For contemporaries this was due to the socio-economic changes mentioned above. In fact the increase was not so much in crime itself as in the improved registration of crimes and in the extension of the criminal law into hitherto untrodden areas (prostitution, drunkenness, poaching, etc.), as we saw with the Vagrancy Act of 1822. According to Gatrell the problematizing of crime from 1780 onwards illustrates mainly public fear about the changes and disorder caused by urbanization, democratization and the industrial revolution.[59] For migrants and travelling groups the changing ideas about foreigners and criminality hardened their stigma, illustrated by the emergence of a specialized policy towards Gypsies, but also by the more general attitude towards alien (im)migrants such as the Irish navvies in England[60] and foreign pedlars in Belgium and France,[61] to mention some examples.

This tendency was reinforced by the specialization within police forces that took place in the last decades of the nineteenth century. In the wake of the general bureaucratization that accompanied state formation in Western Europe, special branches were established for the surveillance of 'social problems' such as prostitution, aliens, vagrants and in some countries Gypsies. Strongly influenced by the general negative ideas about travelling groups, the sections that occupied themselves with these categories could to some extent gain autonomy and the power to define the problem according to their own perception and interest, if only to justify their existence. In the late nineteenth and beginning of the twentieth centuries the two main driving objectives of the policy towards travelling groups were sedentarism and regular work, and – in the case of foreigners – expulsion. The result of this development is that the demarcation line between nationals and foreigners on the one hand and normal and antisocial citizens on the other was more and more stressed.

CONCLUSION

In this chapter we have tried to deal with a paradox: how to explain the repressive policy towards travelling groups from the fourteenth century onwards when we know at the same time that these groups fulfilled a useful and necessary function. How is it conceivable that states and their officials have been blind for such a long time? As a matter of fact, they were not – at least not totally. To start with, this historical overview has made clear that authorities constantly have made divisions within the migrant population between the 'good' and the 'bad', the 'honest' and the 'dishonest', or – in Geremek's words – between migrants with and without an alibi. Here we have only shifted the question, because it still does not explain why most of the time travelling groups have been depicted as bad. The traditional answer is that these groups, especially the so-called Gypsies among them, *were* parasites and that therefore we cannot speak of stigmatization or prejudices. As we argue in the third section of this book, however, generally speaking this image is false. The opposite explanation, along the lines of Lis and Soly, is not convincing either: interpreting the repressive policy as a way to discipline and control people who do not fit the ideal of the dominant classes and viewing the social problems (poverty, banditry, etc.) as social constructions serving as an excuse. Although this approach has valuable elements and is not to be rejected entirely, it does not help us much further, unless we are satisfied with conspiracy theories.

So far the matter has only become more complicated. If the explanation lies neither with the groups themselves nor with the dominant society, are we then stuck with one that is unsatisfactory and middle of the road? Not necessarily, we think, because in this chapter we have argued that the key to our problem has to be found in the development of the system of poor relief in Western Europe.[62] By restricting the poor relief from the fifteenth century onwards to the local poor and simultaneously refusing citizenship rights to poor immigrants, a category of 'vagrants' and Gypsies was created. This poor relief system was based on the restriction of the relief to local inhabitants, and the exclusion of aliens (in Germany known as the *Heimat* principle) had far-reaching effects for the stigmatization of travelling groups who (rightfully or not) were expected to be reduced to beggary. The final transition in the nineteenth century which linked poor relief to the place where one lived could no longer change a great deal for travelling groups. On the contrary, every municipality then ran the risk of becoming liable for their support, which made the authorities more than motivated to prevent their stay, let alone settlement. What makes the history of poor relief so relevant and interesting also in a wider context is that the same mechanisms can be detected which we see in the nineteenth-and twentieth-century aliens policy. In fact, the restriction of poor relief by the cities in the sixteenth century formed a prelude for the later aliens policy at a national level.

For an explanation of the ongoing stigmatization of travelling groups in the nineteenth and twentieth centuries, especially in Germany and France, poor relief has to be linked with the process of state formation. States became more and more dependent on migrant labour (to a lesser extent this accounts for the situation in Great Britain as well), but nevertheless pursued the most repressive of policies towards vagrants and Gypsies. Although we could argue that their policies were still influenced by the anti-migration tradition in the *ancien régime*, this alone is not convincing. We hope to have made clear that the process of modern state formation also played a role. The modern state, characterized by direct rule, has an interest in controlling migration and for general purposes (conscription, taxes, etc.) wants to know where its citizens are. Moreover, the growing fear of the criminality of the underclasses, especially when on the move, contributed to the wish to establish a permanent system of supervision. The foremost control apparatus to perform this task was the police.

This, however, was the general development in Western Europe. In order to understand the differences in repression we have to resort to a new typology that is linked to the *type* of state formation. Strong central states such as Germany and France created a centralized and specialized police force much earlier than the more decentralized states such as the Netherlands and Great Britain. The early professionalization and specialization of the police within the first type led to a reinforcement of the existing stigmatization of travelling groups. This cannot just be explained in a quantitative way by the increase in the number of policemen but also in the *specialization* of the police in types of crime or 'dangerous' groups: anarchists, antisocials, aliens, Gypsies and so on. These developments created a certain autonomous space for police forces and at the same time stimulated the labelling of potential criminals, who had to be watched carefully and if possible arrested.[63] The criminalizing effects have been felt by many groups, but in our case the examples of the vagrants and Gypsies, especially in Germany, are the most instructive. The power of definition and its consequences are far-reaching and were facilitated by new techniques used for tracing and recognizing people. This process of labelling, the fixing of stigmatizing labels such as vagrant or Gypsy to individuals by registering and supervision, is typical of the modern state. Whereas in the *ancien régime* the labelling was quite primitive, modern techniques combined with a proactive policy (registration, fingerprints, photographs) made it a lot more difficult for people to escape registration and stigmatization.

Finally, a last word on the psychological side of the stigmatization process that came about at the end of the Middle Ages. As we have seen the negative images were increased by a process of selective perception and self-fulfilling prophecy. Once the image and category of parasitic and workshy vagrants and travelling groups had been established, people were not only stigmatized as such, but those who fitted (or seemed to fit) this image contributed involuntarily to the hardening of the stigma. Examples of stealing and begging vagrants started to serve as fuel for the stigmatization-engine. However simple and well known this mechanism may be, its influence cannot be underestimated. The final stage in the fixing of the stigma is the self-fulfilling prophecy. People who were treated as riff-raff in some cases started to behave as such and developed their own subculture. Although we do not know a great deal about this process and many questions still remain to be answered (the selection for one thing), it is clear that this was not a linear process or a necessary result of the preceding steps, and the extent to which 'underworlds' did develop must not be exaggerated. No doubt it served as a justification for the stigmatizing policy. Perhaps the best example is the repression of Gypsies and banditry in the eighteenth century. There are hints that a number of these organized criminal bands had a vagrant background. More important, however, is the fact that the authorities associated these people with vagrants and travelling groups and viewed the emergence of these bands as a logical and inevitable outcome of a travelling way of life. Until late in the nineteenth century, when these bands had long become extinct, these associations remained alive.

5 'Harmful Tramps': Police Professionalization and Gypsies in Germany, 1700–1945[1]

Leo Lucassen

INTRODUCTION

During the last decade the historiography on Gypsies in Germany has reached a stage of maturity. Several studies have been published which give important insights into the way German authorities have dealt with people they categorized as *Zigeuner*. Despite this coming of age, there are three aspects which still demand further elaboration and deeper consideration. First of all, while some also cover the preceding Empire and Weimar era, most studies concentrate on the Nazi period (1933–45). For a full understanding of the anti-Gypsy policy of German authorities in the twentieth century, a much longer timespan should be covered. In particular, the decades preceding German unification, about which the information we have is only very scarce,[2] should be analysed much more thoroughly.

A second shortcoming in the German historiography is its failure to problematize the way travelling people have been categorized and labelled over time by the authorities, especially by the police. Instead, almost all authors start from the assumption that the people subsumed under this label form a homogeneous ethnic group. The labelling is thus supposed to conform to the self-definition of the people concerned. This assumption, however, does not hold water when put to the test. Not only in Germany, but also in the Netherlands, the definition of who was to be considered a Gypsy has shifted considerably over time, and at the same time it is not at all clear whether the people thus labelled shared a common ethnic identity.

A third and final weak spot is the isolated approach with which the Gypsy theme has been explored by German historians. In particular, the links with other fields, which are important to achieve

74

a satisfactory explanation for the discrimination against and persecution of Gypsies, are made only sporadically and not very systematically. As a result Gypsy studies have only rarely been incorporated into the more general German history.[3] This lack of integration is thrown into especially sharp relief in the recently booming field of police history.[4] The link with this specialization is relevant, because it was the police who were primarily responsible for labelling travelling people as Gypsies.

Although police historians have focused on the same periods as their colleagues in the Gypsy field,[5] we will not restrict ourselves just to the period from 1870 onwards, the reason being that there are many indications that the process of labelling by the police had already started in the eighteenth century. In this sense, this chapter will also deal with what we could perhaps call the 'proto-history' of the police in the period preceding the unification of Germany. There are some studies about the activities of the political police and the burgeoning labour movement (1848!),[6] but these pay little attention to the more day-to-day police practices involved in the surveillance of 'dangerous' or 'suspicious' persons.

Among the barely used sources which shed a tremendous amount of light on this matter are the numerous police journals (*Polizeiblätter*) which were issued in most German states. These journals, which began to be widespread about 1830, were preceded by more or less private publications in the form of printed warrants (*Steckbriefe*) compiled by highly placed policemen, who gained themselves a reputation as *Kriminalisten* (criminologists), people specialized in the fight with organized crime. Both sources contain numerous descriptions of persons who for various reasons were wanted by the police. The reasons vary from murder to not having the requisite licences to exercise itinerant professions, insulting civil servants or 'disorderly behaviour'. When these sources are analysed three things strike the eye. First of all, most people are harried because of their apparently aimless itinerant lifestyle, characterized as *Umherzieher*.[7] Secondly, in the course of the nineteenth century and especially after 1840, there was a growing tendency to label some of them Gypsies (*Zigeuner*). Finally, the very existence of warrants, police journals and criminologists from the eighteenth century draws our attention to the fact that even before the specialization of the police in Germany in the last decades of the nineteenth century, important developments had been taking place. In this respect we propose to broaden the concept of professionalization somewhat and not restrict it to the process of academization, which is the way it is mostly interpreted in the German literature,[8] but also to include those activities which were aimed at improving police methods.

This approach enables us to get a better insight into the proto-history of the police and at the same time to trace the tradition of Gypsy-labelling. More specifically, in this chapter we will try to discover whether there is a connection between the activities of the criminologists and the persecution and stigmatization of Gypsies and other travellers by the Nazis. This question is especially relevant, as there is a huge body of literature on this matter[9] which tends to overlook the long-enduring tradition of police behaviour, not only towards Gypsies, but also with respect to 'harmful tramps' in general. Finally, we will go into the question of to what extent the Gypsy identity was forged and stimulated by the long tradition of stigmatization and labelling in Germany.

THE ISSUING OF WARRANTS AND THE FIRST CRIMINOLOGISTS (1700–1830)

In the eighteenth century the police in the modern sense of the word were virtually non-existent. Only a few people were responsible for detecting criminals, the power of the state being curtailed by intermediary bodies such as the nobility, the church and cities.[10] This does not imply that criminals and bands of robbers were left in peace. Through the interrogation of suspects and the exchange of information with other civil servants, the attempts of local officials seem to have been more successful than is often assumed. An important method of laying a felon by his heels was the composition and distribution of warrants: lists of names, professions and descriptions of persons who were suspected of crimes, derived mostly from the interrogations of captured thiefs, burglars or vagrants.

The most remarkable aspect of these *Steckbriefe*, which differed enormously in quality, is the great number of petty thiefs and con-men, beggars and vagrants. A mere itinerant lifestyle could be sufficient to be deemed dangerous and to be considered a potential criminal. In Germany this broad category was labelled as *Gauner* (rogues) or *Vaganten* (vagrants) and in some cases as *Zigeuner*. Although there are several examples of high-quality lists containing warrants from the first half of the eighteenth century, after roughly 1750 the *Steckbriefe* became more elaborate, systematic and bulky. This is also the period in which a number of civil servants charged with police work tried to improve the tracing of criminals and pointedly stressed their identity as criminologists. The initiator was the Württembergian *Oberamtmann* Georg Jakob Schäffer, characterized by Bader as *Monomanen der Jaunerbekämpfung*,[11] who can be considered as the first criminologist. In the service of the Duke of Württemberg he was an outstanding example of the eighteenth century enlightened civil servant, who wanted to escape the geographical and social boundaries of the society of estates. Although in practice indirect rule still dominated the administration of European states, his aims were to create a unitary police system that would cross the borders of his own principality, and unite the efforts of judicial authorities in other South German and Swiss states as well.

Encouraged by his activities, the tracing of criminals by way of *Steckbriefe* and cooperation with colleagues in other states was greatly stimulated. Schäffer's meticulous descriptions and the wide distribution of his lists were examples followed by others. One of them was Franz Ludwig Schenk von Kastell, nicknamed 'Malefizschenk', who published the extensive *Oberdischinger Liste* in 1799. He made use of Schäffer's lists and produced some 1,487 descriptions of vagrants and beggars. Among other names which spring to mind is that of Friedrich August Roth from Baden who published an even longer list of 3,147 names a year later. The fourth dedicated criminologist was Friedrich Freiherr von Hundbiss-Waltrams, also from Baden. He maintained close contact with the other criminologists and in 1804 gave an account of his detective work in a modest but qualitatively good *Jauner* list.

The most important aspect of these lists was the professional cooperation between the compilers, which transcended the local or regional significance of previous *Steckbriefe*. All were influenced by the Enlightenment and the ideology of the central state, which was stimulated by the *Reichsdeputationshauptschluß* of 1803, when dozens of small states, especially in the southern part of Germany, disappeared. They tried to achieve a good insight into what they saw as the criminal underworld, with the ultimate aim of making its denizens useful citizens.

During the first decades of the nineteenth century the initiative started by the first criminologists was taken over by others who published their results in so-called *Actenmäßige Nachrichten*, written predominantly for (judicial) colleagues. As we mentioned earlier, the activities of the criminologists have to be seen in the light of the process of state formation which gained momentum during the Napoleonic period and which was superseded by a direct form of government.[12] A more rational and effective 'war on crime' fitted in nicely with this general development. Many criminologists also saw a direct relationship between the fight against criminality and a thorough reform of the system of government.[13]

It has to be said that the criminologists were ahead of their contemporaries. It would take quite some time before the German states realized the consequences of the new approach. Schäffer, for example, had great trouble financing the publication of his lists and others had to sell their *Actenmäßige Nachrichten* in order to pay the printing costs. Another hindrance was that, until the second half of the nineteenth century, there were virtually no police personnel to put the recommendations of the criminologists into practice.

THE CONSEQUENCES OF THE 'GYPSY LABELLING'

In what respect did this general development within the police force stimulate the labelling of travelling people such as Gypsies? The answer in a nutshell is – not very much. In most *Steckbriefe* or *Actenmäßige Nachrichten* Gypsies did not play an important, let alone dominant, role. Far more widely used were labels as *Gauner*, *Jauner* and *Umherzieher*, and in some cases 'Jewish bandits'. The only exception to this rule was Schäffer, whose reputation was to a certain extent established by his *Zigeunerliste* of 1787/8. The main motive was the trial against a Gypsy bandit, named Jakob Reinhardt, better known as Hannickel. This, however, stimulated the sensitivity towards Gypsies only temporarily, so that after 1800 the interest in this group quickly waned. The decline in the stigmatization of Gypsies was probably closely linked to the ideology of the Enlightenment and the efforts made in various German states to integrate them. An initial impulse can be found in Schäffer's 1788 list. He repeated this call in his last *Jaunerbeschreibung* published in 1813, one year before his death, in which he referred to the popular and widely read book on Gypsies by Grellmann.[14]

Between 1820 and 1840 in Württemberg and Prussia (Friedrichslohra) authorities did indeed establish 'colonies' for Gypsies and tried to allow them the opportunity to give up their itinerant way of life and settle down. Although for several reasons these efforts did not bear fruit, for the moment it seemed that the civilization offensive launched by enlightened authorities subdued somewhat the tendency to equate criminals or wandering people with Gypsies and therefore the category was not used as a generic term for all sorts of unwanted wandering people.

POLICE JOURNALS AND THE GROWING OBSESSION WITH 'GYPSIES' (1830–70)

The activities of the criminologists resulted in a more systematic description of wanted or 'dangerous' people. More cogently for our topic, attention shifted from bandits to a much broader category of people without a fixed abode, the so-called *gemeinschädliche Umhertreiber* (harmful tramps). The police journals, which appeared on a regular basis after 1820 and took over the function of the *Actenmäßige Nachrichten*, continued this trend.

The publication of the police journals in various German states was an important step in the professionalization of the police. Although initially it was a private initiative taken by police officers, the state took control after 1840 and turned these journals into official organs. The analysis of these journals shows that the police were in the first place interested in what they called 'harmful tramps'. Contrary to what might perhaps be assumed, this referred not so much to itinerant groups such as wandering beggars, musicians, conjurors, acrobats, tinkers, scissors-grinders and pedlars, but first and foremost to labourers, especially travelling journeymen. With other workers, servants and professions in what we nowadays call the service sector (waiters and hairdressers, for instance) they made up three-quarters of all descriptions.[15] This picture contradicts the widely held image (among both contemporaries and present-day historians) that people with itinerant professions formed the prototype of the *Gauner*.

Maybe even more important than the distribution of occupations are the reasons why these people were wanted by the police. First of all only 18 per cent was suspected of more or less serious offences (several thefts and serious fraud). Apart from these professionals many people were wanted for petty theft and the like. More than 50 per cent, however, were simply listed because of minor offences such as begging, vagrancy and having no clear identity. In themselves these conclusions are not sensational. Other scholars have noticed that in the nineteenth century the police were primarily concerned with the *classes dangereuses* and with what they called vagrants. Likewise, the fact that thefts were common at this time of widespread poverty is not new either.[16] Nevertheless, it is useful, indeed necessary, to stress these insights again, because many researchers allow themselves to be carried away by the contemporary one-sided stereotyping of the 'criminal vagrant class'. Another important point is that it is seldomly recognized that the police were very much preoccupied with checking identity and (closely connected) with the increasing control of migration. Both phenomena gained importance in the course of the nineteenth century in the wake of state formation which required increased monitoring of citizens. People without a clearly fixed abode and without – in the eyes of the police – sufficient means of support were easily criminalized as *Gauner* (villains).

In particular people without or in the possession of dubious passports or identity papers were thought highly suspect. From a criminologist point of view this is partly understandable, as many criminals of course wanted to conceal their real identity. But, pertinent though this is, it is not the only reason. One of the other reasons is linked with the legislation concerning the poor relief system. Most German states adhered to the principle that each citizen had the right to settle in a municipality or to return to it after a period of absence. This so-called *Heimatrecht* also accorded the right to some form of poor relief.[17] The municipal police therefore tried to run away strangers without a claim to their *Heimat*, which was only possible to establish when they could show *where* they belonged. As many itinerants were dependent on ambulant professions, and as these kinds of professions were (partly unjustly) held in low esteem and considered to be a cloak for begging, many of these itinerants often concealed their identity. In such cases the police restricted themselves to taking them to the neighbouring municipality instead of sending them 'home'. Even when the police knew where their *Heimat* was, they often did not have the power to force them to return there.

GYPSY LABELLING

In contrast to the rise of the criminologists some forty years earlier, the police journals did significantly affect the labelling of people as 'Gypsies'. This is immediately apparent if we take a look at one of the first official journals, the *Hannoversches Polizeiblatt*, issued by the royal government, which is representative of other journals.

Notwithstanding the often heard opinion that before the unification of Germany there were virtually no Gypsies in the region and that the policy towards this category only became relevant after 1870, a careful analysis of the hundreds of thousands of descriptions between 1846 and 1870 offers quite a different picture. Long before 1870 the term *Zigeuner* had become dominant and the police started to use it to label all sorts of itinerant families who at an earlier stage had been invisible as such. From the start, *Zigeuner* was used as an important category to classify wandering people. The second issue offered an extensive survey of the families Trollmann and Schwarz, who attracted attention because they were not Hanoverian citizens and were not equipped with the requisite permits to perform their itinerant professions. This description formed the prelude to a much longer article on Gypsies a year later.[18] The anonymous author claims that it was wrong to think that Gypsies had disappeared from Germany. They had only split up their large companies and tried to conceal their true nature and identity. Therefore, so he goes on, it was of the utmost importance that the police drew up genealogical trees in order to discover their real *Heimat* and thus force them to adopt a sedentary lifestyle. This advice was taken to heart, because in 1847 such pedigrees were published for the 'Gypsy' families Brase, Weiss, Trollmann and Tewitz, completed in the years 1851–3 by the families Hanstein, Steinbach, Bamberger, Wappler and Mettbach.[19]

The year 1857 marked an important step forward in the labelling process. Until then the Trollmanns, Steinbachs and others were scattered among other wanted people in the container category 'harmful tramps'. In that year the editors decided to create a separate 'Gypsy' heading. At a glance the reader of the journal could now see who the Gypsies were. The upshot was that the labelling was given greater priority and it became obvious to the readers (mainly lower-ranking policemen) that Gypsies were an important category that had to be closely watched.

Why were some people labelled and others not? Travelling with one's family and carrying out an itinerant trade was not enough to ensure that one was designated and treated as a Gypsy. The remarks in the *Hannoversches Polizeiblatt*, also by no means absent in other police journals, made it perfectly clear that policemen also had an, albeit vague, ethnic image of Gypsies. A dark skin colour ('a Gypsy colour'), for example, is regularly mentioned. When we take a look at all the people who were labelled Gypsies this feature is less obvious. There were also Gypsies with fair skins and, conversely, dark itinerants who were not labelled. Criminal behaviour associated with Gypsies, such as fraud and thefts, was not decisive either. Most Gypsies found their way onto the lists because their identity was vague or just because they followed a travelling way of life. So, although a particular ethnic Gypsy image certainly existed, in practice the application of it proved to be complicated. What is important is that a number of families was traced and their pedigrees researched, thus marking them as Gypsies, and that this information was widely disseminated among German police circles. As we shall see in the last section of this chapter, this growing genealogical database formed the basis for the persecution of Gypsies in the twentieth century.

Another reason to be sceptical of a purely ethnological explanation for the labelling of certain families as Gypsies can be linked to the causes for the sudden upsurge in the labelling process. Although at first glance this seems to be connected with the immigration of strange-looking families from both the Alsace and Eastern Europe, in most descriptions this in fact played no role. Far more important to the categorization was the wandering way of life, the lack of clarity about their *Heimat*, and last but not least the besetting fear gripping the local authorities that these people would lay claim to their poor relief. This, in itself, is not enough to explain why the police were ever more willing to apply the Gypsy label to mark such people. In order to understand the modification of the labelling around 1840, the factors mentioned should be supplemented by two other developments, as follows.

First of all, the work of Willems has unequivocally shown that it is important to realize that the very influential book of Grellmann on the Gypsies, which offered the first detailed ethnographic blueprint, laid the conceptual foundation for both the categorization and the idea that there was such a thing as a Gypsy race or people. The conceptual change can be considered to be a necessary, but by no means sufficient, condition for the stepping up of the labelling. Moreover, it was temporarily moderated by the ideology of the Enlightenment by which Grellmann was strongly influenced.[20]

After the failure of various Gypsy colonies in Germany, the (enlightened) optimism about the possibility of turning Gypsies into decent citizens was replaced by the conviction that the 'Gypsy race' was incorrigible and was afflicted by a hereditary inclination to wander, an idea that we also find in the various articles on Gypsies in the German police journals.

Equally important in the pursuit of categorization seems to have been the general institutional changes within the police force itself and in its organization. In particular, the growing preoccupation of the police with wandering people and the *proactive* policy of distributing descriptions through police journals triggered off the 'take-off' of the labelling from approximately 1840. Within the broad category of 'harmful tramps', these people with unclear family relations created a need for a separate label. Many descriptions refer to the inextricable relationships between Gypsies, deploring the many aliases and false identity papers they produced. Although it is not a simple matter to ascertain whether this phenomenon reared its head more frequently among 'Gypsies' than among others, a connection with an itinerant way of life is conceivable. As we mentioned earlier, many travellers had to use false papers to prevent being sent back to their *Heimat*. Were the authorities to notice this, they were arrested, but the unravelling of the family relationships took so much time that they were left alone, simply being expelled from the municipality. Our strong impression is that it was those people in particular who travelled with their families and who posed grave identification problems to the police who ran a fairly high risk of being labelled Gypsies.

A STRANGE INTERMEZZO (1870–90)

The administrative hunt for Gypsies in which the police journals took the lead was not unilinear in the sense that as time went by progressively more and more people were thus labelled. In the 1860s especially the interest in Gypsies waned somewhat. This can be linked with the developments within the German police. Here we see a whimsical growth of personnel and means. The work of Spencer and Jessen, for example, shows that the growth of the police force in the Prussian Ruhr area stagnated in the 1860s and, measured against the number of policemen per 1000 inhabitants, demonstrates several ups and downs. Only in the 1870s can a considerable and final increase be noticed.[21] At the same time, after the unification we see a paradoxical development. On the one hand the stigmatization by state authorities (through discriminating circulars) increased in most states,[22] while their definition was temporarily restricted to foreigners, a category which from then on meant people coming from outside the German empire. The growing interest in the 'Gypsy problem' by authorities other than the police and the equating of Gypsies with foreigners probably had its roots in the intense contemporary nationalistic fever and the strong feelings thus engendered about the rights attached to citizenship. The importance of the distinction between citizens and aliens, at the foundation of which lay the legislation on citizenship and the right to settle and receive poor relief in the 1860s, became more salient.

Above all, people who came from abroad who might conceivably be expected to become a burden were considered undesirable. From 1865 when small family groups of itinerant coppersmiths and bear leaders from Hungary and Bosnia appeared,[23] in next to no time the central authorities in various states had issued circulars to keep these 'Gypsies' out.[24] As these higher-ranking officials assumed that Gypsies were by definition foreigners, they thought these measures were sufficient to meet their purpose. This focus on foreigners adopted by the central authorities was not to last long, and by the early 1880s the indigenous definition which had been used in the police journals since 1840 was already proving too strong an undercurrent. We are especially well-informed about the southern states, where the rank-and-file police had great difficulties with the restriction of the Gypsy label to aliens.

Finally, the continuity in the labelling of indigenous travellers can be seen in the *Bayerisches Central-Polizei-Blatt*, which first appeared in Bavaria in 1866. Only a small proportion of the people labelled as Gypsies came from non-German states.[25] The others had German names and had been born in Germany or adjoining French regions. In contrast to the Netherlands, the term 'Gypsy' was not reserved for the new immigrant groups from Eastern Europe. It was predominantly the group of indigenous travellers who were increasingly confronted with this label. This development can be traced to the labelling practice pursued in the police journals and, after 1885, it would lead to a strong focus on Gypsies as an internal problem. Before we go deeper into that matter, let us first once more return to the more general developments in the police force.

SPECIALIZATION OF THE POLICE FORCE AND THE SETTING UP OF GYPSY REGISTRATION (1890–1918)

The last decade of the nineteenth century marked an important phase in the development of the German police. More policemen were recruited, but what is even more relevant is that they were better trained and the police forces became more specialized.[26] At the same time, as the German historian Ralph Jessen has shown in a recent article, especially between 1870 and the end of the nineteenth century, the Prussian police attracted more and more welfare tasks. As a result the power of the police to label all kinds of behaviour as deviant and undesirable increased. This full authority to act demonstrated itself, among other manifestations, in the social domain.[27] Alcohol consumption, unhygienic housing, suspect mobility and other 'social ills' were considered to be problems pertaining to the sphere of *Ordnung und Sittlichkeit*. The administrative definitional powers of the police were the result of the mounting intervention of the state which had been growing since the 1870s. Although the police definition also had all kinds of positive effects, this certainly was not always so. Especially when the behaviour of the lower classes was deemed dangerous or at least undesirable, the police were led by class prejudice and often resorted to repressive policies.[28]

This helps us to put the Gypsy policy that emerged at the end of the nineteenth century into context, for it remained entirely within the *Sicherheitspolizeiliche* domain, with the result that the definitional as well as the discretionary power of the police was scarcely subjected to any checks at all. Whereas after *c.* 1890 in many welfare areas the police grew more careful about offending citizens too much and therefore did not penalize every offence, the Gypsy policy went in the opposite direction. The police used every rule and regulation to make matters as difficult as possible for travelling groups, with all the criminalizing effects that were part and parcel of such a move.

The consequences of these general changes in the organization of the Gypsy policy can be best illustrated by the activities of the Munich police. In 1899 this force decided to create a *Zigeunerzentrale* (Gypsy information centre) with the aim of gathering as much data as possible on Gypsies (place and date of birth, professions, whereabouts, offences and so forth), so that the acts and regulations directed against them could be carried out more efficiently. The local authorities, including the gendarmerie, were ordered to forward all relevant data, preferably by telephone or telegraph.

Alfred Dillmann was appointed head of the Gypsy station, as it was soon to be called. For some time he had already been engaged in collecting data from Gypsy families in Bavaria.[29] In doing so, he made extensive use of the Bavarian police journal mentioned earlier. In 1905 he collected his data together in the *Zigeunerbuch* (Gypsy booklet), which contained some 3,350 names and 613 extensive descriptions of people whom he labelled Gypsies. This book (7,000 copies), which was meant for official use only, is especially interesting because the author explicitly addresses the question of definition. In the introduction he clearly states that he uses 'Gypsies' as a sociological category: everyone who travels around with his or her family, irrespective of ethnicity or nationality. Within this broad category he makes a distinction between 'Gypsies' (440 persons) and 'people who live like Gypsies' (173 persons). When we analyse the 613 descriptions,[30] we find that people whose personal details gave rise to some doubt had a bigger chance of being labelled as real Gypsies than others. In the tradition of the nineteenth-century police journals they were primarily associated with people who tried to hide their real identity by giving false information about their names, and place and time of birth. It is also striking that only a few foreign Gypsies are listed and that ethnographic features, such as skin colour or language, played a subordinate role.

These people drew the attention of the police predominantly because of minor offences which were closely linked to their travelling way of life, such as the very broadly defined concept of vagrancy, or offences which were the direct result of the policy of criminalizing Gypsies.[31] It was not so much criminality which caused concern, but the 'disorderly' way of life. The police viewed Gypsies as an annoying travesty of the legal system. This might explain the sometimes utterly unrealistic proposals for putting an end to the supposed danger that they would pose to public safety and order. In this respect, the plan of the policeman Franz Laufer in the

Polizeibeamtenblatt of 1912, for the creation of a special Gypsy police force in order to enable a constant surveillance system to be introduced, is noteworthy. It was around the same time that the Munich Gypsy station tried to expand its activities over the rest of Germany. Other states reacted reluctantly, especially Prussia, because of the costs it would involve. Further, there were disagreements about the definition of Gypsies. Many states opposed Dillmann's broad sociological definition, because they feared that all kinds of 'decent' itinerant traders and artisans would also be hurt. In the end, agreement was reached on the basis of Dillmann's ideas.[32]

An efficient mutual arrangement, however, still had a long way to go. After the First World War the Bavarian Gypsy station tried with renewed vigour to achieve its purpose and monopolize the gathering of data on Gypsies for the whole of Germany.

THE WEIMAR PERIOD (1918–33)

The Weimar period is of interest because it was at this time that the police tried to put into practice the distinction between 'Gypsies' and 'people living like Gypsies', the latter labelled as *Landfahrer* (travellers), and on the other hand honest itinerants. The former had to be treated with the utmost severity, using such tactics as refusing them permits to travel and perform itinerant trades, whereas the latter would be protected. This proved to be far from easy. The problem – and here we touch the very heart of the matter addressed in this chapter – was the result of the following assumptions:

(a) It is possible to distinguish 'real Gypsies' from others on the basis of racist and ethnological criteria.

(b) Gypsies are by definition parasites and their occupations serve as a cloak for begging, vagrancy and crime.

Not only were local authorities unable to see the difference between 'real' Gypsies and other caravan dwellers, but the art of being able to distinguish honest from dishonest itinerants was far from clear cut. Therefore most acts and regulations geared towards a differentiated policy for all itinerant groups failed.

The insuperable contradictions that characterized the *Bekämpfung*

des Zigeunerunwesens (the fight against the gypsy evil) can be best
illustrated by the preparation of the Bavarian act of 1926 against
Gypsies and the workshy. First of all, organizations of itinerant
pedlars and showmen,[33] who supported the act in itself and thereby
strengthened the assumptions mentioned above, complained about
its deleterious effects, for it appeared that notwithstanding the protection that the act offered to 'honest itinerants' by means of a
Schutzvermerk,[34] many of their members were lumped together with
other itinerants and subjected to the same severe surveillance and
controls. The problem was exacerbated as there were quite a few
such members who did not have a fixed abode and therefore were
unable to obtain a *Schutzvermerk*. The boundary between *Landfahrer*
and *Zigeuner* on the one hand and 'decent itinerants' on the other
was not an ethnic one. The decisive factor was the way of life.
Everyone with a fixed abode was excepted from the stipulations of
the 1926 act. Apparently it was assumed that Gypsies could never
meet these criteria.

In view of the foregoing, it is not surprising to discover that the
central police station in Munich was dissatisfied with the
Schutzvermerk policy. They thought that the authorities, both local
and regional, were far too tolerant and flippant, because they forgot
to contact the police first in order to verify if an itinerant appli-
cant was to be classified as a *Zigeuner* or *Landfahrer*. The 1926 Act
was meant to put an end to these abuses, as the Munich police
interpreted it. A distinction between Gypsies and other tramps and
honest itinerants was made, and what is more for the first time
Gypsies were defined in racial terms.

Apart from the 'racial Gypsies' the act referred to people who
lived like Gypsies, and who were by definition even more detest-
able. The provisions of the act made it possible to lock up in work-
houses these categories on the basis of vague and subjective
judgements. Thus, the Bavarian act against 'Gypsies and the workshy' preceded the Nazi regulations a decade later. It is perhaps
superfluous to say that this act resolved neither the definitional
nor the policy problems mentioned above. Again it was left to the
discretion of the local authorities to make a distinction between
the various categories. Moreover, the act – characterized by contemporaries as reactionary and reeking of a police state[35] – chopped
off its nose to spite its face, because it failed to forbid the issuing
of permits to *Zigeuner* and *Landfahrer*. Until well into the 1930s
complaints could be heard about Gypsies with licences *and* a

Schutzvermerk. Effective policing as envisaged by the police was thus frustrated.

WHAT WAS NEW ABOUT THE NAZIS?[36]

In the years following the 1926 act other German states followed the example of Bavaria, thereby the foundation of the Nazi policy was firmly laid. We might therefore ask ourselves to what extent the Nazis added a new dimension to the policy towards Gypsies after 1933 and how important was the weight of police tradition.

As we have seen the activities of the police journals in the mid-nineteenth century for the first time transformed the category *Zigeuner* into a master status, a (negative) category so dominant that it eclipsed all other features of a person who was thus labelled. This practice was intensified by the specialization of the Munich police, which continued the practice developed by the police journals half a century earlier. By this time sensitivity about the term had increased greatly and a growing number of people had been labelled as such. The 3,350 personal files compiled by Dillmann in 1905, among which were those of many *Zigeuner* from other states, increased to 33,524 in 1938, the point at which Munich was recognized as the national centre of intelligence.[37] This increase can be explained only partly by normal demographic causes or by the extension of the Bavarian registration practice over the rest of Germany. Another important cause in the rise of numbers is the application of the Gypsy label to the *Nach Zigeunerart umherziehende Personen* (people wandering like Gypsies).[38]

Only after 1933, when the Nazis engulfed the constitutional state, were the police really given the chance to control the mobility of itinerant groups. Unhindered by democratic checks or constitutional objections, the Munich centre took the lead in solving the 'Gypsy problem', as it was called. The increased power of the police, who worked hand in glove with other authorities, became apparent in the construction of guarded camps in a number of big cities.[39] At the same time, from 1933, the police locked up small numbers of Gypsies, together with other so-called antisocials, in work camps. From 1936 the concentration camps Dachau and Buchenwald were used for this same purpose.

THE INFLUENCE OF THE RACIAL HYGIENIC APPROACH

As Zimmermann and others have shown, during the Nazi era the Gypsies found themselves at the crossroads of deterministic ideas on antisocial behaviour and racist doctrine. The police therefore were confronted with scholars and policy-makers who began to take an interest in Gypsies from these points of view. This led to the question of whether Gypsies were predominantly antisocials who had to be sterilized, or members of a separate race who ultimately had to be exterminated. The answer, so it was thought, should *not* in the first place come from the police, but from scholars specialized in hereditary problems. It is not surprising that a number of these academics seized their chance to dominate this new definitional terrain. In the case of Gypsies the leading role, as shown in Chapter 2 of this volume, was taken by the psychiatrist Robert Ritter, who was appointed as head of the *Rassenhygienische Forschungsstelle*[40] of the *Reichsgesundheitsamt* in 1936. It was up to him to decide on a scientific basis who was a Gypsy and who was not. Soon Ritter was appointed advisor to the *Reichskriminalpolizeiamt* (RKPA), where the files of the Munich Gypsy station were concentrated, because the head of the RKPA, Arthur Nebe, realized that although he had a highly detailed Gypsy registration at his disposal, it had not been compiled primarily on racial grounds.[41]

Ritter's approach was not, as is often assumed, based on ethnological or anthropological methods. No more than could Jews be distinguished from 'Aryans' on the basis of their hair, the colour of their eyes or the shape of their noses was there any clear phenotypical distinction between Gypsies and other Germans. This did not cause Ritter to reflect that perhaps his racial assumptions were flawed; on the contrary, he saw it as proof of the far-reaching extent of mixing that had taken place in the previous centuries. He tried to corroborate this idea by gathering as much genealogical data as possible, which formed the basis for the decision of who was classified as full-blood, mixed or non-Gypsy.

How Ritter and his team operated is not entirely clear. The most probable scenario is that he based his work on the registration of Gypsies by the police[42] and then tried to trace these people back in time. Judging from the smallness of Ritter's staff and the number of Gypsies (*c.* 25,000) that had to be 'weighed', prudence cannot have been their watchword. Pausing to consider how time-consuming thorough genealogical research is, especially with travelling people, our conclusions must be that most *Gutachten* (racial diagnoses) were made on very dubious grounds. Scepticism about the reliability of Ritter's work mounts when we remember that his institute benefited financially from making these racial diagnoses.

CONCLUSION

Gypsy persecution under the Third Reich provides an answer to the main question posed by this chapter: whether there is a connection between the activities of the eighteenth-century criminologists and the persecution and stigmatization of Gypsies and other travellers by the Nazis.

It is widely assumed that Ritter and his team were to blame for the mass murder of some 10,000 German Gypsies in the concentration camps. He offered them as it were on a salver and, moreover, defined who was to be regarded as such. The 'innovative' aspect of his racial-genealogical method would have included a new group of Gypsies: those who had settled in houses and who were not Gypsies in the traditional Dillmannian definition.[43] This view, ascribing a huge responsibility to Ritter and his team, is in itself not unjustified, but it is unlikely that they played such an initial and innovative role as some authors seem to think.[44]

If we take the activities of the Munich Gypsy station into account, which in practice functioned as a national centre from 1931, we see that in 1938, when Ritter started his research, some 18,000 files had already been assembled, dealing with a total of 33,524 persons. Of them the *Reichszentrale zur Bekämpfung des Zigeunerunwesens* labelled 18,138 as *Zigeuner und Zigeunermischlinge*, 10,788 as *nach Zigeunerart umherziehend* and 4,598 as *sonstige umherziehende oder auch seßhafte Wandergewerbetreibende*. Ritter's stocktaking two years later barely deviates from this categorization. Although we are not sure if Ritter had the *same* persons in mind, it is highly probable that he just took over the definitions offered by the police registration and provided them with a 'scientific' stamp. Even the genealogical method was already widely used by the police after 1913.[45] Finally, it would seem that the police had also started gathering data on sedentary Gypsies before Ritter began his research.

This reconstruction shows that in many aspects the Nazi period just continued the traditional labelling of Gypsies by the German

police. The significant change was the means it was offered by the
dictatorial and terrorist regime and the extermination policy. The
Munich Gypsy station especially seemed to be much more important in deciding who was a Gypsy than was Ritter's racial institute.
As a matter of fact the distinction made by Dillmann between
Zigeuner and *nach Zigeunerart umherziehende Personen* was what
laid the foundation for the racial classification used later. But not
even Dillmann worked in a void. As we have seen, his approach
and methods lean heavily on the police practices which were developed at the end of the eighteenth century and which gained
impetus from the police journals in the nineteenth century.

This brings us to the specific contributions of this chapter to the
history of the police in Germany. Most important of these is the
light which is shed on the early beginnings of the professionalization
of the police. In 1984 Siemann had already pointed to the importance of police journals,[46] stressing their preventive and proactive
functions and their stimulating influence on a more structural cooperation by means of data exchange. This chapter adds support
to his provisional suggestions and, moreover, shows that a systematic and proactive approach to the tracing of criminal or unwanted
persons had already started in the eighteenth century with the issuing of *Steckbriefe*. The authors, the criminologists, can be considered as the hinge between indirect and direct rule, or – from a
different angle – between reactive and proactive policing.[47]

The most striking aspect of the tracing is the continuity in the
target groups and the methods used. In the eighteenth as well as
in the twentieth centuries policemen were primarily interested in
obtaining a better insight into the real *and* the potential criminals
(broadly defined), and thus curbing the danger these persons posed
to the public. One of the consequences was the formation of certain categories, such as vagrants, Gypsies, Jews, journeymen, prostitutes and, during the Nazi period, 'anti-social enemies', who were
thus problematized and stigmatized.

Finally, this chapter has dealt with the labelling of Gypsies.
Notwithstanding the multitude of studies on the persecution of
Gypsies in Germany that have been undertaken in the last fifteen
years, the problem of labelling has barely been touched. This over-
sight can be explained by the implicit assumption that historical
sources pose no problem about the question of *who* is a Gypsy, an
assumption that is reinforced by the use of the ethnic term *Sinti
und Roma* instead of Gypsies. This habit springs not so much from

historical considerations, but is the fruit of the actual political (and politically correct) struggle of interest groups from among and for Gypsies.

From a scholarly point of view, the disadvantage of the *Sinti und Roma* approach is that all kinds of contemporary racist as well as present-day ethnic categories are thus used, which easily leads to anachronistic and unjustified interpretations. Assuming that there ever was a clearly ethnically defined *Sinti und Roma* group in the past means that we in fact accept the point of departure (not the enforcement and consequences of Ritter and his team) that it was possible to define who was a 'real' Gypsy.

In this respect it would be interesting to research the question to what extent the atrocities against Gypsies during the Nazi regime – and also in the period before – did stimulate the group formation and ethnicity. What was the relationship between labelling and ethnicity? Did Gypsies always regard themselves as *Sinti* or *Rom* or was this feeling reinforced or even initiated by a long period of intensive stigmatization and labelling?

6 A Silent War: Foreign Gypsies and the Dutch Government Policy, 1969–89[1]

Wim Willems and Leo Lucassen

FOREIGN GYPSIES IN THE NETHERLANDS

In the preceding pages the emphasis has been on historical processes in regard to the representation of Gypsies and other itinerant groups, and government policies towards them. In this and the following chapter we will also focus on more present-day situations. Has anything changed in the attitudes and the behaviour of Western societies towards itinerant groups in the twentieth century and especially since the Second World War? To find out we have enquired into the adventures of so-called foreign Gypsy groups who came to the Netherlands since the 1960s, by using the tools of the stigmatization theory we have expounded in our introduction.

We have concluded that Gypsies and caravan-dwellers in the Netherlands, often seen by the Dutch population as members of one and the same group, have found themselves in an isolated position from the nineteenth century onward. They distinguish themselves by their way of life and housing (a caravan). The most important difference in origin is that most caravan-dwellers are indigenous Dutch, whereas Gypsies have come from abroad. For diverse reasons both groups chose a mobile life in the course of the nineteenth and twentieth centuries. The present-day Dutch Gypsies can be divided into *Sinti* (82 per cent) and *Roma* (18 per cent). The *Sinti*, coming from Germany, France and Belgium, entered the Netherlands in the first half of the nineteenth century. The *Roma* (mostly *Lowara*) arrived around 1900 and originated in Romania and Hungary. Like many other people migrating to 'the new world', they left their country about 1860.[2] They travelled through Germany, France and Scandinavia and also passed the Netherlands on their way to the West. Some of them settled themselves in due course and obtained Dutch nationality.

Apart from these Dutch Gypsies we can distinguish the so-called foreign Gypsies, who left Eastern Europe in the 1960s and stayed some time in Italy and France. From there small groups annually roamed throughout Western Europe, also visiting the Netherlands. Because they were considered undesirable aliens everywhere, the Dutch government decided in 1978 to legalize a limited number. At the moment there are about 800 foreign Gypsies living in the Netherlands. The number of Dutch Gypsies is estimated at 2,700, 90 per cent of whom live on caravan sites. The total number of caravan-dwellers is about 20,000.

In this chapter we concentrate on the Dutch government policy towards the so-called foreign Gypsies, who were legalized in 1978 mainly because they were difficult to expel but also for humanitarian reasons.[3] The government's aim from the beginning was to integrate them into Dutch society by offering them proper houses, having them attend schools and letting them take part in the regular labour market. It was expected that with proper guidance and an extra financial boost, the project would be successful within five years. Thirteen years later, however, we can conclude that the original objectives of the project have not been achieved. What are the reasons for this failure of policy? To find out we looked at the government's position and its ideas regarding these so-called foreign Gypsies.[4] We delved into the emergence of their policy towards this group (or groups), the motives which lay behind it and the reaction of Dutch society.

The structure of this chapter, in which only a few of our findings can be presented, is built along the following lines. We will first outline the positions adopted by the most important implementers of the policy during the last twenty years, their assumptions and the arguments used to justify their position. These are respectively the Ministries of Justice, Welfare etc. (WVC) and Home Affairs and the municipalities which sheltered the Gypsies. Next we treat the reactions and initiatives of the States General, the interest-promoting groups and agents, lawyers and judges. In particular we will show the influence they were able to exercise on the policy. After having considered these actors, we will discuss the image of Gypsies which they took as their point of departure and the diverse functions this image fulfilled. Finally, we will examine the consequences resulting from the policy pursued. Within the spirit of the stigmatization perspective, we will pay particular attention to the extent to which the policy led to the special treatment of Gypsies. In addition, we will spend some time on the 'differentiation' process.

THE ACTORS

The Ministry of Justice

The position on foreign Gypsies adopted by the Department of Aliens' Affairs of the Ministry of Justice shows a large degree of continuity in the period studied (1969–89). Moreover, it agrees with the policy towards all sorts of groups travelling *en famille* which had been pursued since the nineteenth century. These people were always seen as belonging to one ethnic group, that of Gypsies. The image which they bore in the 1970s shows many parallels with that of the preceding century. Gypsies were almost by definition considered undesirable aliens, even though the miserable conditions in which they lived were all too apparent. The idea that they had come to the Netherlands in order to profit from the favourable social system and that once here would harass the population with nonconformist and criminal behaviour was deep-rooted. They were a sad and sorry group of people, but that was not the responsibility of the Netherlands. The Ministry of Justice was well aware of the age-long oppression of the groups which belonged to this category of aliens, especially the oppression they had come across during the Second World War, but that was not considered sufficient reason to grant them the status of refugee or allow them political asylum. The most popular policy was to get them out of the Netherlands as quickly as possible. If that was not (immediately) possible because of the circumstances, then a so-called 'keep them moving' strategy was applied. This meant that they were constantly ordered to move on (frequently from district to district, in the hope that they would end up crossing the border), while at the same time they were offered only a minimum of facilities. In this way the Ministry of Justice hoped to prevent their taking up residence. That was also the reason why the Ministry tried so hard to prevent service-orientated groups, interest-promoting groups or the media from becoming too interested in them. The more visible the Gypsies were, the more difficult it was to have them disappear without a sound.

   The step-by-step legalization of foreign Gypsies in 1978 and 1980 thwarted the prevailing policy towards this group (or groups). New groups of illegal Gypsies were treated as before, but the policy towards the hundreds of Gypsies in possession of a residence permit was (necessarily) adjusted. Nevertheless, the point of departure remained a strict application of the aliens policy, which meant that legalized Gypsies were frustrated for years in their wishes to bring over family members or possible partners from Eastern Europe. The most important arguments on which this standpoint was based were that a more generous policy would lead to:

(a) more and more Gypsies coming to the Netherlands (*specific suction effect*);

(b) more other undesirable aliens coming (*general suction effect*);

(c) Gypsies who were legalized at a later date demanding the special position (residence permit for unlimited duration) of the first group (*specific precedent effect*);

(d) other aliens demanding the above-mentioned special status (*general precedent effect*).

We should not lose sight of the fact that this standpoint cannot be seen as separate from the general restrictive admissions and aliens policy in the Netherlands, which has always aimed at restricting immigration, even when the state is prospering economically, and at keeping the Netherlands clean, as an ex-civil servant from the Department of Aliens' Affairs expressed it. An exception was made only for those for whom there was room on the labour market and for refugees and those qualifying for political asylum. Aliens who did not match up to the prevailing 'idea of clean', for example because they were not expected to contribute to the economy but were expected only to be burdensome, were considered undesirable. The word 'Gypsy' called forth exactly these associations, and it was therefore not surprising that aliens originating from Yugoslavia almost immediately faced a restrictive policy. Their *openly nomadic lifestyle* (travelling with wife and children in caravans or tents) satisfied an image of Gypsies which had come down through the ages. Added to this was the fact that they called themselves by this name.

The political figure in the Netherlands who is authorized to break through prevailing policy by legalizing certain groups is the State Secretary of Justice. In the case of the foreign Gypsies, it was Zeevalking (1975–7) in particular who made a name for himself with the legalization of the Romanovs and, a few months later, the proposal to legalize approximately 500 illegal Gypsies. Driven by both pragmatic and humanitarian motives (they were impossible to expel and Europe needed an example), he was able to make use of the manoeuvrable space within his department which his position offered him. Later State Secretaries, in contrast, followed very strictly the position held by the Department of Aliens' Affairs. They did not use the powers inherent in their post which allowed them to legalize certain contingents of aliens. In addition, we have to admit that attempts made by the Ministry of Justice to reach an international solution within the Council of Europe seem on closer consideration to be mostly based on an illusion. The civil servants responsible never undertook any serious action. The international presence of a Dutch delegation was used, however, by the Ministry of Justice to justify itself to the court. Because an international solution for the 'nomad problem' was lacking, despite the efforts demonstrated, the road was open for the Ministry of Justice to apply the *normal* aliens policy to Gypsies and to reject special treatment, pleading the example of the general minorities policy. The idea that a separate (i.e. less restricted) policy towards Gypsies, when pursued only by the Netherlands, would lead to an unrestrained influx into the country of hundreds of thousands of Gypsies was not to die without a struggle. Nevertheless it is a numerical appraisal which is easily put in perspective and moreover belied by developments since.

The Ministry of Welfare, Health and Culture (WVC)

The second ministry which actively concerned itself with the foreign Gypsy policy was the WVC. In the years both before and after the legalization, this Ministry was responsible for Caravan Affairs and showed itself to be a fierce opponent of any legalization of foreign Gypsies in the Netherlands. The acceptance of such a group meant that WVC would be responsible for shelter (and counselling) and would have to find municipalities which were prepared to take in the Gypsies. In the beginning the government also assumed that Gypsies would have to be placed in caravan camps. In view of the fact that for years there had been too few standing places and because of the difficulties which were anticipated from the indigenous caravan dwellers, such an option was in principle rejected. This stand was kept until the government's decision of October 1977. Only when the Cabinet resolved to legalize a contingent of foreign Gypsies did the WVC drop its resistance and begin to act as an implementing and coordinating department.

With the appointment of a separate civil servant for Gypsy policy to the Department of Caravan Affairs, the position taken by the WVC changed noticeably. It came immediately to the fore in differences of opinion with the Ministry of Justice, which occupied itself with the resident status of the legalized groups and with the matter of what should be done with the new groups of illegal residents. In both issues the WVC civil servant, supported by his direct superiors, argued for a more lenient aliens policy. A second legalization would help the social composition of the first group and thus, at least in his opinion, expedite integration. The Ministry of Justice was told that it was not proper to treat a group which had been recognized in 1978 as having a special position as normal aliens. The consequence of this was that they were in effect denied the right to reunite with their families, which further shook the flimsy confidence that the Gypsies already had in Dutch society and unnecessarily frustrated the integration project. This opinion was shared by most of the 'contact officials' who were involved in the refugee policy as well as by the various municipal governments.

Another point of friction, but this time with the Ministry of Home Affairs, centred around the lack of ministerial consultation with the municipalities which were to put up the Gypsies. The WVC strove for a guiding policy, but could not prevent the decisions of the Ministry of Home Affairs (which has been the coordinating ministry for all minorities policy since 1980) being taken on an *ad hoc* basis. Arguments for a more consistent policy at the local level, and for the application of sanctions where necessary, found no response. This inconsistent approach, which led, for example, to executive civil servants and officials in some municipalities working at cross-purposes, was acknowledged by the Ministry of Home Affairs, but did not lead to any changes. The Ministry – pleading the decentralization policy – confined itself to following the line championed by the municipalities. The WVC civil servant in question thus found himself in an isolated position in the national consultations on the Gypsy policy.

Although a new note was sounded from 1978 onwards at the executive level, this did not automatically mean that the department sang the same tune as other interested parties in the governmental consultations. At essential moments the standpoints expressed inside the department were not adopted and the higher echelons of the WVC (in particular the Department of the Welfare of Minorities) supported the policy of the other ministries. In this way the minister of the above-mentioned Department was closely involved in the preparation of the change in 1984, when it was decided to adopt a more repressive and police-orientated policy. And it was also for this reason that the shifting of financial means which accompanied the change of policy was never openly brought up for discussion. Thus on a higher official level some continuity can be noted also in the WVC's standpoint towards Gypsies. Moreover, it relies on an image of Gypsies shared with the Ministry of Justice.

The Ministry of Home Affairs (BiZa)

This ministry is the third most important party at the governmental level. The position there – referring in particular to the Department of the Coordination of Minorities (DCM) established in 1980 – is less pronounced than in the other two ministries. If we take the Minority Note from 1983 as our starting point – in which Gypsies are put on the same level as refugees – then it seems that the BiZa supports special treatment. In practice little of this is to be seen: the Ministry followed quite passively the trail led by the Ministry of Justice and later that of the representatives of the municipalities which sheltered the Gypsies. Characteristic of the DCM's position is not so much the decisions which were made through the lack of a policy of its own as the constant postponement of planned executive consultations. Only when the conflict between the Gypsies and the municipalities escalated were the concerned parties brought together. As compensation for the acknowledged executive neglect, the minister then confined himself to making police expenses available to the municipalities.

No explanation for the political and executive inertia which the BiZa suffered can be given on the basis of our case study. For this to be possible, Gypsy policy would have to be compared with elements of the general minorities policy of the DCM in the 1980s. We would nevertheless like to make the following remarks. The idea of decentralization which became so popular from halfway through 1980 onwards, is in our opinion at odds with the vigorous approach which the national coordination of the minorities policy, which only became operative since 1979, demands. A number of clear courses to take are given in the Minority Note, but the possibility of policy change was apparently too marginal at the DCM to give form to that policy. It is possible that this has to do with the difficult position of this department within the Ministry. The Ministry had always taken care of contacts with the mayors and local police forces and their idea of administration – relating it for the moment to our analysis of the Gypsy policy – did not mesh with the requirements of a policy of integration. The DCM happened to be the coordinating department, but in practice it did not have the authority to prescribe compulsory measures to the ministries which concerned themselves with the minorities policy. In particular, it was never able to exercise any influence on the aliens policy pursued by the Ministry of Justice. The criticism expressed with regard to the police-orientated approach was only to be seen in internal memoranda; a true change of position towards the Ministry of Justice and the mayors concerned was never discussed.

The Shelter Municipalities

In the 1970s local governments were in general quite worried about being 'saddled' with groups of illegal Gypsies and having to carry the costs they brought with them. The large cities especially, which were the most attractive to these groups, were vehemently opposed. This had not changed by the time of legalization. All the municipalities approached by the government resisted, in the beginning, the idea of taking in the illegal Gypsies. Only after many talks and gentle insistence did some grudgingly agree to shelter a small contingent.

Our impression is that many shelter municipalities finally overcame their reluctance, after months of pressuring from the government, because concessions were made on the part of the ministries and an image was drawn of groups who were prepared to adjust to the new situation at whatever cost. The municipalities had no choice, given the stalemate they were in. Moreover, the WVC would remunerate all expenses and an explicit policy and 'project group' were on their way. In practice it turned out otherwise. As we have seen, national consultations failed to materialize for years and only the WVC, which was the coordinating ministry from 1980 onwards, offered the necessary official support. We have been assured from different sources that, once the decision was taken, most of the shelter municipalities began their 'chore' with zeal and energetically passed all kinds of governmental resolutions. Their good intentions, however, rarely matched reality.

After a year of trying, three municipalities were already convinced that integration had failed and their opposition to the idea returned in full force. It is necessary to distinguish here between the civil servants who were appointed especially for the Gypsy project (contact officials, project leaders and workers in socio-cultural training) and municipal officials who met the Gypsies in another capacity. Whereas the former emphasized in their reports alternative solutions and imperative conditions which had to be fulfilled so that the shelter project would run better, the latter (local government, social services, police) were almost immediately convinced that the project was doomed to fail because of the lack of coordination and, more than anything else, the nonconformist behaviour of the Gypsies. The latter, in all likelihood, did fail to conform to the picture of the average citizen, but some of the requirements which the municipalities demanded of integration (finding work in a short period of time and intensive participation in socio-cultural training) seem to have been far from realistic, given the events of the previous years and the distinguishing features (education, work experience) of the group members in question.

When in the first years of the 1980s some shelter municipalities became more explicit about their dissatisfaction with the Gypsy project, the call for more stringent measures was heard. Cautiously hopeful reports from some municipalities in 1982 were brusquely overruled by the exclusively censorious reports from other municipalities. The changeover to a more repressive approach became national within a few years. The WVC had been urging for a few years before this that Gypsies should on most grounds be treated as all other citizens and sanctioned if they break the law. The municipalities borrowed this idea, but then added the police component (= more money from the Gypsy budget for police) which would play an increasingly dominant role in the coming years. Since the change of policy in 1984, approved by the government, polarization had taken great strides. In 1985/6 the shelter municipalities almost unanimously considered integration an illusion and adjustment guidance a makeshift. They were of the opinion that only a no-nonsense judicial approach would keep under control the problems which had arisen.

The Parliament

Knowing that the government's opposition to the legalization of Gypsies was so great, we must ask ourselves how it was possible that this politically sensitive decision was taken in favour of the Gypsies. As we have seen it was the State Secretary of Justice who took the decision. He (sometimes) found support in social institutions such as interest-promoting groups, jurisprudence and the legal profession, as well as in Parliament, in particular the Lower House. The position which Parliament adopted at the time of the legalization and its critical attitude during the following period was a real source of support to the policy which was in the making. The almost unanimously supported wish to legalize the group gave the government no other choice. The House showed itself to be a critical follower of government policy as far as this group was concerned.

From 1971, members of the House from various political parties regularly denounced the policy pursued by the government, in particular the Ministry of Justice. A closer inspection of these interventions brings to light that most instances concerned *individual* or extreme cases – such as the vaginal body-search in January 1981 at the border or discriminating statements and practices on the part of civil servants. The *general* policy was rarely brought up for discussion. Except in the early years, when the parties in office were also regularly pressed to support a decisive policy and the government was accused of ambivalence and passing the buck, the House tended to be content where cases of principle were concerned with the explanation offered by the responsible cabinet members. The most important example of this was the acceptance of the policy change in 1984: there was extensive discussion concerning respect for cultural identity, participation by the Gypsies and the advantages and disadvantages of a rigid application of the Aliens Act, but the change itself was never made a principle subject of discussion. As a matter of fact, the entry 'police expenses' of 1.2 million Dutch guilders which was then listed for the first time was accepted almost tacitly. It took four years for the Minister of Home Affairs to question the allocation of a part of the Gypsy budget.

How can this, at times aimless, behaviour of the House be explained? In the first place it should be recalled that, generally speaking, a consensus of opinion exists about the generally restrictive aliens policy. Proposals from only a few individuals to depart from it have always had little chance of succeeding. The argument used by the Ministry of Justice was (and is) that this would clash with the general policy. This dilemma was in itself an argument used to reject requests. Furthermore, we must remember that the House is very dependent for its information on certain sources. As was emphasized by various members of the Lower House whom we interviewed, it is easier for administrators to enter the political channels and have their voice heard there. The House is much more reliant on social organizations such as interest-promoting groups. If these are headed by educated staff, who provide information supported by arguments, then the House has much more room in which to move. In addition, because of a full political agenda and information sources which are often widely divergent, the House is in many cases dependent on reports from the media. Many politicians react to current affairs with a certain *Tor Instinkt*. The possibility of getting publicity for certain questions and motions is greater when the media, and certainly television, has spent time on the issue.

The interest-promoting groups

The history of foreign Gypsies in the Netherlands would have been very different without interest-promoting groups and agents, whose activities have been multifarious since the beginning of the 1970s. They laboured for the sheltering of groups of illegal Gypsies who had settled in the periphery of big cities, and approached ministries with the request either to recognize such Gypsies as refugees or legalize their residence. Supporters tried to mobilize the media so that the fate of illegal Gypsies would reach the attention of the public and thus (indirectly) force the Lower House to take some action. Finally, it was they who provided the information and the most important arguments to apply pressure on the government, especially in 1988. Every action in favour of foreign Gypsies originated from an initiative from the interest-promoting groups.

In the period before 1977 it was primarily social-service organizations, such as Humanitas and Release, which called attention to the fate of groups of illegal Gypsies, sometimes in collaboration with highly motivated individuals. Their arguments had in the long run little visible result, but they did meet with some initial response. They helped make others, including some members of the House and lawyers, aware of the problem and thus paved the way for the later interest-promoting tactics. It was primarily the ROM Society which, during the years of legalization and thereafter, championed the cause of groups of illegal Gypsies with (protest) actions, petitions and personal contact with certain members of the government. It took care that the subject of stateless Gypsies was constantly in the news at the end of the 1970s and appeared on the political agenda. This demonstrably helped its case in all the stages of the legalization, but a drawback to its involvement was the controversial status of its most important spokesman. His idea of interest-promoting showed visible signs of patronage. This type of ambiguous behaviour characterized other Gypsy leaders as well. In the 1980s the ROM Society continued to critically monitor the policy. It even threatened legal proceedings a few times and provided extensive written commentary on the political decisions which it thought contestable. Its influence on the policy-making process remained marginal due to its fixation on discrimination and its repeated accusations of 'cultural genocide' – in short, its highly offensive strategy. Another factor against the Society was the uncertainty about which Gypsies it was actually representing. This ambivalence also affected its position as party to the negotiations.

This is less true of the Lau Mazirel Society, which in the course of the 1980s increasingly showed itself to be an agent helping to determine the Gypsies' image. It was not successful – despite repeated attempts – in officially taking part in the government consultations on Gypsy policy, but it did increasingly take over the role of central interest-promoting organization. Its increased influence was due in particular to its expert juridical substructure, the considerable practical experience which it had amassed and the opportunity to publish articles about the Gypsy issue in their journal *O'Drom*. The result of this at the political level was particularly visible in 1988.

Jurisprudence and the legal profession

Jurisprudence and the legal profession together make up the third party which influenced, and still influences, government policy towards foreign Gypsies. The first lawyer appeared in the Romanov case in 1977, urging the Netherlands to take back the group. At the same time, a German colleague petitioned the Council of Europe for an international travelling licence for the group. These initiatives meant the beginning of an intensive effort of legal aid (collectives) on behalf of the legal position of those Gypsies in question, with at first petitions for residence permits and, later on, for licences to establish a business and naturalization. Furthermore, they concentrated on discriminatory and stigmatizing practices by the government.

This is especially true of the jurisprudence, in particular in the matter of expulsions. Diverse pronouncements not only led to expulsions being prohibited but also made it more difficult for the Ministry of Justice to consider such proceedings. Thus the court at The Hague prohibited the expulsion of a group of Gypsies by airplane in 1981 with the argument that they would then be separated from their caravans which were the most important factor in their way of life. The result was that the Ministry of Justice was rendered more or less impotent. With respect to larger groups, the Ministry could only apply the 'keep them moving' strategy.

In addition, the courts influenced judicial policy with respect to family reunification. Whereas from 1982 onwards the Ministry rejected appeals for this by referring to the general aliens policy, the Council of State and two courts of law originally considered such motivation insufficient and, moreover, inconsistent with the specific Gypsy policy. The consequence of this was that the Ministry of Justice took care that, with the policy change in 1984, the official memorandum explicitly noted that the normal aliens policy would from then on apply to Gypsies. When the Council of State considered the new motivation for rejecting family reunification sufficient in 1986, it in effect legitimized the restrictive policy of the Ministry of Justice. This also applied to cases of naturalization: since 1987, the Council of State has interfered only when the Ministry of Justice rejected petitions without grounds to do so.

AN AMBIGUOUS IMAGE

If you ask someone about Gypsy culture who was involved in the above-sketched policy, a number of images dragged up out of the mire of history will make up his answer. In this way a member of the Lower House whom we interviewed told us that Gypsies have always protected valuables, such as jewels, by burying them in the ground. He added that it was important for the police to be aware of these cultural traits so that they know that these objects are temporarily hidden private possessions, and not stolen. To this he added that Gypsies have different views about possession anyway, given their nomadic culture; with this the difference between them and the sedentary culture is finely expressed. We do not doubt this member of government's political integrity, but the simplicity which marks the above statements is characteristic of general notions concerning the difference of Gypsy culture. A reservoir of images of travelling groups is drawn from, although the intentions of the 'image-makers' differ. If they fit, they are used, for example in the case above, to show that a knowledge of the cultural identity of (foreign) Gypsies can bring about more understanding, and therefore increase their chances of integration. But the same notion of nomadism is used by the police or disappointed officials to show that Gypsies are incapable of integrating into Dutch society because of their 'innate' need to travel and because their ideas about 'mine and thine' differ from what is common in the Netherlands.

An image closely related to the above concerns their shiftlessness and inability, or unwillingness, to keep a regular job. Here also the interpretation is dependent on the perspective. Thus some of those involved tend to explain the steady high unemployment among foreign Gypsies by pointing to their lack of means to support themselves in the traditional way. By this they chiefly mean what at present is called 'ethnic entrepreneurship'. The government should be more flexible about diplomas and licences. Here they assume that the Gypsies in question can only support themselves through (traditional) trades or other independent professions. Apart from the fact that we do not know to what extent these groups make use of the possibilities which the 'grey market' offers, this view does not entertain a very favourable opinion of the Gypsy's social skills. It is as if the Gypsy, and his children who were educated in the Netherlands, are unable to orientate themselves in a different direction than in the past. It is possible that the thought lying at the bottom of this is that every adjustment in fact damages the Gypsy culture.

Those who overtly defend the Gypsies argue that they are not able to adjust, whereas many government and police officials accuse them of not wanting to adjust. Both assume a fixed idea of culture. The latter do not recognize that the labour market is practically closed to Gypsies, whom the Employment Exchange regard as incapable of being helped. Gypsies do not take advantage of the employment projects set up for minorities and suffer from discrimination in all sections of society. Moreover, the idea that Gypsies support themselves by begging and stealing, i.e. are not used to working, is widespread. The history of Gypsies in the Netherlands in the nineteenth and twentieth centuries, however, reveals otherwise. Divergent groups were able to support themselves reasonably well with professions such as tinker, bear-tamer, horse-dealer and musician. Documented as well is the fact that they were able to adapt themselves to the changing economic conditions.

Nevertheless, in the domain of employment it is also the case that if the image fits, it is used, which only emphasizes the tendency to blame only one party (either society or the Gypsies).

The image is also found in all kinds of characteristics which are supposed to be specific to the Gypsy culture and which are held responsible for their difficulties in integrating into Dutch society. We will list a few here: they have no idea of time, they cannot handle money, they have no conscience, they are not interested in education, they cannot think in abstract terms, they do not steal but 'find' things, and they are not accustomed to living in houses which results in their being a neighbourhood nuisance. These impressions are not only easily generalized to include all Gypsies, but in general one does not seem to realize that such characteristics are more likely to be related to social environment, educational background, class and suchlike.

Let us confine ourselves to the matter of living in brick houses. There are no extract details available about how foreign Gypsies and their forefathers were housed in their countries of origin. For this reason, all interested parties avail themselves of the prevalent image, namely that Gypsies have always travelled around in caravans, trailers and sometimes tents, so that in principle they fell under the Caravan Act until the 1970s. With legalization, however, the ministries concerned made sedentary housing a requirement, probably because of the scarcity of places in which to set up their homes. Temporary housing was offered first as a transitional measure in order to let them get used to living in a home. When the nuisance problem first arose, the municipalities were quick to produce the argument that Gypsies have never been accustomed to living in houses. In short, it was their culture that was again the problem. Interest-promoting groups in effect used the same argument when they criticized the lack of free choice and argued for the right to live in a trailer by appealing to the 'traditional' nomadic lifestyle. Here also, 'unable to' contrasts with 'not wanting to'. The discussion of the Gypsy policy is dominated by such polarizations in which Gypsies are either excused because of their culture, or accused because of their culture. The image is generally the guiding line here.

THE INEVITABLE PROCESS OF EXCLUSION

With the Romanov group coming to Holland in 1976 it was immediately clear to all interested parties that these were 'Gypsies'. Not only the government but also interest-promoting organizations and the groups themselves used this term. The latter will have meant something different by the term, however, than the former. The Ministry of Justice, the Ministry of Welfare, Home Affairs and police regarded Gypsies as much more of a threat to public order and safety than the average illegal alien. This standpoint arose from the existent stigma which was without scruple projected onto these newcomers. The most important elements of this stigma were that Gypsies were poor because of their lifestyle, and parasitical because they would not work. In addition, Gypsies were believed to be born (petty) criminals who easily slid from bad to worse. It did not matter if the actual situation met these descriptions or not; the stigma was not corrected.

Seen historically, the heart of the threat lay in the openly nomadic lifestyle of these aliens. This was evident in the recent policy towards foreign Gypsies. The Ministry of Justice's biggest concern was that they travelled in groups, were thus very mobile and were therefore difficult to keep under control. Paradoxically, the 'keep them moving' strategy only encouraged this. When the number of illegals increased, the idea grew to set up an internment camp, an idea which was not brought to realization because of political opposition. Then the Ministry of Justice proposed making the houses of detention in Middelburg and Zwolle (two Dutch cities) available for this purpose, but the courts immediately pronounced this unlawful. Even after legalization the question was: How do we prevent from travelling the Gypsies who have not yet been expelled? The second concern was how to *prevent the entry* of new illegal Gypsies. The most appropriate measure was more strict supervision at the southern border. This message was sent by the Ministries of Justice and Home Affairs in divers circulars and telexes to the authorities at the border from 1977 onwards.

Then there was, of course, the problem of *identification*. No travel document listed that a person was a 'Gypsy'. It was therefore necessary to go by identification marks other than nationality. In most instances, appearance, way of living (caravan) and size of group were decisive. In this way the aliens who met these qualifications were also immediately identified as potential criminals. This is apparent from the circulars issued in 1974, in which not only were Gypsies qualified as undesirable aliens but it was also suggested that by definition they were guilty of a crime or of disturbing public order. These directives legitimized a separate and discriminatory treatment of Gypsies, who in practice could be expelled simply on the basis of conjecture.

The *registering* of every alien who was considered a 'Gypsy' turned out to be an aid in identification. Both the Department of Aliens' Affairs and the Central Criminal Investigation Service (CRI) established a system in which the personal details of all foreign Gypsies were recorded. In this way it was hoped that persons who either had no papers or had false papers could be identified by means of photos and fingerprints which were then passed on to the CRI. The same method was used in the case of Gypsies who were suspected of a crime in the Netherlands or abroad. From 1974 onward their fingerprints and two photos were taken before they were expelled. The CRI in particular was able to build up a well-documented registration system in this way. All reports from local police forces which had to do with both offences and identification checks of legal and illegal Gypsies reached the CRI. The person in question did not have to have a record; a simple document check was enough to be entered into the CRI system.

What are the general effects and implications of this stigmatization (an active use of the stigma in the developed policy) by the government? We discern four, namely that:

(a) people who are labelled Gypsies are not judged by individual traits but by (alleged) group traits;

(b) conjectures and suspicions are enough to keep out, expel and register foreign Gypsies;

(c) it is difficult for the persons in question to avoid the stigma of being labelled an undesirable alien and potential criminal;

(d) on the part of the government, much time, attention and money is spent on a relatively small minority group, which is partly a consequence of the prevailing image.

We also see these effects expressed in the policy pursued by the shelter municipalities; they explain in part the changeover in 1984 to a more police-orientated approach. The chiefs of police were informed from the beginning of the legalization by the above-mentioned circulars and telexes that they would be facing potentially criminal residents. In addition, the police forces had intensive contact with each other as well as with the CRI concerning the methods to use with respect to foreign Gypsies. Whereas the first five years of the legalization policy was characterized by a lack of governmental coordination and consultation, the police did collaborate. This undoubtedly led to increased pressure on government officials to provide more financial means as compensation for the police work which was spent solely on Gypsies. The mayors saw in this the chance to urge the government to direct a part of the budget set aside for the sheltering and guidance of the Gypsies to the police. The government agreed to this, with the condition that it would have to be proved that the money was being used for extra detectives. The conviction that the legalized foreign Gypsies would be involved in criminal activities in all the shelter municipalities was deep-rooted at that level as well. The police reports of that time, however, rarely indicate that Gypsies were in fact sentenced more often than others. The police justify this by remarking that the lack of actual sentences has to do with the great mobility of the group and with the numbers of minors. The effect of this discrepancy is that considerable mystification has arisen around Gypsy criminality.

Another aspect of stigmatization is that the groups of foreign Gypsies discussed in this chapter were regarded from the beginning as pitiful and needy people, who would 'rise' to the level common to Dutch society with a little support and guidance. The term 'foreign aid at home' was used. Much of the frustration and disappointment felt by the local municipal government officials stems from this one-sided idea of such a guidance process. The Gypsies' situation was often misjudged because of the lack of knowledge of and insight into their abilities, wishes and interests. A consequence of this – perhaps it is even characteristic of forced integration – is that as soon as the groups in question fall short of expectations and the alternative solutions to the problems have been exhausted, it is quickly assumed that 'they are not cooperating'. Ignorance and impotence lead to 'culprit-hunting', and experience has shown that Gypsies, who are first seen as victims, ultimately end up being accused of having caused the misery in which they find themselves. Their image provides enough leads to 'explain' why they are not able to be included in Dutch society. One explanation is that they are inveterate parasites. Another is that they were forcibly integrated; they should be allowed to travel again. The middle position is given by an ex-civil servant: 'I can't see behind the Gypsy's mask.' In his opinion, they have different interests, but what those interests are remains unanswered. As long as this prevailing image of the Gypsy as a being from another planet is not corrected by other images – for example, of Gypsies who receive a diploma, establish a business or begin something new in the Netherlands – the stigmatization will continue.

A noticeable feature of the literature on Gypsies is that the traits assigned to them (justly or not) are seen as specifically and exclusively 'gypsy-like'. This was true in the eighteenth century and it is still true today, only the emphasis lies elsewhere.[5] Fascinated or shocked by the foreignness of the group under study, attention is chiefly paid to the features which differ from those of groups from a low socio-economic environment instead of to the social circumstances which agree. Here we come up against the appearance of something that also plagues other current minority studies, namely that the nature of the group under study is easily differentiated. We noted this in a number of places during our research. Thus we found that in those cases in which a foreign Gypsy family was accused of being a neighbourhood nuisance, the municipality quickly attributed that to its lack of a 'sedentary culture'. It is only in recent years that a relationship is made in some cases between neighbourhood problems and the socio-economic environment. Absence from school is also easily accounted for by the 'Gypsy culture', which is seen as the reason for the lack of motivation. That some Gypsy children have persevered and graduated from secondary school is left unsaid; the first signs of change go unnoticed. As was noted above, culture is seen as a static factor, instead of one liable to change.

There remains the issue of the much-discussed Gypsy criminality. The first thing one notices is the idea that Gypsies have their own form of criminality, which is practically impossible to suppress. Next is that they are the only minority group for whom separate police have been appointed from the budget meant for their integration. Apart from the stigmatizing effect of this measure, the Gypsies are also singled out in the general minorities policy. It is most noteworthy that this criminality is seldom linked to their marginal position in society, whereas the link is quite obvious. The factor of 'discrimination', which only increases the distance between them and the society around them, can be added to their case as well.

Finally, the differentiation of Gypsies has increased in the past twelve years due to the specific Gypsy policy. The special attention these groups received – both the well-meant care and the more penal treatment – has led to each development, and certainly the problems, being carefully eyed and made much of in both municipal reports and newspaper articles. There was an almost exclusive concentration on the problems, which is not surprising in light of the separate Gypsy budget. More problems as a rule mean more money; the history of the police expenses has made this quite clear. The result is that municipalities which had few problems were ignored, which gave the national integration project a one-sided character. The policy change in 1984, and the marked leaning towards a police-orientated approach, undoubtedly boosted the prevailing image of Gypsies and criminalization. In this connection a general conclusion could be that every form of differentiation carries with it the danger of increasing the stigmatization of the group in question. Certainly in the case of the foreign Gypsies, where for a while a relatively large number of civil servants were assigned to a small number of people, it turned out to be an inevitable development.

7 The Making of a Minority: the Case of Dutch Travellers[1]

Annemarie Cottaar

BECOMING A MINORITY

People often talk about minorities as if they were a fixed idea, a category that never changes and has always existed. History, however, teaches that some minorities (gradually) come into being, but some also fade away, just like the claims for and attribution of cultural rights are forever changing. This is well illustrated by the contemporary problems in the former Soviet Union, the former Yugoslavia and other Eastern European countries. However, the question remains to be answered what the conditions are under which claims to minority rights are formulated. It is often unclear how the groups came into being in the past and for how long they have already formed a cultural or ethnic minority. Many studies, especially those about itinerants, put the emphasis one-sidedly on the group itself: they focus on culture and customs as explanatory factors. By doing so they leave the question aside whether the minority status of a group has anything to do with their (itinerant) way of life. Equally important, however, is the question whether the influence of the authorities – their policies and way of categorizing – has affected the process of group formation.

A striking illustration of the making of a minority is that of Dutch caravan-dwellers. Since 1980 the Dutch government has pursued a special policy towards ethnic minorities, a term covering groups of foreign origin which maintain their own culture and which are socially disadvantaged. There is one group covered by this policy which nevertheless is primarily of indigenous descent: caravan-dwellers. The decision to include them rested not so much on their distinctive form of housing, as on the divide separating them from the rest of society, together with their socially backward position on a number of essential fronts, such as employment, housing and education.

Their situation invoked unmistakable parallels with that of other ethnic minorities in the Netherlands. In defining them as a distinct group, the government was following prevailing public opinion. Caravan-dwellers themselves also, to be sure, emphasize that they are different from 'typical Dutch people' – whom they refer to as *burghers* – and that they have a culture of their own, with values and forms of interaction of which they are proud.[2] In contrast to other Western European states, the Dutch government has always drawn a distinction between caravan-dwellers and Gypsies. From the outset caravan-dwellers have been regarded as natives with a deviant form of housing (and way of life). The term Gypsy was reserved for people of foreign origin who travelled about in family bands and slept in tents or caravans.

As a result of new government policy in the 1990s caravan-dwellers seem to have lost some important privileges, like the exclusive right to live in a caravan. This is why they emphasize more and more that they differ from other Dutch people and accordingly need a different (minority) status with corresponding rights: the right to maintain their own culture, the right to live in an affordable caravan in one of the large caravan camps and the right to travel. Their slogan is 'Our culture is freedom', but very little of that freedom is left nowadays. Since the Caravan Act of 1968 caravan-dwellers have no longer been allowed to travel freely. From that moment on they were obliged to live in large regional camps (fifty to eighty caravans) with many facilities, such as a camp school, a social worker and sanitary provisions. The caravan-dwellers opposed this Act vehemently; they were afraid of isolation, increasing competition and growing tension within their own group. In addition, the people living in the neighbourhood argued against the large camps because they felt intimidated by the vast number of caravan-dwellers. As a result, the caravan site policy failed and government policy had to change course. A draft was therefore made for an amendment to the law. According to the government, the answer to the problem lay in the establishment of small, attractive caravan camps with no more than ten to fifteen caravans. But most caravan-dwellers opposed these new measures as well, as they wanted their friends and family in their immediate environment and this seemed to be impossible in a camp with a restricted number of caravans. An equally important reason may have been that they were given no alternative and were – once again – pressured into moving from one camp to another. This kind of government pressure has been a leitmotif in the history of caravan-dwellers in the Netherlands and has played an important role in the process of minority formation.

THE PROCESS OF MINORITY FORMATION

Throughout Western Europe the first caravans only appeared in the second half of the nineteenth century (see Chapter 10). Nevertheless in the following century their occupants have developed into a separate social category within Dutch society, one which obviously lags far behind. Before delving into the historic roots of this process of minority formation, we need first to define a number of concepts further. This is especially true for the concept of minority itself. Here we refer to the study of minority formation and emancipation in the Netherlands written by the Amsterdam sociologist Penninx.[3] He has made the two-sidedness of the process apparent by including in his analysis both the attitudes and behaviour of the dominant majority as well as the self-perceptions of the minority. In his view a group must fulfil two conditions to be defined as a minority. First of all its members must consider belonging to the group more important than any other social classification. And – by way of the mirror-image of this commitment – (large sections of) society will regard them primarily as a distinct group. These forms of (self-) perception are referred to as the minority's *ethnocultural position*.[4] A second condition is that most members of the group occupy a *low social position*, as manifest in such areas as income (employment), education and housing.[5] By virtue of its numerical position as a minority such a group will have little power or influence in society. When for a number of successive generations these conditions are met, we may speak of *minority formation*.

According to studies about caravan-dwellers in the 1980s and 1990s, they constitute a minority in the strict sense of the term.[6] Their socio-economic position is hardly rosy now and there are few indications it will soon improve, given that a large majority of the group depends upon social welfare and the educational level of the children of caravan-dwellers lags behind that of the rest of society. A considerable distance, spatial and social, separates caravan-dwellers from other Dutch and this gulf appears rather fixed, in part as a consequence of a situation that has developed of mutual distrust. As for the third condition, a glance at statistics shows that,

Gypsies aside, caravan-dwellers comprise the smallest category recognized by official minorities policy.[7] The only unanswered question is how and when this minority position came into being.

To determine which factors have been decisive in the process of the minority formation, the complementary concepts of 'position attribution' and 'position acquisition' are useful. With 'position acquisition' emphasis falls on the characteristics and traits of the ethnic-cultural group itself which can be a special factor in its attaining (an improved) social position.[8] As far as the vocations of caravan-dwellers are concerned, it is assumed that these were marginal and not infrequently amounted to veiled forms of begging. If this is an accurate interpretation, then their way of earning a living has contributed to their minority position and to the negative image that goes with it. This holds true, too, for their deviant form of housing. That is why it is necessary to analyse closely the economic function(s) of caravan-dwellers down through the years, as well as the development of the caravan. The results of an analysis of changes in mobile homes are presented in Chapter 10. Here only economic aspects are reviewed, to the extent that they have influenced the course of minority formation. In addition the degree to which caravan-dwellers have tried to promote their interests by means of their own organizations is investigated. The participation of their children in education, on the other hand, is only touched upon indirectly, not simply because we know that prior to 1945 this was slight (especially at the height of the travel season) but primarily because, according to the Compulsory Education Act of 1901, the children of caravan-dwellers were exempted from having to attend school if their parents remained in a municipality for less than 28 days (after 1921 reduced to eight days).

With 'position attribution' other factors are involved over which, in principle, the group itself can exercise little or no influence. With respect to their social position, we should take into consideration division of labour, housing and education, regulated by the government and other institutions, including private organizations.[9] What interests us most of all is when the government started to treat caravan-dwellers as a distinct category: from the moment people began to live in caravans or perhaps even before (although in the last event, one could not yet actually speak of caravan-dwellers)? Should categorization, i.e. group formation, have preceded the time when people moved into caravans, then form of housing would not offer an adequate explanation for the process of minority formation.

Their form of housing, however, did determine the name given to caravan-dwellers as a category so that it is of importance to ascertain what influence such housing had on their ultimate emergence as a minority. In this context what matters especially is how various government agents acted towards them, bureaucrats from the relevant ministries and provincial and local authorities. In an analysis of the ethnic-cultural position of caravan-dwellers, the individual persons who make up the category are central: who were they, where did they come from and in what respects did they differ from other Dutch? It might be that their group identity developed as a response to the negative attitude manifest in Dutch society. Therefore it is important to find out what place caravan-dwellers were relegated to by dominant institutions. Also of importance is the way in which the group, possibly by way of reaction, maintained its own distinct ethnic identity.

THE CARAVAN-DWELLERS' PERSPECTIVE

At the outset of the twentieth century there did not yet exist a separate, homogeneous group of caravan-dwellers. As far as their origin and vocational activities were concerned, there were significant differences among themselves and at the same time countless similarities with the so-called sedentary population. The only two respects in which they already differed from 'citizens' were their itinerant way of life and their housing. At a certain moment a wagon with a wood cabin on top offered people whose way of earning a living required travel the chance to take their family with them on the road. After 1900 we see people using these wagons to an increasing degree, not only to travel, but also to live in. They offered, especially in cities, an alternative in an era plagued by a shortage of housing. Urban caravan-dwellers have always confused the government because they were not supposed to live in caravans. But then what determined who did?

An obvious factor seems to be the special nature of itinerant work and related services. What caught our attention when looking into their economic activities was the enormous diversity. The heart of their economic activities consisted of trade. As a rule there was little initial capital required and as traders they met a need, for not only in the countryside but also in towns there was a vigorous demand for inexpensive goods. In addition trade activities could

readily be combined with other more artisan-like work and with the seasonal exploitation of fairground attractions.[10]

To determine just how group-specific these vocations were and how atypical the incomes which they yielded, comparison with equivalent vocational categories among the sedentary majority of society was necessary. Were the discrepancies striking enough to consider caravan-dwellers occupying a social position of their own? This question can be answered – without any reservation – in the negative. For most vocations practised by caravan-dwellers, there was a sedentary version. This was least true perhaps for travelling showmen, knife-grinders and chair-bottomers, despite the fact some of them also settled permanently in a big city. In any event innumerable sedentary hawkers worked the streets and alleys of big cities, carrying out their vocations where they lived. The extent to which they travelled about was insignificant compared to the itinerancy of caravan-dwellers, but this appeared to be the only major difference, which also was true for many (street-) musicians and singers.

Further, there was rather a lot of variation in the economic position of the caravan-dweller population, which found expression not only in divergent earnings but also in the condition of the caravan and the number of horses one owned. What can in any case be demonstrated is that, on the whole, before the Second World War caravan-dwellers were no worse off than many in the working-class population, where housing, employment and income are concerned. Although in the prewar situation caravan-dwellers enjoyed the freedom to move about unhampered, that is not to say they were continuously under way. When travelling, moreover, they seldom ranged widely. During the winter months, when the roads were only passable with difficulty, they usually remained in one place, for the most part in a large municipality, a location which guaranteed them a large pool of potential customers. In the spring they set off in the caravan again.

THE GOVERNMENT'S PERSPECTIVE: WHO'S GOING TO PAY FOR IT?

When people first began to live in caravans during the second half of the nineteenth century, there was certainly no 'open situation'. From the beginning they were confronted with the already existing

negative image of itinerants in general. A dominant part of the stigma against dwellers stemmed from the suspicion that they possessed insufficient means of subsistence and only managed to survive by begging and stealing. The rise of the caravan simply reinforced this stigmatization. Thanks to their unique form of housing, the itinerants became more conspicuous in the eyes of the world at large which made it easier for governments to adopt a specific, stigmatizing policy towards them.

Research into the fear of municipalities of admitting these people within their boundaries leads us to the nineteenth-century changes in the poor laws, which provide us with a key to understand the process of social exclusion and the formation of the minority group of caravan-dwellers in the Netherlands. Even before caravans were passing with some regularity along Dutch roads, it was already determined that their future inhabitants would have to contend with authorities who rejected them. The leading actors are to be found at the municipal level. What had happened? With the alteration of the Dutch poor law in 1870 municipalities were made financially responsible for the support of all impecunious persons within their areas, not just their own residents but also those who stayed only temporarily. At first this change appeared a welcome improvement in their position, especially for smaller municipalities, since place of birth had previously determined domicile for purposes of poor relief. In other words people who left their birthplace to settle elsewhere became a burden on the budget of their municipality of origin as soon as they became impoverished.[11] For smaller municipalities which witnessed the migration of many of their inhabitants to cities in search of work, this arrangement represented a considerable potential drain on their resources.

With the alteration of the poor law in 1870 this imbalance appeared to have been set straight. There was a new danger for smaller communities, however, lurking in the provision that they must also support people who were only stopping for a while within their boundaries, should these be needy. This is why they began to regard itinerants as a threat to their relief funds and mobilized themselves against their visits. Their antagonism derived from the long-standing popular notion that people who travelled as a way of life were, by definition, poor. It certainly looks like the small municipalities were eager to eke out every last advantage they could from the revised law. We should remind ourselves, however, that their treasuries were usually only moderately filled and that conse-

quently their capacity to provide assistance was limited. Nonetheless the conclusion is justified that the municipalities were led more by their anxieties than by rational considerations. Until the Second World War at any rate they were unable to demonstrate that they suffered severe financial strain owing to relief extended to caravan-dwellers within their territory. They may have handed in claims to this effect to the Ministry of Justice, but the ministry dismissed their statistics, both shortly before and after the war, as so much trumpery. Even when the unavoidable concentration of caravan-dwellers during the war began to be burdensome to the budgets of a number of municipalities, bills were passed along to the Dutch government with remarkable speed. During the war, to be sure, expenses incurred were not for poor relief, but for setting up and outfitting compulsory camps.

The next question is whether it was predominantly the concern over the poor relief funds which determined municipal policy before the Second World War. It must be pointed out that there were also other complaints about caravan-dwellers and it is highly possible that this too influenced municipalities in their stigmatizing policy. They, for example, informed higher-level authorities that the public order was jeopardized by the stationing of caravans along public roads. Horses let loose to graze, moreover, were said to poach grass, while the way caravan-dwellers scrounged meals and clothing at times seemed close to begging. And what about the criminality ascribed to the group? Were these arguments cumulatively of sufficient weight to turn caravan-dwellers away?

To improve our grasp of what motivated the municipalities, a comparison with itinerant groups of foreign origin – the so-called Gypsies – is meaningful. Just as caravan-dwellers, from the mid-nineteenth century onwards they were confronted with a repressive government policy, but in their case it was the national government rather than the municipalities which worked in opposition. One explanation for the comparatively tolerant way municipalities behaved towards Gypsies is, possibly, their foreign status. Not only were municipalities not obliged to take care of them if they were poor, they could even oblige them to move on.[12] Gypsies were probably tolerated because their presence didn't cost the municipalities any money. The crux of the matter is that caravan-dwellers – being Dutch citizens – were entitled to make demands. This difference inspired municipalities to be more stand-offish towards them. Protective feelings towards the poor relief funds were decisive.

WARDING OFF AND DISCOURAGING CARAVAN-DWELLERS

From the end of last century municipalities had been exerting pressure on the Ministry of Justice to issue a general prohibition against caravans. In the beginning their complaints fell on deaf ears which obliged them to derive alternative strategies to keep away caravan-dwellers. The first possibility for achieving their goal was to call for police action on the grounds of Article 135 of municipal law. To activate this procedure they had to file a complaint about a disturbance of public order, morals or health. Right from the start their purpose was to forbid the parking of caravans locally, expecting that the inhabitants of the caravans would inevitably then stay away. This approach misfired owing to a competing law, Article Four of the Dutch Constitution, which offered caravan-dwellers protection by assuring everyone in the Netherlands the freedom, in principle, to stay wherever he or she wished. Thus, with police ordinance in hand municipalities were able to get rid of the caravans, but they were not satisfactorily armed to keep the *dwellers* outside their boundaries.

Administrators quickly realized that without help from higher officials they were powerless in their own municipalities. So they began to urge the national government to pass a law in the hope that in this way restrictions could be imposed on itinerants. Their arguments homed in on areas of relevance to the state. It was no longer emphasized that caravan-dwellers presented a threat to public order, instead they stressed that their way of life conflicted with three new laws. First of all the Compulsory Education Act of 1900: 'They hardly go to school, if at all'; the Housing Law of 1901: 'They live in immorality too close to each other'; and, finally, the Law to Control Contagious Diseases which had become operative in 1872. With these new arguments the municipalities hoped to show that policy towards caravan-dwellers was not really their affair, but rather the direct concern of the national government which should occupy itself more with the supervision of this special group. The pleading of the municipalities ultimately culminated in the naming of a state commission in 1903, one of whose tasks was to consider specific legal measures aimed at caravans. Their final report, published in 1913, led after the First World War to new legislation.[13]

The passing of the Caravan Act of 1918, which limited the number of caravans, ushered in an important phase in the process of minority formation, not, however, because this state law promoted, in principle, the (further) segregation of caravan-dwellers but because it did not lead to the result that the municipalities had anticipated. What happened was that the number of caravans appeared to increase appreciably – the law thus had the opposite effect to that which was desired – while municipalities no longer had the authority to turn them away. The law took precedence over all local ordinances, so that caravan-dwellers were better protected than ever before against arbitrariness. What the situation amounted to in fact was that townships had to tolerate not only the occupants, but their caravans, too. From 1918 onwards municipalities were obliged to equip a location where caravan-dwellers could stay. To reverse what they considered an unfortunate turn of events, local authorities thought over new strategies for fending off caravans. One of the most obvious of these was to select a place with little allure for the obligatory caravan grounds: a plot on the municipality's outskirts, for example, or next to a garbage dump or graveyard. Such ploys are illustrated vividly by the policy pursued by the municipalities of The Hague and Zwolle where camps were improvised in isolated spots and for as long as possible maintained with a minimum of expenditure. The number of facilities remained limited to prevent the premises from attracting other caravan-dwellers. The municipal authorities, moreover, promoted the idea that the caravan-dwellers were themselves responsible for the filthy, run-down state of their camp. The sight of a dirty camp reinforced the image the officials wished to project. This accounts for one of the most persistent prejudices with which caravan-dwellers have had to contend, and still encounter today. Today, immaculate interiors and countless hygienic measures easily offer contrary evidence. A half-century ago things were different.

That with their policy of rejection these municipalities were in line with a national trend appears with crystal clarity from interviews and comparisons with other local studies. The thread running through different accounts was invariably the municipality's fear that a well-furbished caravan camp would attract additional travellers. Thus, structurally, no investments were made in such facilities and most decisions were reached on an *ad hoc* basis, so a consistent municipal policy towards caravans never took shape. After the introduction of the Caravan Act in 1918, the hidden agenda of municipalities was without exception to deter and discourage caravan-dwellers from stopping within their boundaries, with all the predictable consequences for living conditions in the camps so reluctantly provided.

Up to the Second World War caravan-dwellers usually managed to escape from their spatial isolation and kept in touch with members of sedentary society by availing themselves of their right to travel freely. As more and more caravans came to stand in close proximity to each other in pre-selected locations in each municipality, however, under ever-deteriorating living conditions, it became more difficult to avoid segregation. Looking back, we can see how the concentration of caravan-dwellers in remote camps – which, through the neglect of the local authorities, grew progressively shabbier – contributed strongly to the stigmatization of the entire group. What's more, in 1938 for the first time a proposal began to make the rounds to bring caravan-dwellers together in vast, central camps. The Ministry of Justice at once opposed the notion, arguing that since, like other citizens, caravan-dwellers were at liberty to choose their temporary domicile, assignment to central camps would clash with the law. The proposal disappeared into a desk drawer. German occupying forces on the other hand had fewer scruples and bit by bit deprived caravan-dwellers of their mobility, though not in the first years of the war. At this time, caravan-dwellers were already listed separately (in the Central Population Register) and were subjected to checks by the State Identification Service which suspected that all sorts of people had gone into hiding, among them persons whom the occupiers considered dangerous to the state. But as of 1 July 1943 their freedom of movement was over: throughout the country caravan-dwellers were no longer allowed to circulate. In addition so-called assembly camps were designated to which they were required to bring their caravans. Each municipality was informed to which assembly camp it had to send its caravans, with a precise specification of the number. Employees of construction companies and showmen who were members of the professional fair association were exempted from this deportation. Many caravan-dwellers, however, abandoned their wagons to go underground in a house or what passed for one. What before the war the Dutch government had never been able to achieve was now realized: the number of caravans diminished drastically.

THE RISING WALLS OF POSTWAR POLICY

The roots of the process by which caravan-dwellers became a minority are thus embedded in the period preceding the Second World

War when the group was segregated progressively from the rest of the Dutch population. Yet, at that time they formed nothing like a minority in the strict sense, owing to social and economic diversity within the group. We therefore must look for decisive factors in the process of minority formation after 1945. Here we will examine the period up to the new Caravan Act of 1968, for although in the years which were to follow the government would summon to life innumerable regulations to realign its caravan policy, it could no longer counteract the negative effects accruing from the previous decades.

After the Second World War caravan-dwellers, whose freedom of movement was rapidly restored, once again fell under the law of 1918.[14] They could go wherever they wanted and many who went into hiding during the war resumed their old lives. It would not be for long, however, before the freedom they recovered would be threatened a second time. The German occupier's measures had opened the eyes of Dutch administrators at different levels to possibilities for curtailing caravan-dwelling. Furthermore, the Ministry of Justice insisted on a revision of the Caravan Act because of the large numbers who after the war began to live in caravans although such housing was not intended for them.[15] A proposal was made to divide the caravan-dweller population into a sedentary and a non-sedentary part. The first category included the homeless who deserved as quickly as possible to be provided with housing. For the non-sedentary, itinerant caravan-dwellers, there was a wish to streamline existing laws, but also to apply laws more resolutely. Roadbuilders were not covered by the legislation, nor were showmen mentioned in the proposal. The support of indigent caravan-dwellers would in the future be left up to the state, for experience had taught that municipalities usually proved undependable. The Ministry of Justice, however, took a strong stand against the concentration of caravan-dwellers (a 'smudge on our culture') since it was contradictory to the fundamental principle of the Caravan Act which, to be sure, had been drafted to apply to an *itinerant* population group. Meanwhile outspoken ideas had also been developed concerning the moral upbringing of caravan-dwellers. And it was this very subject which would cause feelings to run so high in the 1950s.

Attention to the themes of social care and the raising of children was central to the approach of the Roman Catholic Vereniging van Woonwagen Liefdewerken (Society of Caravan Charities) founded in the Netherlands in 1946.[16] Before the war this was also the terrain of charity committees and church organizations, especially those

of Roman Catholic signature. The new society, however, found it
time to change course and called upon the government in 1948 to
shoulder its responsibilities.[17] They offered to work closely with the
ministries, in exchange, to be sure, for subsidies.[18] The Ministry of
Justice felt the proposal should be taken seriously. The first step
in a new direction was taken.

A direct consequence of the Society's report was that a subcom-
mittee of the State Commission for Replacement of the Poor Law
turned its attention in 1948 to the future of the caravan-dwelling
population.[19] The most important recommendations in its report
which came out in 1952 were a ban on aimless travelling, the concentration of caravan-dwellers in regional camps with adequate
supervision, better physical facilities and proper schooling for young
people. The suggested draft legislation floundered, however, because the government opposed, primarily, the travel prohibition. It
did nonetheless agree that the idea of regional camps should be
worked out in more detail.[20] In anticipation of a new Caravan Act,
in the mid-1950s a number of changes were made in the law. Thus
from 1956 on the education of caravan-dwellers' children became
the concern of Buitengewoon Lager Onderwijs (BLO – Exceptional
Primary Education) and a year later permission was granted to open
the first large regional camps. In these years the government also
began to become more actively involved in the welfare of caravan-
dwellers. A real shift took place in caravan policy from emphasis
on public order to social welfare. In 1957 this was accomplished by
a transfer of responsibility in this policy area from the Ministry of
Justice to the Ministry of Social Welfare.

In addition to calls to concentrate caravan-dwellers in regional
camps, discussion during the 1950s was dominated by the ideas,
fashionable at the time, of re-education and adaptation. In the end
this combination culminated in far-reaching changes of policy towards
caravan-dwellers. First and foremost was the idea that their adaptation to sedentary society should be stimulated so that the time
would come when they would achieve full participation. This view
was strongly coloured by the premises of the struggle waged against
antisocial behaviour in those years. In government policy with respect to families considered social misfits, to adopt the vocabulary
of the period, segregation, concentration in their own neighbourhoods and re-education were considered suitable means.[21]

In 1968 the long-awaited new Caravan Act came into effect which
was intended to promote caravan-dwellers' adaptation to sedentary

society. By design it called for fifty regional camps each with stands for fifty to eighty caravans and all furnished with special facilities including their own schools, doctors and social workers. The controversial ban on travelling was smuggled into the law in disguised form. Caravan-dwellers kept their right to move about but they were no longer allowed to station their homes anywhere outside a regional camp. From then on, moreover, official permission was required to change camps. Not only spatial segregation, but also the size of the caravan population was regulated by the introduction of the principle of descent (*afstammingsbeginsel*). Retrospectively considered, the contours of the group were only formalized with the adoption of this principle in 1968. So-called *burghers* no longer had the right to live in a caravan unless they married into the group. Only the offspring of caravan-dwellers retained the right, on the condition that a stand was available. The result was that when living in a house proved disagreeable, the road back to the caravan camp for those who rued their choice was a hard one.

The Caravan Act of 1968 aspired to improve the social position of caravan-dwellers but it had almost the opposite effect. Accordingly it furthered the process of minority formation. Caravan-dwellers had always kept a certain distance from the rest of the Dutch population, but this segregation was now reinforced, both spatially and legally. The most crucial impact of the law, however, was that it cut down the possibilities for caravan-dwellers to earn their living. The anxiety of such long standing that these 'drifters' would prove a drain on poor relief funds proved a *self-fulfilling prophecy*. In the 1970s and 1980s we see steadily larger numbers of caravan-dwellers becoming dependent on welfare payments. This brings us to an important point in the discussion of the declining survival options for caravan-dwellers in the postwar period. Some blame the government policy, others point to the fading demand for traditional products and services. In this view of things, caravan-dwellers proved unable to adapt to mutations in the labour market. Future research on caravan-dwellers and official policy from the 1950s to the 1970s will have to determine what factors weighed most heavily. As part of such a study special attention should be paid to the government measure instituted in 1965 to make collective welfare payments in the hope to get more grip on the caravan-dweller population.[22] In any event, due to the law of 1968 caravan-dwellers were actually set apart. This raises the question of how they themselves have reacted to the policy of exclusion during the last 120 years and to what degree, and when, they began to present themselves as being different.

CARAVAN-DWELLERS AS AN ETHNOCULTURAL GROUP

Study of the process of minority formation of Dutch caravan-dwellers has shown that position attribution was decisive and preceded position acquisition. What are the implications of this conclusion for the ethnic-cultural position of the group? It is not unlikely that to a certain extent caravan-dwellers were already conscious of themselves as a distinct group before the Second World War. With the passage of time, indeed, they had been relegated to a spatial position of their own in combination with an ever-increasing distance from others. Municipalities shunted them off to isolated camping grounds and in addition they had to contend continuously with a negative image of themselves propagated by the government. In the eyes of many house-dwellers, moreover, given caravan-dwellers' deviant form of residence and way of life, they would have appeared as aliens.

Expressions of ethnocultural self-projection, however, were unknown previous to the Second World War. It may have been incidentally true that caravan-dwellers united to protest against abuses in certain camps, but then invariably only small numbers were involved. What's more, in the process they never referred to the norms and values of their own group, but only pointed out the negligence of the culpable municipality. One subcategory of caravan-dwellers constituted an exception to this pattern: the showmen. In the course of the first half of the twentieth century they started to portray themselves as different from other caravan-dwellers with the goal of safeguarding their own social position. This also had consequences for the general process of group formation.

At the outset of this century caravan-dwellers in general and showmen in particular certainly did not live in separate worlds. In part they had the same occupations and usually stayed at the same caravan camping grounds. When after 1910 preparations were made to regulate living in caravans by law, showmen realized that to protect their own interests they needed to project an image that would distinguish them from the rest. Therefore in 1899, they created Ons Belang (Our Interest), the first society in the Netherlands for travellers connected with fairs. To be convincing in their public relations they had to distance themselves from other caravan-dwelling subgroups. Up to this time there were unmistakable ties among them all, both through the work they performed and through family relations. In the 1920s, however, the first signs became visible of a division which in the following years was to grow steadily deeper.

Comparison with international literature teaches us that a similar development occurred in England and, probably, also in Germany.[23] To combat pending legislation regarding caravans, in England in 1889 the Showmen's Guild was founded.[24] The points of departure for the proposed law (the Movable Dwellings Bill) were more or less parallel with those underpinning the Dutch Caravan Act of 1918. Essentially at stake were the registration of caravans, prescriptions for facilities and hygiene, and obligatory schooling for children.[25] Resistance in English caravan circles concentrated in particular on how the authorities were going to see to it that the law was lived up to: civil servants were to be given the right to enter and inspect any caravan between six in the morning and nine at night in total violation of the individual rights enjoyed by British subjects.[26] The Showmen's Guild, however, wasn't out to block passage of the law, but rather to protect the interests of its membership. For this purpose they considered it necessary to draw a distinction between the *showmen class* for whom it considered the legislation superfluous, and the *Gypsy class*.[27] The various bills failed to carry the vote. From that time on the Showmen's Guild had assured itself a privileged position. Their objective was to distance themselves from the Gypsy stigma by denying a common origin. To do so they targeted Gypsies as a scapegoat.[28]

In the Netherlands a similar reaction can be observed. To avoid stigmatization Dutch showmen began to emphasize that they were different. That they succeeded in their design can be deduced from the privileges which they succeeded in acquiring in the course of time. To the extent that showmen still live in caravans, these are stationed on private plots and not in an official caravan camp. Many – though not all – showmen even avoid contact with other caravan-dwellers.[29] A good number can still be found who do not disown their common past. From their stories we know that before the Second World War various categories of caravan-dwellers intermingled far more than they do today.[30]

When travelling showmen tell how their (grand-) parents made a living, street performers pop up in their accounts with regularity, as do merchants and people who went from fair to fair with some small attraction.[31] Through the winter fairs were quiet and show-men had to support themselves selling umbrellas or Christmas and New Year cards, repairing chair bottoms and doing other jobs which kept caravan-dwellers afloat.[32] Nevertheless a time came when show-men and other caravan-dwellers parted ways, although the process of their alienation from each other is not easy to reconstruct. Show-men did not form the only category that managed to avoid stigma-tization. For road-workers it was altogether unnecessary to distinguish themselves in such a way from the group as a whole, for they were usually not considered to be the same as caravan-dwellers. This probably had to do with the fact that they did not live in caravan camps; their mobile homes were stationed close to their work sites which were usually outside the built-up centres of municipalities. (Factory) workers as a rule were housed only temporarily in a caravan so that for them as well there was no compulsion to distance them-selves from caravan-dwellers.

With regard to the ethnic indentity of caravan-dwellers, it ap-pears highly likely that this was above all a response prompted by Dutch government policy in the 1950s and 1960s.[33] To prove this argument we will sketch some of the dominant images they now-adays have of themselves in relation to Dutch society. They blame, for example, the government for their social isolation, the restric-tion of their freedom to travel and the fact that they are not longer able to be self-supporting. They see the government as chief offender in their development into an autochthonous minority, always bracketed together with Turks, Moroccans and other foreigners with a law socio-economic status. In nearly every conversation with re-searchers they put forward the grudge they bear towards The Hague (the city where the government resides), specially the elderly among them, who still remember the time when they used to travel in order to sell their goods and services. They are aware of the fact that the freedom to travel has been taken away from them step by step. In their opinion, the aim of government policy has always been adjustment to sedentary society and in the end transforma-tion into an average citizen. The aversion to governmental inter-ference is so profound that caravan-dwellers regularly make a comparison between the policy of the Dutch government and that of the German occupier in the Second World War. They also make a clear distinction between the time before and the time after the occupation. In their opinion, the postwar policy boils down to a continuation of German actions during the war.

Another often-heard saying is: 'They put us away in the jungle.'
The isolated location of the camps, the high concentration of many
different families who did not always get along very well and the
diminishing contact with *burghers* caused an increasing stigmatization of the group: 'When you live in such a large camp in the jungle
and someone commits a crime, they blame us all. Everywhere in
society there are bad guys and good guys. Caravan-dwellers are no
exception to that rule, but that doesn't mean that we *all* are criminals.' The fact that they could not travel around any more was a
great blow. The Caravan Act of 1968 stipulated that it was no longer
permissible for a caravan to be sited outside a regional camp. If
people wanted to move to another camp, they had to announce
their arrival and wait for approval before they could leave. In the
view of caravan-dwellers, in particular, this measure caused a break
with their past and frustrated their way of life. The feeling that
they had become prisoners increased. If there were conflicts in the
camps, they could do nothing else but stay. There was no longer a
way out.

Elderly caravan-dwellers often refer to the good old days when
they could earn a living by travelling and selling their goods. They
admit that life was not always easy and they know what it is to be
poor, but at least they had the freedom to live and work wherever
they wanted. Freedom and independence are two concepts which
are inextricably bound to living in a caravan. It explains the lack of
enthusiasm for wage labour. Working for a boss and between four
walls is considered inhuman by most caravan-dwellers. After the
Second World War it became more difficult to continue their trades.
As a result of increasing prosperity, used utensils were easily replaced by new ones and no longer needed to be repaired. At the
same time consumers became more critical. Products had to com-
ply with strict requirements and for their purchases they went to
shops which carried a broad selection and were able to guarantee
quality. It also became harder to find seasonal work. Caravan-dwellers
say they see no problem in changing circumstances. In the past
they have always been flexible and have become used to adjusting
to circumstances over and over again. For instance, they became
involved in the trade in second-hand cars and waste products. But
in that business as well it is very hard to earn a living these days.

A final noteworthy image concerns the skill and good judgement
of human character. Caravan-dwellers think that in this respect they
distinguish themselves favourably from *burghers*, and they ascribe

these qualities to their experience of surviving in many different situations. The function of these images is in the first place an ideological one, namely to stress the identity of their own group. The fact that they do not mention any other differences between themselves and *burghers* has to be ascribed to the short history of the group as a separate minority and the similar cultural background between them and the rest of Dutch society. Nevertheless, as a minority in their own country, they feel more entitled than ethnic minorities to a special status. Through such reactions the idea is strengthened of belonging to a distinct group, one which needs to defend itself against others. The culmination of this development, as mentioned, was the new Caravan Act of 1968. With its enactment the population group of caravan-dwellers was sealed off from 'outsiders' – except for entry by marriage. In combination with a century of negative stereotyping and stigmatizing policy minority formation has turned out to be the inevitable outcome.

Part III
Socio-economic Functioning

8 A Blind Spot: Migratory and Travelling Groups in Western European Historiography[1]

Leo Lucassen

INTRODUCTION

During the last few decades the negative image of travelling groups among professional historians has only changed slowly. It is not strange to see that in more general overviews of the socio-economic history of Europe this image is repeated time and again. A good example is the recent book by Henri Kamen on Western European history in the sixteenth and seventeenth centuries, in which 'poverty', 'beggary', 'vagrancy', 'seasonal migration' and 'criminality' are lumped together point blank.[2] More or less the same mixture can be found in Wehler's overview of German social history. Travelling people are depicted as aimless wanderers, whose criminal behaviour forced authorities to adopt cruel repression.[3]

In this chapter we will try to explain how this interpretation came into being and to what extent it is tenable. Because of the fact that ambulatory professions and travelling groups are mostly indirectly studied in the context of vagrancy, poverty, criminality, marginality, and linguistic peculiarities (secret languages), the criteria for the selection of studies have to be broad. To provide an answer to the two questions stated above, we will first give a brief sketch of the historiography, where emphasis is laid on the underlying assumptions and sources used. In order to structure the huge amount of studies the literature has been subdivided into three perspectives: criminality, marginality and poverty. The criterion for this subdivision is their main focus, mostly reflected in the sources used. The subdivision was not always easy, because in most works all three, or at least two, aspects are dealt with. When this happened, then the most important issue was decisive. For practical reasons we have restricted ourselves mainly to studies on France, Belgium,

Great Britain, Germany and the Netherlands in the period 1500–1950, many of them focusing on the eighteenth and nineteenth centuries. In the third section of this chapter a new perspective is presented, having a greater explanatory power than the ones used in most studies.

We would like to clarify the nature of our (critical) comments. As most of the studies to be reviewed only deal partly, or even marginally, with the main theme of this chapter, we will restrict our analysis to these passages. The reader should therefore bear in mind that criticism of certain authors only applies to their statements on migratory and travelling groups, and not necessarily to their entire work or line of thought.

A final remark about the terms used: in this chapter a distinction is made between *migratory* and *travelling* groups.[4] The first includes *all* people whose occupations make it necessary to travel. Travelling groups, on the other hand, relate to people practising ambulatory professions and who travel in family groups. The latter form therefore only a (small) part of a much wider category.

TRAVELLING GROUPS IN THE EYES OF THE AUTHORITIES: FROM THE TOP DOWN

The criminological interpretation

In past centuries the lower strata of society have been studied primarily as a criminal group, resulting in a pathological image of crime among *les classes dangereuses*. This biased approach has been criticized at length,[5] but the pathological and partially racist explanation has remained tenacious, especially in Germany. Here the influential works of Arnold on travelling groups (such as Gypsies) set the tone till the middle of the 1970s.[6] His view differed only slightly from scientists such as Ritter who had laid the theoretical foundation of the racially inspired[7] policy of extermination of 'Gypsies' and 'antisocials' by the Nazis.[8]

Arnold is quite unambiguous about the character of travelling groups. In his book on *Vaganten* from 1958 he defines his subject explicitly as an 'antisocial problem'. Travellers are regarded as a 'disease of the national community' whose behaviour is to be explained mainly in biological terms. In his more recent book (1983) on all sorts of travellers (pedlars, showmen, tinkers, circus people, etc.) in Germany and other European countries – a mixture of contemporary observations and historical and genealogical research – his main thesis is that travelling is caused by hereditary traits, i.e. by a certain mixture of the lower sedentary German classes with Gypsies who are believed to be of 'foreign blood'. Thus a contrast is created between the sedentary and the nomadic population, the latter being partly of Gypsy descent. The consequences of this mixture are far-reaching, according to Arnold. Travellers are unproductive, primitive and criminal. Just as nomadic hunters and gatherers they only 'find' things and produce nothing, thus remaining on the lowest level of human civilization.[9]

According to the influential Arnold this is not only the case in Germany, but with all 'vagrant groups' in Europe. In a short overview he rejects socio-economic explanations for travelling and tries to prove that travellers are all partly of Gypsy descent.[10] The existence of pedlar communities in Germany is not due to the poor soil and lack of employment. Explicitly, he states that 'the composition of the blood is decisive'.[11]

The first serious attack on Arnold's biological and racist interpretation was made in 1976 by the social historian Küther.[12] In his favourably received book on bandits in pre-industrial Southern Germany, in which he uses Hobsbawm's ideas on the function of social bandits, he rejects Arnold's position by stressing socio-economic changes were responsible for the formation of vagrant groups. The problem with his study, however, and this holds true also for his book on 'vagrants' that appeared seven years later,[13] is the very general statements on migratory and travelling groups (which include all kinds of people with ambulant occupations, such as knife-grinders, tinkers, showmen, pedlars, etc.), whereas his sources are mainly on bandits. His explanation for the pariah position of vagrants may be different in principle from that of Arnold, but the image is more or less the same: he assumes without further ado that they formed a closed social group that was despised by the rest of sedentary society. His division of pre-industrial Germany into productive (farmers and craftsmen) and unproductive (vagrants) members is not only simplistic, but, as we shall see, also highly questionable. In the wake of German criminologists a picture is given of vagrants doing nothing but robbing, stealing, intimidating and begging. Even in his definition Küther follows without comment the highly negative image of earlier criminologists.[14] This mixture of critical and traditional attitudes is also evident in his treatment of Arnold's idea that criminal behaviour was an individual predisposition. He rejects this pathological approach, but does not exclude the possibility that genetic traits can explain the parasitic way of life of the 'racially pure Gypsies'.[15]

Although in Küther's research traces of the traditional criminological approach can be found, his work marks a break with the past and must be considered as an important step forward in German historiography. The same can be said of several other studies on 'bandits' and 'vagrants' in pre-industrial Germany that have appeared in the past decade.[16] A good example is the work of Schubert on *Arme Leute*.[17] He also mainly used criminal records, leading him to conclude that migratory groups in general were criminal and poor. His main argument is that in the list of wanted persons so many ambulant professions were mentioned. Notwithstanding this bias, however, Schubert definitely has an eye for criminalizing processes.[18] He shows how distrustful central authorities were, trying therefore to forbid and criminalize ambulant professions. The people involved were regarded to be of a low moral standard and the professions as a cloak for begging 'and criminal behaviour'. Schubert shows that in practice many local authorities were tolerant because they knew that this image did not completely hold true. In his section on migratory groups he therefore gives a nuanced sketch of all kinds of ambulant professions, stressing that many of these were functional, especially in the countryside.[19]

During the last decade approaches such as that chosen by Schubert have been followed by others, leading to a less stereotypical image of migratory groups. Finzsch, for example, points out that it is wrong to assume that all the people concerned were poor and deviant, and that it has to be realized that the lower classes only appeared in the sources when they were seen as a problem.[20]

A second important field of research within the criminality interpretation is the Tudor period in England. The reason for this interest is the well-known repressive policy of the authorities against what they saw as the threat to orderly society posed by vagrants. From the nineteenth century onwards this resulted in a number of studies that have become known as the 'rogue literature'.[21] The main argument here is that vagrants formed large bands of workshy and idle rogues and were organized in a separate criminal anti-society. This picture is due to a particularly uncritical approach of the sources which breathe an outright hostility towards vagrants.

An important turn in the historical interpretation of these 'rogues', comparable with the reorientation of Schubert, was caused by the publications of Beier and Slack,[22] which have convincingly debunked the idea of an anti-society. Just what kind of people are behind the label 'vagrant' remains in both studies for the most part in the dark. Due to the selectivity of the sources used – only those who have been arrested are known – it remains unclear to what extent they were representative of the entire group of migratory people. Conclusions are only valid for 'vagrants under arrest', not for 'vagrants in general'. This selectivity has another disadvantage, namely that it is assumed too easily that people labelled as vagrants were poor and that travelling was at the bottom end of society. This may be so, but the evidence put forward by Beier and Slack does not support such general conclusions. The result is that contemporary characterizations of the professions of 'vagrants' are easily reproduced.

To conclude: as we have seen, the criminality perspective has been very strong in Germany, although not only there. This approach is valuable for our knowledge on travelling groups, certainly as far as the attitude of the authorities is concerned. In particular the more recent studies by Beier, Schubert and Finzsch have showed how far-reaching the criminalization of migratory groups and their travelling existence could be. On the other hand, however, the survey makes clear how difficult it is to break loose of the traditional negative interpretations of the socio-economic functions of travelling groups. The racist interpretation of Arnold may not attract many followers any more, but his picture of the workshy and criminal traveller is still very much alive and kicking.

The marginality interpretation

The second important point of departure in studies on travelling groups is marginality. Instead of economic status, the social position is highlighted. The 'founding father' of this perspective is the well-known Polish historian Bronislaw Geremek. His attention to the stigmatizing policy of the authorities is an important addition to the criminological perspective, but at the same time relics of the traditional criminality perspective can be found, leading to an ambiguous and inconsistent explanation. Thus he *also* considers marginalization as an inevitable outcome of the objective growth of the vagrancy problem and the existence of an 'anti-society' in which crime, beggary and theft are the core values. This is based

on the unproven assumption that marginal people placed themselves outside the social order, retreating into their own 'society'.
Nevertheless Geremek's stress on the stigmatizing role of church
and state meant an important step forward in the historiography.

Another important representative of the marginality approach is
the Swiss historian Graus who wrote a fundamental article on
marginal groups in the late Middle Ages, thereby focusing on the
attitude of the dominant society and the reaction of the stigmatized groups.[23] Although in the case of Jews and Gypsies Graus is
not free from primordial assumptions,[24] he justly criticizes the inclination of many historians to make use of all kinds of stigmatizing terms, such as vagrants, paupers, beggars, dishonest people,
etc., and the use of a linear model of society, placing these categories
at the bottom. To break loose from this way of thinking he pro-
poses the term 'marginals' (*Randgruppen*), to be defined as people
who have been labelled as being on the edge of society. With this
fresh approach, in which all kinds of 'marginal' groups are from
the start not regarded as down-and-outs, Graus creates the possibility of escaping the linear scheme.

To summarize, we can say that the contribution of the second
interpretation is that migratory groups, now defined as marginal,
have been dissociated, at least in principal, from criminality and
poverty. Not all marginal groups are poor and criminal, they are
only different. The primordial idea that lies underneath, however,
can be problematic. Other important contributions are more or less
the same as the new direction in the criminality approach: systematic analysis of the authorities' attitude and not taking for granted
contemporary opinions and categorizations. Because of the amount
of attention paid to the (changing) attitudes, the socio-economic
function of migratory groups is only treated in a superficial way.

The poverty interpretation

In the search for the socio-economic functions of migratory people,
books on poverty offer a useful starting point. Most of these, however, do not deal with travelling groups and are not very useful for
the argument in this chapter. We therefore selected only studies
that go deeper into their history, to start with the influential work
on *The Poor of Eighteenth-century France* by Olwen Hufton. In this
study ambulatory professions, seasonal labour and migration are
considered as signs of social decline. Seasonal migrants barely dis-

tinguished themselves from down-and-outs. They are pictured as poor and unskilled wretches who, when they were lucky, earned some money in the high season. The socio-economic position of people with ambulatory professions is described in an even more negative way. More critical of their contemporary sources are the studies of Gutton and of Schwartz on poverty in the *ancien régime*.[25] In his search for the vagabonds Gutton used the archives of the *marechaussée* and the poor houses and ends up more or less with the same conclusions as Hufton a few years later. People who started wandering, especially pedlars, had a great chance of ending up as vagabonds. In many places in his work Gutton puts these general remarks into perspective. To start with, he shows that the authorities made an exception for seasonal workers because they were indispensable for the farmers, especially during harvest time.[26] For the *marechaussée*, whose main function was to repress beggary and vagrancy, the difference between a seasonal worker and a vagrant was often unclear, however. A good example are the so-called *scieurs de long*, men specializing in sawing planks out of trees using huge sawhorses. Although they earned enough money and worked regularly, they were arrested on many occasions, because they used to beg for food travelling to and from their work in order to maximize their income.[27] A second illustrative example are the pedlars who were also often arrested on suspicion of vagrancy. In many cases they could prove that they earned enough money to make a living and, just as the *scieurs*, they were soon released. Although Gutton holds the view that most ambulatory travellers were poor and close to vagrancy, his analysis of the *marechaussée* archives leads him to the conclusion that 'real vagrants', people without any occupation, formed a small minority.[28]

An important contribution to the study on poverty has been made by the neo-Marxist studies of the Belgian historians Lis and Soly. Building on the work of Hufton and Gutton among others they offer a broad overview of the history of poverty and poor relief in Western Europe from the Middle Ages onwards. The innovative aspect of their approach is mainly that they reject the vision of Abel and Le Roy Ladurie that poverty in the *ancien régime* was more or less a natural and therefore inevitable situation.[29] They give a class analysis of the socio-economic developments in Europe, explaining the attitudes of the governing classes as a means to control the labour force in order to keep wages down and labour available. The main idea is that the growth of capitalism has increased poverty by the proletarianization of the mass of the population.

The interesting part of their book for our theme is their analysis of the increasing criminalization of begging and wandering from the fifteenth century onwards. They show that poverty is no longer deemed normal and is now equated with vagrancy and criminality. At the same time an elaborate stereotyping of the alleged criminal anti-society came about. The 'social problem' was associated with idleness, criminality, etc., to be solved by the creation of work-houses. In order to regulate the labour-market the cities created a system of poor relief. In this climate the idea of vagrants could easily become the symbolic apogee of antisocial behaviour and it was extended to everybody who refused to work for a (low) wage. The aim was not so much to catch the real criminals, but to stigmatize the wandering poor as disorderly and antisocial. The church did the same and the middle groups soon took over the hostile attitude. Especially from the seventeenth century on, the alleged resistance of the poor against wage-labour was regarded as structural. Marginal groups were thought to be extra dangerous because they could persuade others to go astray.

A weak point is that it is too easily assumed that proletarianization can be equated with impoverishment, at least where the pre-industrial period is concerned, and that migration has to be regarded in the first place as a phenomenon of poverty.[30] The possibility that travelling was sometimes a positive choice, for example to escape poverty, is not considered. Migratory groups, who strictly speaking need not be proletarians,[31] are thus reduced to victims of capitalism and state formation, and this explains why Lis and Soly refrain from a thorough analysis of their economic functionality. This does not mean that their thesis is not useful; the contrary is true. The stigmatization of migratory groups, regarded primarily as people who resist wage-labour, explains the hardening policy towards them. Very important, and in need of elaboration, is the observation by several historians that all kinds of alternative strategies have to be regarded as rational economic behaviour and not as signs of a *carpe diem* mentality.[32]

THE ECONOMIC FUNCTION OF TRAVELLING GROUPS: FROM THE BOTTOM UP

The labour migration approach

Recent theoretical developments within all three approaches dealt with so far have in common an important progress in our knowledge of the attitude of the authorities towards migratory groups. A highly critical study of the sources in the past few decades has focused attention on the stigmatizing and criminalizing policy of many state institutions. As we have seen, however, this did not change fundamentally the general image of the socio-economic place of migratory groups in society. The reason for this is that the socio-economic history of these groups is in general not the main object of study. Most authors have other preoccupations, such as crime and poverty. This makes it understandable why the sources used may be suited for their research, but are highly selective and therefore produce a biased analysis in the case of migratory groups.

In order to produce a more balanced analysis we therefore have to use the new insights of the three approaches and combine these with a study of the socio-economic history of ambulant professions. This implies more attention to the importance of labour and mobility. To what results such an interpretation can lead is illustrated by several studies of the group around the French historian Goubert, who has pleaded for the use of quantitative and serial sources. The results of his research on vagrancy in eighteenth-century France (in the departments Brie and Bicêtre) are much more balanced than the studies mentioned in the poverty approach. They show that most of the people arrested by the *marechaussée* did have genuine professions and the increase in the number of 'vagrants' in the first place has to be explained by the fact that the *marechaussée* was offered higher bounties. Criminality and begging only played a minor role. The majority of the people arrested as vagrants were labourers, not beggars, vagrants, thieves or bandits.[33]

The idea that labour mobility – especially seasonal labour – is not only a functional but also an essential element within the labour market and therefore necessary for economic development has been elaborated further and more thoroughly in the study by Jan Lucassen on migrant labour in Europe between 1600 and 1900.[34] In this mainly (socio-)economic analysis of migrant and seasonal labour the emphasis is laid not on marginality, poverty or criminality, but on the labour factor. Compared with the works mentioned in the first part of this chapter, the interpretation of ambulatory professions (which make up only a minor part of this study) is here radically different. By concentrating on their actual function the author makes clear that they cannot in general be seen as a cloak for begging or just as marginal. In spite of the often bad reputation of tinkers, knife-grinders, hawkers and pedlars, their work was important for the distribution of goods and services and many could make a reasonable living out of it. Hawkers and pedlars in the seventeenth and eighteenth centuries, for example, specialized in areas with a weak infrastructure and economically backward conditions. They were well organized, had considerable financial reserves and made agreements on the coverage of certain territories. Although their home base was situated in areas with few economic possibilities, it would be wrong to consider them as poor. During their lifetime, many accumulated a modest capital with which they bought a farm or a small working place.[35]

The study on migrant labour not only shows that the existence of migratory and travelling groups was primarily economically based, but also that migration in general was a widespread phenomenon. This fits very well with recent studies that emphasize the structural character of migration in the pre-industrial world.[36] Applied to people working in the retailing and amusement sector this migrant labour approach proves to be promising, as is shown by a few monographs on certain ambulatory professions in the nineteenth century.[37] A good example is the study by Demetz on the hawkers from the Austrian Grödenthal.[38] She shows that the negative image of the hawking business (*Hausierhandel*) cannot be maintained. The accusations that these hawkers were workshy and only sold products of inferior quality and thereby deceived the simple country folk were mainly uttered by sedentary shopkeepers who were afraid of competition. Demetz argues that these allegations were generally false. Many of these hawkers also operated in larger places, where people could compare the quality with that offered by the shops. Moreover, in the smaller villages they returned regularly enough so that they could not afford to cheat the villagers.

The more positive interpretation of Demetz and others is supported by the results of a research into the hawking business initiated by the German Verein für Sozialpolitik (Society for Social Policy) in 1895.[39] The overall image arising from the enquiry was that of a hard-working, resourceful and economically functional group that not only operated in the traditional countryside, but increasingly in the ever-growing working-class neighbourhoods of the cities.[40] It appeared that many workers preferred to buy from these pedlars instead of going to the more expensive and snobbish stores. Most contributions to this enquiry stress the good and regular contacts between pedlars and customers and reject implicitly the idea that the sedentary population is mostly the victim of deceitful pedlars.

The conclusions of these monographs are supported by the results of several smaller contributions to the socio-economic history of hawkers in the nineteenth century.[41] Although opinions on the chances for upward social mobility greatly differ,[42] a *communis opinio* exists on the indispensable function of pedlars. Moreover, these studies show that the negative attitude towards ambulant professions was more differentiated than is often suggested. Notwithstanding the authorities' distrust of pedlars (especially from abroad) in France, Belgium and Great Britain, they recognized their economic functionality and therefore refused to give in to pressure from shopkeepers to restrict the competition of hawkers. In France the policy of many local authorities to restrict ambulant peddling required the Minister of the Interior in 1816 to instruct the prefects that the law of October 1798 (guaranteeing freedom of trade) had to be enforced.[43] Restrictive regulations were only issued towards aliens and in some cases towards indigenous groups such as Jews and Gypsies. General instructions were rare and were seldom enforced.

The studies mentioned so far mainly deal with single men or women who normally did not travel with families. Although they give reason to assume that the negative ideas on itinerant groups are highly questionable, they still do not teach us very much about *travelling groups* (people practising ambulatory professions and who travel in family groups). For this we have to turn to the recent historical research on groups labelled as 'Gypsies'. The results of these studies can be regarded as the ultimate test, as all the works that mention Gypsies depict them as the workshy and vagrant group *par excellence*.[44] Historical research on Gypsy groups from a labour migration angle is not easy to find. In the past decade most authors in this field have begun to attack the criminological and racist interpretation for the marginal position of Gypsies, especially in Germany, but this analysis is restricted to the attitude of the authorities. Exceptions to this rule are the studies of the historians Fricke on Württemberg,[45] Mayall on the Gypsy-travellers in Great Britain in the nineteenth and twentieth centuries[46] and Lucassen's dissertation on the history of Gypsies in the Netherlands during the same period. These studies show that when the activities of people labelled as Gypsies are set in labour migration perspective, the highly negative image is refuted to a great extent.

These conclusions agree with the recent anthropological research on 'peripatetics' or 'service nomads', since that also focuses on their economic function within society.[47] Most students no longer depict them as rare and exotic beings or as parasites, but stress their organizational flexibility and willingness to move and to switch occupations, which enabled them to fill gaps in the host economy.

ALTERNATIVE SOURCES

In the preceding section we have made clear that for a more balanced approach to migratory groups three conditions have to be fulfilled: (a) they must be treated as a normal part of the general labour migration; (b) research should be aimed at a detailed analysis of their economic functions; and (c) a different and more diverse use of historical sources should be applied. As the first two conditions have already been discussed at length, we will here dwell on the third condition. In the following, four categories of sources are proposed:

General economic and statistical sources

If we consider the possibility that not all migratory and travelling groups were poor and criminal, and that most performed useful functions in society, than they must have left traces in government records concerning the regulation of ambulant professions. The nineteenth and twentieth centuries have produced a wealth of such sources. As a result of state formation and national economic policies from the Napoleonic time onwards, all kinds of permits, patent registers and taxes were introduced for people with ambulant professions; in many cases these records have withstood the ravages of time. To reconstruct the economic history of the Grödner pedlars, for example, Demetz used lists of permits containing all sorts of social (name, place of birth, age, etc.) and economic (income, destinations) information. A similar German source in this respect was the travel permit for ambulant professions introduced in 1869 in order, among other reasons, to guarantee that the holder did not use his or her profession as a cloak for begging. The fact, for example, that local authorities in many cases kept providing 'Gypsies' with these permits, notwithstanding continued instructions from central authorities not to, can be an important indication that Gypsies could not be differentiated from other travellers and therefore were not as parasitic as is generally assumed. A more specialized source for travelling groups, producing more or less the same information as the records used by Demetz and others, are records of caravan permits, which exist in the Netherlands from 1918 onwards.[48]

Apart from these records in some countries (government) enquiries into ambulant professions are available. The most elaborate is the French enquiry of 1811, which formed the main source for Jan Lucassen's study on migrant labour.[49] Other important enquiries were undertaken at the end of the nineteenth century in Germany, Italy and Belgium as a reaction to complaints by shopkeepers and delegates in Parliament on the alleged unfair competition of pedlars. The best known is the already mentioned publication of the German Society for Social Policy of 1898 on the situation of ambulant professions in Germany.

A last important statistical source for migratory groups operating outside their native country is the passport registers for alien as well as indigenous travellers, foreigners' registers and population registers. As a result of state formation these can be found in most European countries, as well as in the United States, on several levels (local and national) from about 1815 onwards and in some cases also for the *ancien régime*. Such sources make it possible to reconstruct to some extent mobility patterns, occupational shifts and methods of operating.

The traditional 'repressive' sources

The fact that most letters and reports by authorities dealing with 'vagabonds' (especially the police and gendarmerie) are in many cases biased does not rule them out as an important source. As we already saw in the review of the first three approaches (cf. especially the work of Gutton), neutral information can be deduced from them.

On a *macro* level long series of correspondence between various authorities concerning 'Gypsies', 'travellers' or 'vagrants' can be established. The advantage of such series is that for a longer period cycles can be found in the attitude towards and ideas on the categories concerned. Moreover, a large collection of such documents enables us to differentiate between the various branches of the state (Justice, Foreign Affairs, Domestic Affairs, Industry) as well as the several hierarchical levels (local, provincial, national). Let us illustrate this on the basis of the history of Gypsies in the Netherlands. On analysis of the long series of correspondence and regulations concerning this group during the period 1868–1944 (3,000 documents), the general parasitic image does not hold and the attitude of local authorities and the population does not appear entirely negative. This can be deduced from the fact that despite numerous and repeated exhortations from central authorities to expel Gypsies without exception, all kinds of permits were issued to them and people continued to make use of their services.

On a *micro* level documents from the same series show that even in the letters of the most rabid anti-Gypsy official in the Netherlands, the Administrator for Border Control and Aliens Service (AGVD), neutral information can be found. Thanks to his registration passion, for example, it is possible to calculate how many horses an average horse-dealer took with him. This helps to determine the relative importance of these horse-dealers to the Dutch and Belgian horse fairs. A second advantage of this source is found in the often very detailed descriptions of Gypsy activity. The numerous letters of the AGVD on certain groups of Silesian coppersmiths contain data on their way of operating, customers, earnings, skill, etc.[50] In Germany and Great Britain no systematic serial research has been undertaken yet, but the available studies give reason to believe that with a similar approach more or less the same conclusions will be reached.[51]

Apart from correspondence between various officials, 'repressive' sources can contain other valuable information. A good example is the police reviews that were published in most German states from 1800 onwards and in the Netherlands half a century later.[52] The Dutch review, for example, published weekly lists of people who had been expelled because they were unwanted aliens. These lists not only give their names, but also their places of birth, ages, occupations, means of transportation and family members. These make it possible to reconstruct the migration and economic specializations of the four main Gypsy groups that came to the Netherlands during the period 1850–1920,[53] but these lists can also be used to gather information on other migratory groups, such as the Italian street musicians or French bear-leaders.

Other qualitative sources

It is not only in government sources that a wealth of information can be found. Newspapers, specialized reviews, literature, contemporary descriptions and iconographic material[54] can also be important in reconstructing the socio-economic and cultural history of migratory and travelling groups. In most Western European countries the migration of Gypsies from Eastern Europe, for example, has been reported in a very detailed way in newspapers. Numbers, dress, carts, tents, occupations, wealth, destination, attitude of the population and authorities: all these subjects have been dealt with and these newspaper accounts can help to fill the gaps left by other sources. The same holds true for certain colourful itinerant groups such as Italian child-musicians, who attracted much attention from politicians, civil and police authorities, philanthropic agencies, Italian diplomats, newspapers, magazines and contemporary writers in cities such as Paris, London and New York. Zucchi has shown that a careful and critical analysis of the various sources that were the result of this attention can produce a balanced description. Being aware of the stereotypical image of the wandering musicians (the 'little slaves of the harp') of his middle-class sources, he is able to discount many negative exaggerations and generalizations and reconstruct the economic reason for their migration.[55] Less conspicuous groups, such as German musicians, remained more in the dark, but a creative combination of various sources enables a reconstruction of their professions and mobility.

Specialized (economic) reviews can be crucial for our knowledge of the economic functions of travelling groups. If one entertains the possibility that certain Gypsy groups played an important role in the horse market, for example, one should study reviews such as *The Horse, The World of Horses* or the economic archives of places with important horse fairs instead of police reports. These are sources which may not seem obvious at first, but which nevertheless do contain valuable material.

Interviews

A last important source is interviews with travellers. The use of interviews by now is widespread among historians, especially in social history (history of women, labourers, etc.). In historical studies on travelling groups this source is seldom called upon. Anthropologists and sociologists, however, have shown its potential. For the research of Acton and Okely into the economic life of English travellers after the Second World War, the core of their material was gathered by interviews and participating observation.[56]

The critical reader may argue that most examples given above concern the nineteenth and twentieth centuries, whereas the historiographical review was mainly restricted to the *ancien régime*. We cannot, of course, reproach other historians for neglecting sources that were non-existent for their period. Historians of the *ancien régime* must manage with what they have, and in many cases this means highly selective sources. Although their job is definitely more difficult than that for students of the past two centuries, they also can escape the dominating contemporary anti-migratory opinion. The research by Baulant, Goubert and others into French parish records in the seventeenth and eighteenth centuries has made this clear. Moreover, Goubert – and to some extent also Gutton and Schwartz – showed that the repressive records of the *marechaussée*, when analysed as a socio-economic source, also lead to different conclusions than when only information regarding poverty or criminality is selected. Although less abundant than in recent centuries, the *ancien régime* also offers economic and statistical sources. In the study by Lucassen on migrant labour in Europe between 1600 and 1800, for example, the transport of migrant labourers and the recruitment of sailors was reconstructed,[57] whereas Spufford in her search for the petty chapmen in seventeenth-century England combined (qualitative) information from wills and inventories with quantitative data from the register of licences under the 1696–7 Act, enabling her to give a balanced impression of the chapmen's economic function.[58]

CONCLUSION

In the introduction of this chapter two questions were posed. To begin with, how do we explain the negative image of travelling people in European historiography? As we have seen, the answer is partly of a methodological and technical nature and therefore relatively simple. Most historians are in the first place interested in criminality, marginality and poverty where migratory and travelling groups are concerned. The consequences for the overall image are far-reaching.

Travellers are only treated when they appear within the context of these themes: when they are suspected of theft, aimless wandering, deviant behaviour or vagrancy. In this light it is tempting and therefore conceivable that on the basis of these selective sources authors implicitly or explicitly jump to conclusions on travellers in general. The reason for this is perhaps not so much the prejudices in their, mostly criminal, records – most historians nowadays are aware of this bias – but primarily the omission of other sources.

The tenacity of the negative image is further strengthened by a strong *communis opinio* on migratory and travelling groups among historians. It is notable that it makes no great difference whether the ideas are inspired by Marxism or liberalism. In both cases the outcome is more or less the same. 'Leftist' historians such as Hufton and Hobsbawm seem to be strongly influenced by Marx's idea of the lumpenproletariat, which includes everybody without (regular) wage labour, i.e. pedlars, showmen and others.[59] In his famous study *Bandits* Eric Hobsbawm differentiates between social bandits and criminals.[60] The first category presumably is recruited from farmers, whereas the second comes from the vagrant and nomadic population. This picture may be due to Marx's characterization of the lumpenproletariat as an untrustworthy underclass that – susceptible to populism – by their lack of class consciousness could easily be used by reactionary forces as their stormtroopers. In the 'historical process' of the proletariat they did not play a role.

The linear perspective of society, in which travelling is seen as a sign of being uprooted and vagrant, is shared by non-Marxists, and as a result travelling groups are predominantly studied in the light of criminality, deviancy and poverty. It seems as if both 'left' and 'right' are so strongly influenced by the nineteenth-century cultural offensive of the bourgeoisie against groups such as travellers that the negative ideas concerning them are often reproduced in contemporary sources.

Notwithstanding this *communis opinio* several studies offering the labour mobility approach have made clear that the dominating image is not tenable in general. In particular, studies with an economic perspective supply quite different conclusions. 'Gypsies' are the ultimate test in this respect, and they are often presented as the parasitic and criminal group *par excellence*. As we have seen, recent historical and anthropological research shows that this image cannot be maintained. They were not aimless wanderers, living from day to day and earning their money by theft, deceit or begging.

Most of them, as did all travellers, tried to make a living by using the possibilities and advantages that ambulant professions offered. Some were quite successful, others had to be content with a more modest income, and there were people who now and then resorted to crime – more or less the same picture as can be drawn for a group of wage labourers or the population in general. These conclusions agree with the new insights into the field of the history of migration, namely that migration (be it internal, seasonal or permanent) has to be considered as a normal drive and motivated by an urge for upward social mobility, and therefore not automatically a symptom of crisis.

This conclusion, however, leads to the paradoxical situation that although monographs on certain migratory groups draw a fairly favourable picture of their economic function, these results do not influence the dominant criminality/marginality/poverty paradigm. Conversely, historians who undertake this kind of economic research do not seem to realize that their results implicitly contradict the outcome of many studies mentioned in the first part of this chapter. Why have the studies based on the labour migration approach not fundamentally influenced the interpretation of historians working with other perspectives? One might think that this lack of communication is caused by the ongoing specialization of the historical discipline. However tempting and partially justified this explanation is, it is not sufficient. The reason for the cohabitation of contradictory knowledge is more complicated. Reviewing most studies one cannot escape the impression that the students involved are often aware of the existence of other approaches, but do not realize that they plough the same field. The contrast between 'honest' and 'dishonest' travellers, as continually propagated by authorities from the fifteenth century onwards (comparable with deserving and non-deserving poor), is thus maintained.

9 The Clink of the Hammer was Heard From Daybreak till Dawn: Gypsy Occupations in Western Europe (Nineteenth– Twentieth Centuries)[1]

Leo Lucassen

INTRODUCTION

Many children's books in Western European countries portray people living in caravans and performing those trades associated with fairs and circuses, but services provided by knife-grinders and chair-bottomers also appear regularly in literature written for children. People have been and still are confronted with all kinds of itinerant occupations in their daily life: showpeople who go from fair to fair, musicians, conjurers, jugglers, acrobats and others who perform their activities in the streets of big cities, collectors of scrap metal, and so on.

These kinds of occupation have existed for ages and been practised by all kinds of people, of whom the most well known are those who travel in groups. They performed a wide range of functions, which have in common the spreading of goods and services that mostly could not be offered, or not at such a low price, by the sedentary professional class.[2] The demand for the mending of kettles or street musicians in many cases was simply too low for inhabitants of cities and villages to earn a living. Therefore a small class of people specialized in itinerant occupations, thus complementing the functions of their sedentary colleagues.

Because of their travelling lifestyle, however, they were more vulnerable to negative treatment by groups who distrusted them. For example, authorities often thought Gypsies practised their occupations in order to beg and steal, while sedentary competitors now and then accused them of unfair competition. In both cases itinerant groups had great trouble defending themselves properly. They lacked the organizational strength of the guilds and the privileges of most sedentary occupations.

Gypsies and others had, and many still have, an economic and social function and were able to adapt to major economic changes. The Industrial Revolution did not make their occupations and services obsolete, but created a range of new possibilities. It is therefore a myth that itinerant groups were passive victims of modernization, and that their archaic nomadic culture was unable to adapt to change.

THE ESSENCE OF GYPSY OCCUPATIONS

It may seem odd, but Gypsy occupations did not differ essentially from economic activities by sedentary people. One of the most confusing concepts used in this respect is 'nomadism'. This idea refers to societies of hunters and gatherers, and is often used as proof of the Gypsies' traditional and specific culture. Gypsies, however, differ as much from pastoral nomads – wandering in a certain area with their herds – as do other members of Western European societies. Although Gypsy occupations have some specific features, on the whole the similarities with other ('normal') occupations are much greater than is often assumed.

Let us have a look at the main characteristics associated with the 'Gypsy economy'. The *family as work unit*, where all members (men, women, children) contribute to the family income, is a phenomenon that can be found all over the world. Most people followed this model in the past and only in recent times has individualization become more general. But even in modern highly industrialized societies, the family as work unit is still valid, particularly among immigrant or ethnic groups. A second feature often mentioned with regard to the Gypsy economy is their *mobility*. Here, again, Gypsies are not unique. Well into the twentieth century, European agriculture and industry made use of tens of thousands of seasonal workers who left their homes every year for months at a time to earn a living abroad or in other parts of the country. Irish labourers went to England, Germans to the Low Countries, French inhabitants of mountainous regions to the Basin of Paris, while Italian musicians and animal tamers wandered all over Europe and even to other parts of the world.

A last crucial element is *self-employment*. Many studies have stressed that Gypsies prefer to be their own boss. Wage-labour is looked upon unfavourably and is considered to have a lower status. This preference is explained in cultural terms which stress that Gypsies are self-supporting because in that way the necessary boundary between their own culture and the world of the non-Gypsies can be upheld. This may be so at the moment, but it remains to be proven whether the choice for independent occupations is rooted in their culture. Moreover, the ideology expressed by many Gypsies does not deviate much from the arguments put forward by most self-employed people. It can be argued with as much plausibility that the preference for self-employment has economic roots and that the present, extremely negative attitude of Gypsies towards wage-labour is a reaction to discrimination and stigmatization. One argument in favour of this interpretation is the fact that Gypsies in the past worked as wage labourers on a temporary basis. Moreover, they were not the only self-employed itinerant people in the past. From the Middle Ages onwards many took to the road as hawkers, pedlars, musicians and so on. The reason for this was mainly economic: a living could be earned by filling up the gap between supply and demand.

In many rural areas it was difficult for people to buy products because of the lack of shops. Besides, there was a need for entertainment and all kinds of services. The possibilities these economic niches offered were not only used by Gypsies. In all Western European countries people specialized in independent itinerant functions, the only exception being that – as in the case of the seasonal wage-labour migrants – in most cases they left their families at home.

The *specific* character of Gypsy occupations consisted of a combination of the three elements mentioned above: a mobile way of life in family groups aimed at self-employment. Unlike the seasonal migrants or itinerant traders and craftsmen mentioned above, Gypsies took their families along with them, on foot, in carts or in caravans. Therefore there was little necessity to have a house, although in practice a combination of house and caravan occurred. In England, for example, a significant number of Gypsy families settled from time to time in houses, particularly during the most severe period of winter. Having thus defined the character of occupations of people who have been labelled as Gypsies through time, we propose to take a closer look at the different specializations and their function within society.

THE MAIN GYPSY OCCUPATIONS

For the purpose of analysis we have divided the economic activities into four separate categories. Consequently we will deal with trading, crafts, entertainment and seasonal wage-labour.

Trading, hawking and peddling

Trading was perhaps the most important economic niche for Gypsies, and within this category hawking – going from house to house trying to sell products – seems to have been the principal activity. Gypsies did not have a monopoly on hawking; on the contrary, many people tried to earn a living in this way. In particular, members of the working class undertook itinerant activities, among other things, in order to increase their low wages. For these 'penny capitalists' retailing continued to be popular for a long time. The low costs made street-selling or hawking attractive to the ambitious and destitute alike and provided a possible escape route for the working man.

Especially in the first half of the nineteenth century we see predominantly single hawkers operating in the countryside selling light hardware toys and other goods. In only a few instances are 'Gypsies' mentioned in this respect. The 'Gypsy awareness' of authorities increased after the middle of the century when more people started travelling in families and took their own housing with them. In Great Britain the most well-known groups, the 'princes of the itinerant trade', were some thousand pedlars known as 'cheapjacks'. They travelled with their families to fairs, markets and towns all over the country, selling cutlery, firearms, saddlery and other sorts of manufactured goods. The transition of single hawkers to hawkers who took their families with them was stimulated by the wider use of caravans after 1870, although in some countries (especially Great Britain) tents were also used quite frequently from the beginning of the nineteenth century onwards. A caravan made travelling with one's family not only easier and more comfortable, but also more visible. In most countries many of these travellers were quickly stigmatized and often 'gypsified' by the authorities.

Due to industrialization the demand for cheap items such as brooms, baskets, fancy goods and earthenware increased enormously. This was not only a result of population growth, but also because more and more people began to work for wages while at the same time cities were growing and becoming more important. Consumers neither had the time nor the ability to manufacture many of these goods themselves. Moreover, hawkers often offered cheaper products. The travelling group of potters in the beginning of the nineteenth century in England, for example, used to buy 'seconds' from the pottery industry for sale either at fairs or on the doorstep. This example further makes clear that, as stated in the introduction, it is impossible to consider Gypsies as a clear-cut ethnic group, not only because travelling groups have been given different labels, but also because various itinerant professionals had close contact with one another.[3]

The demand for earthenware and other products sold by hawkers and street-sellers was created by the jerky development of modernization. In particular the increase in shops did not keep pace with the growth of the population, the purchasing power of the masses and urbanization. The importance of hawkers and pedlars must not be underestimated because many customers depended on them.[4] Even where several shops did exist people often preferred buying goods from hawkers, many of whom were women.[5] Most hawkers had a regular circle of customers and were therefore trusted. Moreover, they offered cheaper goods and did not show the contempt that many workers were confronted with in middle-class shops. Consequently some shopkeepers were not all that popular with the working man.[6]

Not only the demand, but also the supply stimulated itinerant trade. Wholesale businesses in particular used hawkers for the distribution of their wares. The development of modern transport systems, e.g. railways, enabled pedlars to have goods sent to places in their work area from where they started hawking. For some time hawking and industrialization therefore went hand in hand and performed a retailing function among the rapidly growing urban population. Itinerant traders were not an anomaly, but a buffer and a stimulus to industrialization.

Accusations that hawkers were workshy, only sold products of inferior quality and thereby deceived the simple country folk were mainly uttered by shopkeepers who were afraid of competition. We know now that these allegations were often false. Most hawkers also operated in larger towns, where people could compare the quality with that offered by shops. Moreover, in the smaller villages they returned regularly so that they could not afford to cheat,[7] otherwise it would not have been possible for many pedlars to return again and again to the same areas and customers.

Only with the energies of large department stores did the function of urban hawkers gradually diminish. In the countryside modernization sometimes took much longer, so that hawkers, among whom were the Gypsies, were able to earn a living for a long time. A good illustration is the protest in 1941 of the French Minister of Industrial Production and Labour against the internment by the Germans of travelling groups, with the argument that the provision and distribution of food, clothing and utensils in the small villages would be endangered.[8]

Some industries were entirely dependent on hawkers. This was the case with products that could not easily be distributed by regular shops because there was not enough demand and their value was too low, so that the costs of keeping them in stock were too high. An instructive example is the sale of jute carpets, manufactured in the German province of Silesia. From the beginning of the twentieth century the manufacturers engaged Romanian hawkers (who brought their wives and children with them) in order to ensure that a constant supply of goods reached their markets. After the coming to power of the Nazis in the 1930s, the company received complaints from German officials who accused these Romanians, whom they suspected of being Gypsies, of dishonesty and cheating and urged the company to replace them with 'honest' Germans.[9]

Other examples of a complementary relationship between industry and itinerant occupations are the rag-and-bone business and the trade in animal and human hair in the nineteenth century. In the former case industries were dependent for a long time on travelling groups that collected old rags, needed for the production of paper. In Germany these collectors were among the few for whom an exception was made in the very restrictive policy on itinerant occupations. The men who collected animal hair often travelled great distances in the course of visiting butchers to collect their raw material. When they eventually returned home with sacks full of animal hair worth hundreds of German marks the women would sit and grade the hair which was subsequently sold by the men to the manufacturers.[10]

Some industries needed itinerant traders to ensure a constant supply of raw materials. In more recent times Irish, Dutch, English and American Gypsies have found reasons to collect items regarded as worthless by the settled community.[11] With regard to the scrap metal business we are especially well informed about the

Irish travellers, who – at least till the 1980s – played an important role in the supply of scrap in some industrial areas.[12]

The emergence of many new industries also created a demand for repair and maintenance work for which the specialist experience of itinerant occupations was sometimes used. Hawkers could play a role when they offered specific (traditional) articles needed for the cleaning of new machinery. This was particularly the case in the food sector, which regularly required brushes for the cleaning of kettles, casks and dips in which beer, milk, jam, etc. were manufactured. Only when other cleaning techniques were introduced (in the 1930s) did the demand for brush-hawkers diminish.[13]

Apart from hawking with machine-made goods, Gypsies also sold self-made products, such as sieves, baskets, brooms, pegs and flowers. The production of these items fitted well in the family economy of Gypsies, because the various tasks could be divided among the members of the household.[14] Gypsies not only traded from door to door, but also on streets or at fairs. One of the best-known activities is the horse trade, which together with kettle-mending and the making of music is regarded as a typical Gypsy occupation. The role Gypsies played in this field is made clear by the history of Gypsy horse-dealers in the Netherlands. The first horse-dealers appeared around 1900 and came from various parts of Europe, especially from Scandinavia. Although they were only a small group (at most some 500 people), they quickly managed to get a firm grip on the at that time expanding trade in cobs, small but tough horses which were indispensable for commerce and transportation until the Second World War. At horse fairs these Gypsies were very much at home and during the First World War they almost managed to monopolize the important trade in cobs. Mostly Gypsies bought horses from farmers and then sold them at horse fairs; in the Netherlands this took place by choice in the town of Utrecht, which formed the centre of the horse trade.

The trade was in the hands of the men, who sometimes left their wives and children for days to exercise their occupation. For the buying and selling of horses they used small carriages in order to be more mobile.[15] Their operational area covered the Netherlands, Belgium and the northern part of France, for which they had to cross the national borders frequently. The authorities invariably interpreted these movements as an invasion of their country by hordes of Gypsies. In fact, only concerned relatively small groups (thirty people) were involved, whose business required constant travelling. Apart from the recurring difficulties at the borders, they also had to face other kinds of opposition. This had to do with the well-known stereotype of the ever-cheating Gypsy, especially where horses were concerned. Gypsies were accused of transforming old and worn horses into elegant animals by a process of clipping, singeing and beautifying.[16]

There are, however, powerful arguments against the impression that Gypsy activity at horse markets was characterized by deceit. To begin with, it does not explain why customers kept dealing with people with such a bad reputation. Trading between Gypsies and others suggests a relationship of trust and respect rather than intolerance and abuse. There can be no doubt that 'trickery' formed part of horse trading (and trading in general), but it was not peculiar to Gypsies, nor can it have been a general phenomenon. Nevertheless this stereotype was used to incriminate Gypsies and obstruct their occupation. In Germany we know of attempts by sedentary traders to protest against what they regarded as unfair competition, proof in itself that Gypsies already played an important role. In 1911, for example, Hannoverian horse-dealers asked the authorities to exclude Gypsies from their trade because they only aimed at deceiving their customers.[17] The dealers' plea was not met, but authorities shared their opinion and promised to hamper Gypsy horse-dealers. A circular published in the German state of Württemberg in 1903 ordered local officials to prevent Gypsies from attending horse fairs as much as possible. In Bavaria, finally, Gypsies were in 1921 indeed excluded from horse-dealing because of their 'dishonest' competition.[18]

Despite the restrictive and even repressive policies pursued in many countries, making it more and more difficult for Gypsies to practise their occupations, most of them managed to earn a living until the Second World War. In the Netherlands as in Germany they were known for their riches. Especially after the First World War many German authorities depicted them as being wealthy, possessing expensive caravans and substantial amounts of money.[19]

This short survey of the role of Gypsies at European horse fairs not only contradicts the idea that they were parasites and poor, but also shows their economic adaptability. To clarify this we have to keep in mind that for most of these Gypsies the horse trade was a new occupation. Their fathers, working in the second half of the nineteenth century, were predominantly copper- and tinsmiths. The transition around 1900 was caused by the decreasing demand for mending pots and pans and the growing importance of the horse trade in the period 1870–1940. Although industry was increasingly replacing animals with mechanical means of power, it must be remembered that this was a gradual process; due to the impressive growth of the population and the economy in Europe, the demand for horses in transport, agriculture and industry increased dramatically. Numerous carts for the transport of vegetables, petroleum, milk, etc., as well as trams and omnibuses were to be dependent on horse power until the Second World War. In agriculture the use of horses was stimulated by the introduction of machines that were drawn by horses. Tractors only appeared in great numbers after the Second World War. It is no exaggeration to say that in Western Europe more horses were used in the period 1870–1940 than before. Although in Great Britain and the United States horses were gradually replaced by lorries, automobiles and buses after the First World War, this process was much slower on the continent.[20]

Crafts

A second important economic niche comprised itinerant crafts, especially repair work. For most people occupations such as kettle-mending, chair-bottoming and knife-grinding come to mind when Gypsies are concerned. Most of these craftsmen travelled in a relatively small area because there was enough demand for their services. In such areas, however, they travelled constantly – for example, the German knife-grinder Gerd Wendeln covered some 1,700 kilometres in one year.

Only when these kinds of professions were more specialized and aimed at a smaller circle of customers, like industries, did the area become larger, as is the case with broom- and brushmakers in the Netherlands who in the twentieth century provided dairy industries with brooms to clean their kettles. These people had regular contacts and the factories depended on them. The example shows that it would be wrong to depict these occupations as traditional and belonging to the pre-industrial world. As with trading we see that industrialization could also be a stimulus to service occupations, itinerant services in particular. As a result of the increase in population and spending power, the demand for mending and renewing commodities increased accordingly and new crafts emerged. Good examples are the mending of umbrellas and the fabrication of artificial flowers, skewers and clothes-pegs, crafts that became more popular in the course of the nineteenth century,[21] and of which some have continued to the present day.

It is important to bear in mind that the shift to an industrial society was very gradual. In the agricultural sector, for example, many traditional crafts, such as sieve- and basket-making and rat-catching remained economically viable well into the twentieth century. Finally, many crafts were constantly adapted to changing circumstances and demand. This can be well illustrated by the history of Gypsy copper- and tinsmiths, known in the literature as the 'Kaldarash'.[22] Coming from Hungary, at least according to their passports, the first groups appeared in Western Europe around 1860 and were immediately stigmatized as Gypsies. In contrast to the popular image their economic behaviour appears to have been quite regular. These coppersmiths were well organized in companies of some forty people (men, women and children). Before coming to a certain country, these groups sent a few men ahead to explore the possibilities and make arrangements for camping places and residence permits. When the authorities made objections, they frequently used the services of their respective embassies and consulates, which in some cases pleaded their case with the authorities. According to the clients of the Kaldarash – and local authorities as well – their skills were impressive, and despite regular price-fixing problems, they were often asked back year after year by the same customers. Sometimes even authorities with the most negative Gypsy image, ad whose task it was to get them out of the country, e.g. the gendarmerie, were impressed by their skill.[23] As specialists the Kaldarash earned a good living; some possessed impressive amounts of money, which enabled them to have pictures taken by professional photographers.

More detailed descriptions of the professional activity of this group were offered by members of the English Gypsy Lore Society (founded in 1888). Eric Otto Winstedt's accurate and detailed accounts of these Hungarian Coppersmiths, as they called themselves, were based on a visit they made to Great Britain and France during the years 1911–13. One of the remarkable conclusions from this *petite histoire* is the economic flexibility of these craftsmen. Due to a lack of demand from private consumers, they concentrated more and more on the industrial sector. In Great Britain they tried to get assignments from breweries, and jam, biscuit and chemical factories. To overcome suspicion and distrust they often offered to repair a kettle for free and when the client was satisfied, the ice was broken and a contract signed. Later they often asked a higher price and in some cases a mediator was called in to reach a compromise. Notwithstanding this bickering, most of the times both parties came to an amicable agreement and it did not prevent clients from asking the same men back another time. The quality of their work was of such a standard that clients put up with the conflicts about the price. In contrast to indigenous coppersmiths, these Hungarians mastered a technique that was highly valued by industrial clients.[24]

Their methods were closely connected to traditional craftsmanship; their tools were modest and consisted mainly of a big vertical anvil (*dopo* – coppersmith dialect) on which the kettle balanced. By patiently and skilfully hammering the entire surface of the kettle, a time-consuming activity, its strength and durability was greatly increased. Furthermore, they made use of an old-fashioned pair of bellows, by which (in contrast to modern bellows) the power was regulated so that the temperature could be kept under control at all times.

Although this equipment was only suitable for relatively small kettles, it did not prevent the Hungarians from carrying out bigger projects. During their stay in Great Britain, for example, they made a two metre wide pan, using a hired set of mechanical bellows. Winstedt concluded that these groups were not prejudiced against modern methods as such, but kept traditional, i.e. smaller, equipment because this fitted their itinerant way of life better. This interpretation is confirmed by the fact that they bought most of their materials and equipment such as hammers, pincers, files, etc. in shops and thus did not differ very much from their sedentary British colleagues.

The shift from consumers to industrial clients can also be observed in the work pattern of Gypsy coppersmiths who visited the Netherlands. Whereas in the second part of the nineteenth century they predominantly mended kettles for domestic use, in the course of the twentieth century they specialized more and more in industrial work. Tinsmiths from the German province of Silesia who visited the Netherlands after the First World War worked mainly for dairies, bakeries and laundries. For bakers they plated tin for their troughs and dough mixers and for dairies they repaired milk cans. As in Great Britain problems often arose about the price clients had to pay. This kind of incident caused the Administrator for Border and Aliens Control to demand severe measures against these 'Gypsies', but a letter from the Rotterdam Chief of Police makes it clear that the activities of the tinsmiths cannot be seen only in the light of fraud or deceit. It was rather a consequence of the prevailing anti-Gypsy sentiment. The offering of a very low price could be one of the means to overcome suspicion.[25]

Repairs to metal objects were not only carried out by Gypsies from Eastern Europe. Also in the West some travellers and Gypsies specialized in this craft, as shown by the example of the Scottish and Irish tinkers.[26] Irish tinkers repaired old vessels at farms and in villages as well as selling new ones. Broken kettles were mended with the aid of solder. Here, again, there existed a relationship of mutual dependence between Gypsies and their clients. Irish farmers before the Second World War expected them to repair the earthenware coolers that kept their milk from deteriorating. Several of the same families of tinkers would also undertake specialist repairs of broken china, earthenware or glass.[27]

These highlights from the occupational history of Hungarian, Silesian and Irish itinerant metalworkers once again show that Gypsies were perfectly able to adapt to changing economic circumstances and did not stubbornly hold on to their 'traditional' ways. The biggest threat to their position was not industrialization, but the authorities who did everything they could to get rid of these foreign Gypsies, developing in the long run a very restrictive alien policy. The constant surveillance of the police was particularly damaging to the confidence of potential clients. The coppersmiths therefore were not very pleased with such attention. In 1868, for example, they left a Dutch town saying that 'there was too little work and too much police'.[28] This stigmatization increased in the twentieth century, when official messages were issued by the police in local newspapers warning bakeries against these Gypsies.

In the course of the 1930s not much was heard anymore about these copper- and tinsmiths in Western Europe. Most of them had taken up other occupations or had emigrated to the United States and other parts of the world. This is not to say that the trade disappeared with them. Other groups, who stayed in Western Europe, continued to offer these kinds of services. A good example were Gypsies who in the 1960s visited major building sites at certain times of the year and collected concrete scissors and other utensils. Temporarily hiring space in local forges they sharpened and hardened these and then moved on.

Entertainment

A third important economic sector for Gypsies and other itinerant people was entertainment. Wandering musicians, animal-performers, acrobats, owners of freak shows, showmen and the like have always played a role in European history.[29] Although for most of that time they were treated with a good deal of suspicion, their activities have always been valued too highly for them to vanish. Not only did they bring distraction, they also introduced all kinds of novelties. Thus, at the end of the nineteenth century, the telescope, cameras and cinema were introduced and made popular by itinerant entrepreneurs.[30] By Easter some of them had already travelled large distances.

Others brought in strange animals, such as bears, camels and lions. Many of them were not labelled as Gypsies since they did not travel in family groups. Very mobile groups were Italian (child) musicians and organ-grinders, French bear-leaders from the Pyrenees and German itinerant orchestras.[31]

In this section we will discuss three groups in particular: bear-leaders from Bosnia, musicians from various countries and animal-performers from Parma (Italy). At the same time as the coppersmiths from Hungary moved west, small family groups of bear-leaders from Bosnia (at that time part of the Turkish empire) appeared. The labelling of them as Gypsies was not as general and quick as with the Kaldarash, but in most countries they were stigmatized as well. These bear-leaders are known in the literature on Gypsies as Ursari, from the Romanian word *urs* (= bear). Most of them came from the area around Banja Luka. Like the Kaldarash they travelled great distances and did not restrict themselves to Europe. In the 1880s many emigrated to the United States.[32]

The occupation of bear-leader required a lot of experience and training. To begin with, the bears had to be caught in the Balkan mountains and taught all kinds of tricks. Not only was there the bear dance (called *oursareasca* or *tânână*), but imitations of human behaviour also belonged to the standard repertoire. The performance began with singing and the jingling of a tambourine to attract the attention of the public, after which the bear would start performing. A Serbian author from about 1900 gives an interesting description of the repertoire: the bear acts as a newly married woman and holds his paw to his head. The bear rides a horse and uses for this the bear-leader's stick. The bear moulds dough and hits his paw repeatedly on the ground. The bear sifts flour and moves his bottom. The bear lies on his back and spreads his paws as a bride for a groom. After this the bear collects money with the tambourine. In the United States, finally, we know of bear-leaders who offered money to people who thought they could beat the bear in wrestling (catch-as-catch-can or Greek-Roman).[33] In the twentieth century more animals were added and small circuses were created with horses, monkeys and camels. Another alternative was barrel organs and street pianos on carts. Why bear-leaders began to disappear from the streets in the course of the 1930s is not clear. It may have been the result of competition from other forms of entertainment, but there may also be a link with the growing opposition from authorities and private societies for the protection of animals against (alleged) cruelty. In Germany the occupation was forbidden altogether in 1933.[34]

The income of the Ursari was not as impressive as that of the Kaldarash, but most Bosnians nevertheless seem to have earned a good living. Many of those who left the continent had considerable sums of money and were able to buy houses in England and the United States; Dutch sources corroborate this observation. At the time he was expelled from the Netherlands in 1887, the Bosnian Peero Geergovitch possessed over 2,000 francs, at that time three times the annual wage of a skilled worker.[35] Another piece of information, this time concerning the bear-leader Giovanni Nedilk, was found in the archives of the Dutch gendarmerie, where his working book was preserved, listing 229 performances between April 1923 and August 1924, most of them authorized by local authorities. This unique source shows that a bear-leader without competition from others could stay a considerable time in a relatively small area, visiting some places more than once. When the military police (charged with the supervision of aliens) 'discovered' him and immediately labelled him as a 'Gypsy', however, he was soon expelled because he was considered to be 'without a means of existence'.

A second group of bear (and animal) leaders came from Parma in Italy, in particular from Bedonia. More often than their Bosnian colleagues they also travelled with other animals, especially camels and goats. The history of these groups is still quite obscure, but we know that some of them created famous circuses in France, such as Bouglione and Amar.[36] Similarly the small German village of Alsenborn in the Palatinate has generated some world-famous circus families such as Bügler and Althoff. These small circuses are of special interest because their being labelled as Gypsies was far from consistent. In the Netherlands, for example, they were considered unwanted aliens, but never Gypsies. German and French officials, however, were of a different opinion, as the following short excursion makes clear. In the afternoon of the 4th of July 1905, in the Bavarian municipality Mühldorf, a group described as 'Gypsies' and accompanied by monkeys, a bear and a camel was stopped on the road. The five men had no identification and were arrested for begging and mistreating animals. Only the leader, Luigi Sozzi from Bedonia, had been given a licence to practise his itinerant profession, but because the 1896 Law on Itinerant Occupations did not allow permits to be issued to Gypsies, this was taken from him.[37]

The second occupation, which we will go into in more length, is that of Gypsy musicians and performers. This is probably the profession that is most associated with 'Gypsies'. On the continent especially, many people who were labelled as Gypsies worked as musicians, often in combination with other performers: acrobats, comedians, showmen, magicians and puppeteers. With these occupations many wandered through Western Europe. In contrast to coppersmithing these occupations were not monopolized by men, for women are also regularly found in historical sources as independent professionals.[38]

After the turn of the century we can discern an occupational specialization. Whereas in the nineteenth century many Gypsy performers combined music with other showmanlike activities, trading and crafts, in the twentieth century they began more and more to concentrate on the making of music. This shift may have been caused by increasing professionalism within the world of showmen. From the end of the nineteenth century we see in all countries the emergence of more capital-intensive attractions, such as carousels, merry-go-rounds and cakewalks. At the same time the policy toward small street performers became more repressive and since they lived in caravans these people were marginalized as Gypsies. This combination of economic and socio-political developments caused the more successful operators, who also lived in caravans, to organize themselves into guilds and thus try to escape the Gypsy stigmatization.[39]

The 'losers', however, cannot simply be depicted as passive victims. A number of them still found a modest niche as small showmen, but others decided to concentrate on music, like the Welsh Woods brothers, Cornelius and Adolphus, using modest home-made instruments from chocolate boxes. Others were better equipped and formed professional bands. In the Netherlands and Germany (and probably France), string instruments (violin, guitar, harp and lute) dominated. A number of musicians managed to earn their living by forming small orchestras and some even became famous. The numerous cafes and restaurants offered enough possibilities.[40] Apart from making music, many Gypsies became skilled in the building, repairing and selling of musical instruments, especially violins.[41] Others were less successful and had to content themselves with playing music door to door and on the streets, combined with other activities (mostly hawking).

In some cases Gypsy musicians settled down in cities because the demand for their work was so great that they could give up travelling altogether. This was especially the case in Eastern Europe where Gypsies had, and still have, an important function in the daily social life of the sedentary people. Gypsy orchestras are called upon for many weddings and burials. Some musicians – primarily those who have settled in cities and play in hotels and restaurants – have become respected members of the city they live in. But even the more humble musicians who travel in the countryside, although regarded as less respectable, have a clear social function.[42]

In a survey of occupations within the entertainment field, fortune-telling is probably the most 'Gypsy-like' of all, having been associated with Gypsies since the fourteenth century.[43] In eighteenth-century French encyclopaedias, it was even part of the definition of 'bohémien'. This is not to say, however, that fortune-telling was monopolized by Gypsies. Others (sedentary and itinerant people alike) also engaged in this sort of activity, often combined with magic and sorcery.[44] Although many Gypsy women have earned money in this way up to the present day, little is known about this activity except that there was a regular demand from all classes in society and it was often combined with hawking or entertainment.[45]

Many of these women not only operated in holiday resorts, but also in the countryside, where they offered all kinds of 'emotional services'. Some gave advice in the case of theft and bewitching, but most of them talked with their clients about the highs and lows in life, such as marriages, travels (emigration), the possibility of evading conscription, accidents or death. Although many fortune-tellers lived at a fixed place waiting for people to visit them, a good number travelled. As said before, they used to combine their occupation with peddling. The techniques differed. Palm-reading, which used the lines in one's hand as the point of departure, is of course well known. Other means to predict the future were astrology or cards, in which case every fortune-teller used her own systems.

Fortune-telling also provides a good example of how the family economy worked, because in many cases it served more than one purpose. When coming to a village the women used to visit as many houses as possible in order to earn money by selling goods and telling fortunes, but at the same time they would ask whether the inhabitants had other (repair) work to be done. This information was used by the men for their line of work. In modern terms, the women had the function of 'exploring the market'. As fortune-telling was for the most part forbidden in Western Europe the women had to be careful. Some simply kept a deck of cards in their peddling basket so that it was in clear view of the housewife. If she rose to the bait, the Gypsy would act.

On average the income derived from fortune-telling was modest, but some women were quite successful, like the famous Lucy Lee who worked in Great Britain around 1915.[46] As with all professions, itinerant or not, abuse was possible and occurred now and then. Some fortune-tellers used their skill to 'lift' their clients, for example in cases of illness or bad luck (sick cattle), by suggesting that a spell had been put on the unlucky farmer. In offering to lift the spell they would advise their clients to gather all their valuables and bury them. After a set period of time the client was to dig these up again, after which the situation would be normal again. It needs little imagination to realize that in such cases the fortune-teller was ahead of the superstitious client. However, treasure digging was not a common phenomenon.[47] Most fortune-tellers offered their 'emotional services' without cheating the population upon whom they (and their families) depended.

Seasonal wage labour

From the preceding overview one might have been given the impression that most Gypsies had only *one* occupation. For some this was true (the coppersmiths and bear-leaders), but most Gypsies used to combine all kinds of crafts and services in order to react to seasonal changes in demand and supply.[48] History offers numerous examples of this economic flexibility. In nineteenth-century England, as we have seen, many Gypsies settled down during the winter months and made all kinds of products (clothes-pegs, skewers, flowers, etc.).[49] At the beginning of spring they started to travel and sell their manufactured wares, as well as offer all kinds of services; during the summer many of them were hired as seasonal labourers, whereas during the autumn fairs were visited and trade was resumed.

Another instructive example is the work cycle of Swiss travellers in the twentieth century, known as Jenischen. These groups did not just wander about during their 'tour of Switzerland' but followed a distinct route. In March they travelled through the Rhineland going from village to village and selling all kinds of products. In the autumn, when the farmers returned with their herds to their villages, the Jenischen came to the peasants' villages in order to make and repair their baskets, especially the big baskets used to feed hay to the cows, where special expertise was required to make effective repairs. Furthermore, umbrellas and kettles were mended. It is clear that these peasants counted on their services and lived with these travellers for some weeks till the work was done.[50]

Seasonal labour in agriculture was one of the few occupations that did involve wage-labour. In England agricultural employment was found chiefly in the South and the East. Seasonal workers, including Gypsy families, used to go from farm to farm following the ripening of the crops: hay-making, turnip-hoeing, pea-picking, wheat-fagging and strawberry-picking. The cycle was completed with the picking of hops.[51]

How large the number of 'Gypsies' within the seasonal workforce in England was is not clear. According to a government report of 1907, between a quarter and a third of those picking peas in England were 'Gypsies'. For hop-picking this number seems to have been much lower and here Gypsies were only a small minority; the bulk of the workers were Irish. Hiring Gypsies, especially women for fruit, could be advantageous for farmers because they brought their own accommodation with them. Remarkably enough the same report states that Gypsies had a standard of living and level of health far above that of the ordinary seasonal labourer.[52] In Germany and France Gypsies are also reported as 'hoppers'. From a letter from the Bavarian community of Pfaffenhofen in 1913, we can conclude that every year in the months of August and September an 'international army' of hop-pickers visited the area. Among them were many people with carts and caravans, generally labelled as Gypsies. A number of them were also basket-weavers. They arrived some weeks earlier, not only to assure themselves of a spot to put their caravans, but also to make the baskets that were needed for the harvest.[53] In other cases (potato harvest) farmers depended on (Gypsy) basket-weavers as well. They even used to save twigs so that the Gypsies would have enough material for the basket needed and therefore not lose time.

CONCLUSION

This chapter has made clear that specific 'Gypsy occupations' do not exist. All the occupations mentioned, including fortune-telling, were also practised by non-Gypsies. Even itinerancy was not peculiar to them. As we have seen, tens of thousands of people were itinerants without being labelled as Gypsies. Finally, all the characteristics listed in the second section (the family as working unit, mobility and self-employment) are general phenomena and can therefore in the end not be explained by reference to a 'Gypsy culture'. The specific feature of Gypsy occupations lies only in a combination of the three: being self-employed and travelling with one's family. People who chose such a way of life were very likely to be labelled by the authorities as 'Gypsy' (or something similar) in Western Europe. This power of definition, that has been in force since the fifteenth century, was so strong that it was very difficult for people to escape from it. Moreover, it could easily lead to the development of ethnicity: people began to feel that they were different from others and so began to cultivate their own way of life and the symbols attached to it.

This question of ethnicity and group-formation is inextricably bound up with Gypsy occupations. For it was the economic choice of an itinerant profession *with* the family, an overt travelling way of life, that set off the stigmatization. Cultural characteristics such as dress and language seem to have been less important in this respect. The stigmatization can partly be explained by the mistrust towards itinerant occupations in general. Most accusations against Gypsies were similar to those against hawkers, entertainers and craftsmen who left their family at home. These ideas were reinforced from time to time by sedentary economic organizations such as the guilds, which tried to defend their privileges and monopoly. The combined stigmatization, however, never led to the disappearance of itinerant professions. Notwithstanding their distrust many authorities realized that itinerants fulfilled a necessary economic function and they therefore restricted themselves to fighting the alleged abuses.

These abuses were especially associated with people who took their families with them: 'Gypsies'. Invariably this category is put forward as *the* example of people who took undue advantage of the legal possibilities for itinerant occupations. The only way to escape the Gypsy stigmatization and labelling was by stressing one's distinctive character as a professional group. The most successful in this respect were the showmen – as we have seen in Chapter 7 – but the same process can be discerned with German organizations of hawkers from the beginning of the twentieth century onwards, who in all Western European countries managed to be excluded from stigmatization.[54] Their organization and lobbying convinced the authorities that they were 'honest' businessmen, who could not be compared with the 'dishonest' Gypsies. Occupations where the need for organization was less pronounced, however, did not lose the Gypsy label and faced many legal and social difficulties.

The relation between stigmatization and group-formation brings us to the two assumptions on which this chapter is based. The first has to do with the economic function. On the whole we can say that the restrictive and often outright discriminatory policy towards 'Gypsies' did not make their economic activity impossible. Although Gypsies did not play a key role in the sectors discussed, their work cannot be disposed of as 'parasitic' or 'begging in disguise'. Even the most repressive authorities from time to time admitted that Gypsies *could* be useful and in some cases (seasonal work) indispensable. As a matter of fact, in economic terms Gypsies can very well be compared with the lower and middle classes: there were outright beggars and criminals among them, but most of them earned a modest living, while – notwithstanding the stigmatization – some groups were rather successful. The examples of the coppersmiths and horse-dealers have made that clear.

For the second assumption we also found enough evidence. Itinerant occupations in general and Gypsy occupations in particular could only exist if they adapted to the changing economic situation. The widespread ideas that industrialization caused the decline of itinerant occupations and that Gypsies always hold on to their traditional occupations can both be dismissed. To begin with, the process of industrialization and modernization had divergent effects and its development was far from uniform. Industrialization may have made a lot of (itinerant/'traditional') occupations obsolete, but then others emerged instead and 'Gypsies' as well as 'non-Gypsies' reacted accordingly. Only after the Second World War do we see that in many countries 'Gypsies' were forced into a rather hopeless social and economic position. The issuing of explicit legislation on them, e.g. the Dutch Caravan Act of 1968 that made travelling virtually impossible, combined with a strong anti-Gypsy feeling and attitude in the surrounding society has created a dead-end street. Deprived of their itinerant occupations, discriminated against in the regular labour-market and unable to escape their own group and thereby their stigmatization, it has become very difficult for many Gypsies and other itinerant groups to cope with the situation in economic terms.

10 Dutch Travellers: Dwellings, Origins and Occupations[1]

Annemarie Cottaar

A NEW CATEGORY OF TRAVELLERS

In the international literature there exists a vague notion of the differences between indigenous travellers (*Jenischen, Landfahrer,* tinkers, ambulants) and (foreign) Gypsies. As far as the first group is concerned the idea prevails that they descend from vagabonds who, in the course of time, intermixed with Gypsies. There is, however, hardly any historical research available to prove or refute this assertion. The study by Heymowski is a favourable exception.[2] He not only aimed at tracing the developments in the way of thinking about the Swedish travellers or *Taters* (Tattare), but he also tried to find out if, as most researchers thought, they were different from the Swedish people. Therefore he looked to see if their language, habits and looks indicated a descent from Gypsies. Heymowski, however, concluded that *Taters* were different not in an anthropological, but rather in a sociological sense. Besides their own ideas of belonging to a different group, it was the attitude of the majority of the population that was decisive for their distinct position within the Swedish community. Our historical research into the origin of Dutch travellers has led to the same conclusion.

While Dutch authors on this subject usually draw a distinction between foreign Gypsies and indigenous travellers, the notion that the latter boast a distinctive tale of origin from the majority of the Dutch people also appears to enjoy general currency.[3] Their roots are said to reach back to the west of Germany (knife-grinders from Westphalia), the southern regions of the Netherlands (discharged mercenary soldiers) and the Gypsy population. Especially about the two geographical regions of origin many stories circulate, without being tested on their historical tenability. That's why we decided to take a close look at these stories and their narrators. We compared the ideas with the results of our own genealogical research on Dutch

174

caravan-dwellers. Only in this way do we think it is possible to judge their historical value.

From the moment that people in the Netherlands began to live in caravans in the second half of the nineteenth century, they were categorized as a distinct group within Dutch society. We saw in previous chapters of this volume that analysis of the history of Gypsies in the Netherlands did show that, although for public opinion it was obvious who belonged to this category of people, in practice it turned out not to be such a simple matter. To qualify for the label 'Gypsy', someone needed to meet the conditions of visible permanent itinerancy with the entire family and a foreign origin. Ambulant groups which failed to fit this image were *not* branded as Gypsies.[4] Among indigenous Dutch caravan-dwellers the criterion of 'foreign origin' played no part and categorization was determined on grounds of their deviant housing. Everyone who inhabited a caravan thereby also immediately became, in principle, a caravan-dweller. Form of housing and the identity of residents were coupled with each other inextricably, as we saw in Chapter 7. Yet, the reality of the situation was more varied. Showmen, for example, managed to separate themselves from caravan-dwellers, and thus escaped the stigmatizing government policy. In addition, a distinction is commonly drawn in Dutch literature between travellers, or caravan-dwellers of long-standing, and citizens with a sedentary history who only after the Second World War moved into a caravan.

If we concentrate on the form of housing the different groups share in common it might be possible to track the development of subgroups within the population of caravan-dwellers (Gypsies excepted), and reactions to them. Ideas prevailing in government circles about caravan-dwellers and official lines of action towards them have already been discussed. What concerns us here are aspects of the group itself. First of all, naturally, this means their form of housing. When did people in the Netherlands first begin to make their homes in caravans and what (technological) development did these homes undergo up to 1945? Subsequently we will redirect our attention to the caravan-dwellers. Were their origins indeed remarkably different from those of the rest of the Dutch population, and what were the motives behind their choice of this form of mobile habitation? Thus we arrive at the vocations which Dutch caravan-dwellers practised prior to the Second World War.

THE CARAVAN APPEARS ON THE SCENE

Before the first caravan appeared on Dutch roads in the second half of the nineteenth century, itinerant salesmen and artisans looking for a place to lay their heads after their day's work could choose from various sleeping accommodations. If they were staying for a longer time in a large city, at times they rented a room, but usually they stayed in a lodging house. In the countryside farm sheds provided shelter overnight. This explains the terms common at the time: sleeping peasants and shed sleepers for such paying guests. They also on occasion would sleep in the warm areas of factories which produced bricks and roof tiles.[5] In addition, there were barracks in which primarily fieldhands stayed, but which provided short-term shelter at night for chair-bottomers as well. Tents were never popular in the Netherlands. Only those who made their living at fairs might in season spend the night now and then in the tents where by day their performances took place. The most well-known tent campers were tinkers from Hungary who came to look for work in the Netherlands during the last quarter of the nineteenth century.[6] Finally the small boats should be mentioned which, in a country with as many waterways as the Netherlands, were much sooner pressed into service as abodes than their equivalents along the roads. Along with travelling showmen and navvies, among those living aboard boats we find the same vocations characteristic of caravan-dwellers, including chair-bottomers and petty traders, which resulted in their being called skipper-scroungers or boatmen pedlars.[7] Some part of the houseboat population probably made the transition to caravans as the twentieth century unfolded, lured by the greater area brought within reach thanks to the considerably improved network of roads.[8]

In the 1879 census we encounter the first mention of 'inhabited caravans', 16 of them, in the Netherlands.[9] Although the count here is hardly reliable, it is not likely that more than a few dozen residential caravans were riding the roads in the Netherlands at this time. The first municipal ordinance concerning 'mobile homes' of which we are aware, also from 1879, was passed by the town of Deventer in the Province of Overijssel. This serves as an indication that before the 1870s there weren't any caravans in the Netherlands. Research in the population register of Amsterdam supports this hypothesis. In those years Amsterdam registered caravans in what was known as the *Keeten Register*[10] which recorded in particular the names of labourers and navvies who lived in barracks. During examination of these registers for the period 1874–92 the following caught our attention: there were no caravans before 1879, but in that year two caners registered who lived in an unnumbered barracks. A year later the first three caravans appeared and until 1883 these few remained the only ones. Subsequently the definitive shift to caravans took place, these also being called simply wagons or travelling wagons. To be sure, these caravan-dwellers were not restricted exclusively to this form of habitation; from the same register it can be concluded that a number of them also – mostly for a short time – lived at divers addresses in the city where other members of their family had already settled previously. Those who worked the fairs at the time still primarily made use of houseboats to transport their gear and sleep in because they were able to reach more areas in the Netherlands by water than overland by road.[11] That prompts the query whether there was a connection between the condition and extent of the road network and the point in time when the caravan arrived on the scene. In that connection a comparison seems called for with surrounding countries. Here we immediately confront a number of gaps in our knowledge. Thus only a limited number of empirical studies are available about road infrastructure,[12] and what has been written about the development of carts and (covered) wagons is superficial.

ROAD NETWORK AND CARAVANS: AN INTERNATIONAL COMPARISON

The paving of roads in the Netherlands began comparatively late, just as in Prussia and Bavaria. Through the absence of any strong central authority and the complete lack of initiatives on the part of cities, private individuals or provincial governments, little road building took place. After 1700 the Republic had been obliged to wrestle with economic stagnation which reduced the demand for transportation. What also influenced events was that a system of waterways was already accessible which was well enough developed to support brisk traffic. In the Netherlands it was only after the French conquest that the state assumed responsibility for improving the roads. It was about all King Willem I, whose reign lasted from 1813 to 1840, who emerged as the great initiator of roadworks and under whose administration the most important land arteries were strengthened within a few decades, first with rubble or gravel, later with smaller bricks and then paving stones. By roughly 1850 this network of major roads had reached completion.

To test the premise that the paving of roads ushered in the arrival of the caravan, comparison is necessary with countries where such roads were available earlier than in the Netherlands. What was the road situation, for example, in France or England? The literature reveals that a strong central authority made improvement of the roads in France possible at an early stage. Political and military-strategic goals meant that the work was tackled with success. As early as the end of the eighteenth century an extensive system of paved main roads linked Paris with the far reaches of the country and with France's provincial capitals.[13] Economic prosperity in England in the eighteenth century led to an increase of road traffic and a burgeoning demand for roads. Measures taken to improve roads were primarily private initiatives which resulted in what came to be called 'turnpikes' where tolls were levied.[14] What's more, at the beginning of the nineteenth century, many British roads were macadamized, which enabled people to move about readily with a small caravan.[15]

The caravan first found its way onto Dutch roads in the 1870s, after the completion of a road system that was crudely paved. A causal relationship here could be possible. It is indeed beyond dispute that driving about with caravans, relatively heavy objects, was only possible on hardened roads, for otherwise their owners needed too many horses to pull their vehicles. On poorer surfaces lighter covered wagons or dog carts were likely to be used. From England we know that after 1820, by which time most of the principal roads were macadamized, it was in theory possible to keep a caravan rolling with a single horse up front.[16] The same held true for France. It is crucial to note, however, that the first paved roads were the main thoroughfares connecting provincial capitals. Providing a hard surface to the secondary roads which were intended to end the isolation of rural areas took a back seat for some time. And it was precisely these roads which were by far the most vital ones for itinerant travellers, since they had to penetrate the smallest of remote outposts with their trade and services. The paving of such roads in the Netherlands only commenced after 1850.[17] Differences among Western European countries as far as fixing the surfaces of secondary roads is concerned might thus have been less appreciable. This leads to the question of whether the appearance of the first caravans can be linked to the hardening of secondary roads in England, Germany, France and Belgium.

In Dutch sources, and in foreign literature as well, we search in vain for technical data about the development of this so highly visible form of habitation.[18] In England the first caravan probably materialized mid-way through the last century.[19] Before 1840 Gypsies, tents aside, primarily made use of covered carts and wagons.[20] Only later did the first wooden caravans take to the road, inhabited by performers at fairs, to be followed by others with itinerant vocations. This reconstruction may be anything but iron-clad, but, for the moment, it's the best we can do. For Germany we know equivalently little; no empirical studies are available and we have only impressions at our disposal. The picture that emerges is that the first four-wheel wagons with covered arches for roofing in which people actually lived only began to circulate at the end of the nineteenth century.[21] Earlier *Zigeuner* and *Jenischen* in Germany passed the night in tents. From the research in German police journals it also appears that from 1840 onwards the *Planwagen* received regular mention as a means of transportation for itinerant families. The German police used this term for covered carts or wagons with a top of green linen or leather.[22]

For France our source material is a section of photographs in Vaux de Foletier's book on the nineteenth century.[23] Yet it also appears possible, on a basis of illustrations in divers international publications, to compile a chronological overview of the advent of the first caravans. De Vaux de Foletier included 14 plates in his book, 11 of which offer an impression of the living quarters of travellers. In five instances tents or tent-like accommodations appear and in two covered wagons: in 1847 in the Alsace and in 1852 in Saintes-Maries-de-la-Mer.[24] In four illustrations the first 'real' caravans are portrayed, that is to say four-wheel wooden frames supporting wooden living quarters. The earliest mention dates from 1869 and concerns an illustration by Émile Bayard for the novel *La maison roulante*.[25] Subsequent drawings are from 1872, 1880 and 1890 and all have French settings. International literature thus teaches us that no images of wooden caravans have been discovered dating from earlier than 1869. In England the first reports date from 1879 or shortly before.[26] In one illustration there appears a caravan camp in the Notting Hill district of London and in another we are afforded a glimpse of the interior of a caravan, complete with a cabinet-bed, table, chair and stove. These two drawings by W.H. Overend appeared more frequently in the international literature as examples of the first caravans in divers countries. Vaux de Foletier indeed describes the caravan at the camp in London as a 'roulette dans un faubourg de Paris en 1880', but he borrowed the illustration from the French magazine, *L'Univers illustré*, a year after the *Illustrated London News* had published it. The actual location of the camp was therefore London. It seems likely that German authors relied exclusively on English drawings, because there are no images of German caravans from the nineteenth century. Only Arnold's book includes a drawing from the 1880s, even though it shows a group of French showmen beside their caravans. Furthermore he names no source. It might thus very well be a French drawing. In Mode and Wölffling's richly illustrated book only illustrations of tents and covered wagons (from 1861, 1876 and 1884) are printed, culled from such German publications as the *Illustrierte Zeitung*. In the Netherlands there are no sketches known of caravans (four wheels) before 1900; the earliest illustrations are photographs of carts in which people lived (two wheels) dating from about the turn of the century.[27]

On the basis of this sifting of international literature we can place the first caravans in the 1860s, in France and England.[28] The Netherlands and Germany followed later. If caravans were already in use in Western Europe prior to mid-century, they can only have appeared sporadically. A network of major paved roads was in any case not a sufficient condition for their emergence. These findings lead us to the conclusion that the Netherlands did not differ much from other European countries and that a path for caravans was cleared with the extension of the system of hard-surface roads to rural areas.

FROM DOG CART TO CARAVAN

In the Netherlands the so-called dog cart (a small cart pulled by one or more dogs) served for a long time for the transport of goods. Not only did bakers and dairy farmers, but also itinerant traders used them. A time came when these people also began to use their vehicles to sleep in. Among older caravan-dwellers in the Netherlands there are still those who had their first experiences of living on the road in a dog cart. Travellers rebuilt them into a kind of covered wagon by setting up arched ribs over which they stretched a cloth cover and then sprinkling some straw on the bottom. Thus a place where a few people could sleep at the same time was created.[29] If the weather turned too cold or wet, one would park the dog cart on a farm and the family members would be dispersed between the cart's sleeping area and the haystack. Even after larger wagons began to circulate, the dog cart continued to be used to carry merchandise.

The first four-wheel wagons were intended, just as their predecessors, to carry wares by day and to sleep in by night. Covered wagons, which we have illustrations of in the Netherlands from 1900 onwards,[30] were already a bit more spacious, but you couldn't stand up inside them. These were, in fact, farmers' wagons which carried goods in Germany and Eastern Europe. It was characteristic of this kind of wagon that the side panels, held in place by iron pins on their outside, slanted outwards. Iron bands were stretched around the wooden wheels and most wagons were equipped with springs to cushion the worst shocks from riding on roads that were not yet paved.

At the end of the nineteenth century carts and small wagons also appeared which conformed more closely to what we think of as caravans.[31] Usually an existing vehicle was used as a base on top of which to build living quarters, a sort of wooden barracks with supporting ribs on the outside. These as a rule had no more than two wheels. Before entering the cart, a prop had to be put in place underneath, both in the front and in the back, to keep it from tipping over.[32] The carts served not simply as sleeping quarters, but people lived inside them as well, which we can deduce from the chimneys visible in many illustrations. In addition, there would be a window on opposite sides of the cart, two in the somewhat larger ones. To keep out the rain, the cart-dwellers as a rule covered their wooden roof with tar paper or white heavy-duty linen impregnated with water-repellent white lead paint.

In areas where caravans were permitted to stand in the period 1910 to 1920 different types of such wagons were to be found alongside each other. In addition there were also the more luxuriously fashioned caravans of showmen with a small front porch and wooden railings with their 'sticks' crafted by a cabinet-maker or turner.[33] In the course of the twentieth century wagonmakers played an increasingly important role in the building of caravans. Before the Second World War these were primarily made from tongue-and-groove wooden planks, while thereafter plate wagons, first constructed from compressed wood but later from large steel plates, became popular. The caravans acquired names descriptive of their type from the place where they were first built by skilled artisans who really went to town decorating the wood- and glasswork. At present most Dutch caravan-dwellers live in stationary caravans which can only move to a new location by conveyance in a deep-loader.

One of the intentions of the Caravan Act of 1918 was to put an end to the use of caravans that were falling apart and to regulate their quality and size. This led to countless regulations all meant to prevent ramshackle caravans from obstructing the roads. A caravan had henceforth to rest on at least two axles and four wheels, so that carts became forbidden as habitations. The minimum dimensions allowed by law were 4.5 × 2.1 × 2.1 metres.[34] As for the interior, it had to be split into a room for day and a room for night, the two separated by a partition with a sliding door or a door on hinges. When a caravan under inspection met all requirements, it received a permit which bore the name of the municipality where the permit had been applied for and a serial number. Next a registration number was supposed to be painted on the left and right sides of the caravan. Completely consistent with procedures for automobiles at that time, this licence plate consisted of the letter of a province and the number of the acquired permit.

Tables 10.1 and 10.2 show the number of caravans and people living in them up to 1960. At the close of the last century, the number of caravan-dwellers began to increase and this growth went on uninterrupted until the Second World War.[35] The decreases in 1911 and 1918 are probably to be attributed to the unreliability of the relevant counts. These were conducted at the height of the travel season so there may have been caravans which escaped the notice of the census-takers.[36] After 1938 the total number of caravan-dwellers fell slightly because in the war many of them left their mobile homes. Had we a census available for 1944 or 1945, in all likelihood it would show a still sharper decline. After the war, the number of caravan-dwellers climbed more rapidly than ever before. In the period from 1948 to 1960 an increase of no less than 84 per cent could be observed. If we express the caravan population as a percentage of the Dutch population, then although between 1889 and 1960 the figure rose, it nevertheless remained remarkably low. In 1889 caravan dwellers constituted 0.007 per cent of the Dutch population and in 1960, despite a surge in absolute numbers, still not as much as 0.2 per cent. The growth of the caravan population in the period before and after the Second World

Table 10.1 Number of caravans in the Netherlands, 1879–1960

1879	1889	1899	1909	1911	1918	1920	1930	1938	1942	1947	1948	1960
16	93	429	817	584	988	1418	2261	2722	2719	± 2696	2631	± 5616

Source: Cottaar (1996), p. 33.

Table 10.2 Number of caravan-dwellers in the Netherlands, 1879–1960

1879	1889	1899	1909	1911	1918	1920	1930	1938	1942	1947	1948	1960
–	326	2189	3984	2800	4884	7391	10 795	12 070	11 457	11 955	11 651	21 403

Source: Cottaar (1996), p. 34.

War cannot be accounted for exclusively by natural increase. There were also people who time and time again left their houses for a caravan. Who were these people and what motivated them to go and live on wheels?

THE ORIGIN OF DUTCH CARAVAN-DWELLERS

According to Dutch studies, caravan-dwellers or, more generally still, itinerants descend from people who themselves had no fixed abode and who, moreover, in considerable measure were of foreign origin. In the literature there is also recognition of the possibility that the ancestors of some contemporary travellers had led a (semi-) sedentary life for generations on end, but the conviction is strong that their genealogies are dominated nonetheless by countless drifters, and these are alleged to have been resistant to sedentary influences. In a genealogical study which we carried out assertions about foreign roots and descent from rovers were tested against factual data on the social and geographical origins of Dutch caravan-dwellers. The study was of modest design and covered only a limited period, never extending back further than the second half of the eighteenth century and heavily emphasizing the nineteenth.[37] On the grounds of two selection criteria, two groups of 20 caravan-dwellers about whom sufficient information was available were compiled for the genealogical study. First of all non-contiguous *geographical* locations were chosen. In order to assess the possible influence of big city or rural roots, one study area had to be countrified and the other more urban. The Provinces of Overijssel and South Holland – and within it especially the city of The Hague – satisfied our geographical demands. As the second criterion for selection we used the caravan-dweller's vocational group. Only by making the vocation of central importance could we discover in particular to what extent work was decisive for travelling, and, in turn, for living in a caravan. Also in this way we could find out to what extent sons (or daughters) adopted the trades of their parents, or if certain vocations perhaps dominated in particular families. A final reason for proceeding in this way was that only by doing so could we make sure that we did not immediately lose sight of – and thus exclude from the study – seemingly less obvious activities of caravan-dwellers, such as the work they did as field- or factoryhands, an omission that is common in the literature about them.[38]

Table 10.3 Size of vocational groups among caravan-dwellers in
The Hague and Overijssel (1921 to 1941)

Vocational groups	The Hague 1921–41		In sample	Overijssell 1921–7, 1931, 1941		In sample
I Artisans	133	(17%)	5	64	(12%)	5
II Tradesmen	377	(47%)	5	259	(48%)	5
III Showmen	137	(17%)	5	119	(22%)	5
IV Wage-labourers	125	(16%)	5	76	(14%)	5
V Miscellaneous	30	(3%)	0	22	(4%)	0
Total	802	(100%)	20	540	(100%)	20

Source: Cottaar (1996), p. 46.

In our study of Dutch caravan-dwellers four vocational groups were differentiated: artisans, tradesmen, showmen and wage labourers.[39] A schematic representation of the percentage distribution of caravan-dwellers among these various occupational categories reveals that The Hague and Overijssel did not differ notably (see Table 10.3). The prominence of those who sold things for a living has to do with the fact that tradesmen often did other work as well and so selling was reported as a vocation comparatively frequently.[40] For research into the descent of caravan-dwellers from each vocational group five persons were chosen in both The Hague and Overijssel, which amounted to, nationally, ten informants per vocational category.

Research results provide an impetus to adjust prevailing ideas. Thus it turned out that caravan-dwellers and their parents in the northeast of the Netherlands exhibited a strong attachment to the region. Down through successive generations we come across mostly individuals who were born in this region and nearby Germany and who for most of their lives lived and worked there. By way of contrast it emerged from the sample in The Hague, a (large) city, that only the youngest generation of caravan-dwellers was born there, while their parents, for the most part, came from the south or northeast of the Netherlands. By taking a closer look at their places of residence, we discovered that it was especially the preceding (second) generation which took the step of moving to the city. Eight of them were born in the west, while 20 members of this generation had lived for a shorter or longer time in the Hague. The most plausible explanation for this pattern is the general migratory movement from rural areas to major population centres in the second half of the nineteenth century and first decades of the twentieth. After 1875, as a consequence of critical economic circumstances, many (farm) labourers gravitated to large cities like The Hague, Rotterdam and Amsterdam and it is probable than many parents and grandparents of later caravan-dwellers were part of this migratory pattern too. Many appear to have relocated in urban settings irreversibly. The Hague was clearly not a transit stop, as most members of the second and first generation died there.

We acquired deeper understanding of the descent of these travellers by investigating the vocations which caravan-dwellers and their parents performed. Petty trade was by far the most important way of earning a living for those in our sample, albeit often in combination with all sorts of other income-generating activities. Not much capital was needed to begin and until well into the nineteenth century there were hardly any village shops so that travelling tradesmen met a need. Their services were not confined to rural areas, however, for since industrialization demand for inexpensive products had also increased in towns. Industrialization had led to rising wages with enhanced consumption following, partially as a result, too, of population growth in the nineteenth century. The wares of caravan-dwellers were either self-made or procured from a wholesaler. The tradesmen's self-made goods included slippers, artificial flowers, pegs, umbrellas, trivets, brushes, brooms and baskets.

Although in population registers we may seldom find a vocation listed after the name of a married woman, this by no means implies that they made no contribution to the family income. A man's earnings were regularly supplemented by what his wife's vending yielded. Were their children old enough, they too did their little bit. Peddling of fancy goods in the caravan world was a woman's affair.[41] They made use of a light basket and, after the war, shopping bags.[42] Such dealings were not a matter of selling self-made items, but supplies bought from a wholesale supplier. The women vendors, moreover, functioned as intermediaries between caravan-dwellers and the settled citizenry. Apart from selling things, they enquired whether there was any work for their husbands or a good place to station their caravan. Included in the standard assortment of the hawkers' fancy goods baskets were thread, needles, ribbons and buttons. The rest of the inventory was constantly in flux depending on the vendor's purchasing power. At one time or another she might have on offer buttermilk soap, shoe polish, stove polish, combs, razor blades, handkerchiefs, chamois-cloths, sticking plasters, elastic and (tooth-) brushes.

Just as did tradesmen, artisans (mostly knife-grinders and caners) lived in a caravan because their vocation made travelling necessary. If we take a look at caners from the village of Loon op Zand (in the Province of North Brabant), who used dog carts to bring their services to their customers, we see that until the start of this century they always returned to their home base. In the long run, however, their absences from home grew more and more protracted until most finally settled elsewhere. Cities such as Tilburg, Rotterdam and The Hague offered them more of a market, and living in a caravan these caners could also increase their sphere of action. The distances which they covered with their wagons were limited and restricted to certain regions. For caravan-dwellers who worked in the entertainment sector, showmen and musicians, the situation was different. They covered a significantly larger area with their activities than others did. No doubt this was connected to the brevity of the festivities and fairs, for example, which were held in succession throughout the entire country.

Labourers made up the smallest vocational category. They comprised an exceptional group within the caravan-dweller population, since for their work (factory) workers did not need to travel about. Why did they nevertheless live in a caravan? We must seek the incentive for their choice in the major problem of cities in the period before the Second World War: a shortage of affordable housing. On the other hand there were labourers who actually needed a mobile home because they were employed by some large road-building, land reclamation or dredging concerns. Shifting among work sites they covered many times greater distances than the average caravan-dweller, only they relocated less frequently, stationing their wagons for longer periods, sometimes even for several years at a time, on a single construction site.

Let us finally have a look at what our genealogical study brought to light with regard to the performance of itinerant vocations. Did itinerants indeed descend from people who themselves had no fixed abode or remained, as their forefathers, in the course of time in one and the same place? For an important part of the ancestors of caravan-dwellers in the sample we could indeed trace a sedentary past: they were farmers and fieldhands. These vocations were found not only among the previous generations of the labourers in the sample, but also among the ancestors of the tradesmen and showmen.

Finally there remained a group of families about whom it must be said that all four generations included in the study were, more or less, itinerant. These were primarily knife-grinders and caners. A closer look at the work performed by caravan-dwellers during the period between the world wars reveals that the percentage of travelling artisans was only 12 per cent in Overijssel and 17 per cent in The Hague.[43] When we then consider that it was pre-eminently the family trees of knife-grinders and caners of the first generation which were dominated by itinerants, we have to conclude that not even a fifth of all Dutch caravan-dwellers had ancestors who belonged to the 'hard core' of travellers. Foreign origin also turned out to play no significant role.

In fact each era generated its own travellers. In a number of periods a transition took place from a sedentary to a travelling existence because people in agriculture or industry could no longer earn enough to live on. This can be illustrated by developments in Loon op Zand, the village in Brabant mentioned above. The surrounding area was of low fertility consisting of woods, wild terrain, shifting sands and farmland.[44] In the west and north, for centuries, there were fens and swamps and the mining of peat in the fens was, until the seventeenth century, the leading source of income for the municipality's inhabitants. After that the peat was exhausted. In the ensuing generations poverty struck and people cast about for alternative means of subsistence. Farmers added to their earnings from their land and animals by spinning wool and weaving, while others turned to making mats, baskets and matches and fabricating shoes and slippers for which they sought customers in the (wide) surrounding area. In the last quarter of the nineteenth century we see a number of them travelling further afield to capitalize on their products and services, snapping their ties with Loon op Zand for good.

ONCE A CARAVAN-DWELLER, NOT ALWAYS A CARAVAN-DWELLER

Finally it is important to point out that certainly not all pre-Second World War caravan-dwellers chose this form of housing for good. Thus the twenty people in our sample from The Hague turned out to have spent an average of 16 years in a caravan, with extremes ranging from less than a full year to up to 59 years. Among the seven persons who lived more than twenty years in a caravan, we discovered five itinerants, one travelling showman, and a labourer. To the group of nine who inhabited a caravan for less than ten years belonged the four remaining labourers and five respondents from the category of those whose ancestors had been both itinerant and sedentary. Also falling within this group were two showmen who didn't relinquish their caravans for a house, but for a houseboat. The remaining four, two itinerants and two showmen from the category of 'mixed' descent, lived in caravans for between ten and twenty years. This leads to the conclusion that during the interim between the wars – and afterwards as well – caravan-dwellers did not form a closed group. The arrival of many newcomers into the group and the departure of many others constitute the foremost support for this assertion. A very large part of the sample changed their form of habitation on a number of occasions, even those who lived for an extended period in a caravan. Of those who lived for more than twenty consecutive years in a caravan, five itinerants formed the core. Three of these lived out the length of their days in a caravan, which sets them apart from the rest. They spent 41, 36 and 59 years, respectively, as caravan-dwellers, while the other two resided on wheels for 21 and 22 years. This might mean that people whose families before them were travellers, if they once began to live in a caravan, more often stayed in it than those where the preceding generations were split between itinerant and sedentary living patterns.

Before the Second World War anyone in the Netherlands was free to live in a caravan, as long as the residents and the vehicle met certain legal requirements. It is therefore conceivable that there was considerable movement into and away from the ranks of caravan-dwellers. An end came to this situation only in 1968 when the Dutch government introduced the principle of descent as a prerequisite. From then on descent from caravan-dwellers determined whether someone might live in a caravan. The heterogeneity of the pre-Second World War caravan-dweller population became a thing of the past. At present it appears that the principle of descent is at its last gasp. That caravan-dwellers themselves are distrustful of its pending demise is closely connected to their disheartening social position. There is not a single caravan-dweller who looks forward to competition from 'citizens' in caravan camps, where an acute shortage of space is the usual state of affairs as things now stand. After more than a century of stigmatizing government policy and actual segregation, the Dutch caravan-dweller population is now, of its own volition, closing ranks.

Notes

CHAPTER 1 INTRODUCTION

1. See, for example, the bibliographies mentioned by Fraser (1992), pp. 319–20.
2. Tawney (1967), p. 275, quoted by Beier (1974), p. 3.
3. For example Danker (1988) and Finzsch (1990).
4. L. Lucassen (1996).
5. Geremek (1980); Geremek (1991).
6. See, for example, Le Goff (1979), who points to the state and the church as responsible for the growth of marginal groups. See also Chaunu (1981) and Agulhon (1990). Recently the stigmatization concept was used by Moore (1987) in explaining the persecution of heretics, Jews and lepers in the Middle Ages.
7. Hufton (1974), pp. 71, 83–102 and 120. See also Hufton (1972), pp. 100 ff. A similar description can be found in Braudel (1976), Vol. II, pp. 80–3. His explanation ('cette silencieuse et épouvantable armée des prolétaires', p. 83) fits well in the poverty interpretation.
8. For example Schwartz (1988).
9. Lis and Soly (1979).
10. Notable exceptions being: Mayall (1988); L. Lucassen (1990); Fricke (1991); Cottaar, Lucassen and Willems (1995); Cottaar (1996); Schubert (1995); L. Lucassen (1996); and Fricke (1996).
11. See, for example, Refish (1975); Okely (1983); Gmelch (1986); Sway (1988).
12. On the role of the Gypsy Lore Society, see Mayall (1992) and Willems (1997).
13. See, for example, Green (1996).
14. Members of the Gypsy Lore Society, founded in England in 1888. It is no coincidence (confirmed personally by Fraser) that his book bears the same title as that by one of the founding fathers of the GLS, Charles Godfrey Leland, published precisely 110 years earlier.
15. See Lucassen and Willems (1995).
16. For an analysis of Grellmann, the founding father of 'gypsiology', see Willems (1997) and Chapter 2 in this volume.
17. Said (1978).
18. Examples are Kenrick and Puxon (1972); Hancock (1991), pp. 11–30. For German studies see L. Lucassen (1996).
19. L. Lucassen (1990), pp. 15–17; Willems and Lucassen (1990), pp. 19–20; and L. Lucassen (1991).
20. Especially Mayall (1988) and Fricke (1991 and 1996).
21. We confine ourselves to refer to the work of Miles (1989).
22. Noiriel (1991); Moch (1992); for an overview of the recent literature on this subject, see L. Lucassen (1995b).
23. See, for example, Demetz (1987); Zucchi (1992); and Fontaine (1996).

CHAPTER 2 ETHNICITY AS A DEATH-TRAP: THE HISTORY OF GYPSY STUDIES

1. This chapter is a modified version of a paper presented at a conference of the Gypsy Lore Society in Leiden, 29–31 May 1995 and at the European Social Science History Conference, Noordwijkerhout, 9–11 May 1996.
2. Grant (1995).
3. Acton (1974); and Salo (1979), pp. 73–96.
4. Take Germany, for example, the classic setting for Gypsy studies. In the eighteenth century some 8 per cent of the population there still belonged to the so-called 'vagrant marginal classes'. They survived through such diverse activities as rat-catching, chimney-sweeping, and selling books and almanacs to peasants. See Fertig (1997), pp. 271–89.
5. See our Introduction and Chapter 8 in this volume.
6. That studies based on an ethnographic perspective are inclined ultimately to explain the policy of persecution by pointing out that Gypsies were (conscious) outsiders, we observe as well in German postwar studies which have analysed the roots of such harassment during the Nazi regime. For a critical discussion of the consequences of this approach, see Chapter 5 in this volume.
7. See Grellmann (1783, second edition 1787). For a sketch of his life, works, the reception of his book on Gypsies and his influence on later authors, see Willems (1997), chapter 2.
8. Fraser (1992), p. 196.
9. This discovery, which we made in the National Library of Austria in Vienna, is recently confirmed by the Hungarian ethnologist Viera Urbancová. She has in addition prepared a complete dual language (Hungarian/German) edition of the series of articles on Gypsies: Samuel Augustini ab Hortis, etc. (1994). See, too, her introduction and afterword in which she urges the restoration of this 'forgotten monograph' to the respect it deserves.
10. See Willems (1997), chapter 2; also Ruch (1986), who was the first to come up with a critical analysis of Grellmann's works.
11. On Johann Gottfried Herder and the roots of nineteenth-century national myths, see Mosse (1978), pp. 1–35, and Poliakov (1979), pp. 155–82.
12. It is very probable that Herder had a direct influence on Grellmann, since he was a close friend of his father-in-law. See on this topic Walter (1908), pp. 36–59.
13. The most well-known is Johann Christoph Wagenseil, *De civitate Noribergensi commentatio* (1697), pp. 435–50. See also Gronemeyer (1987) for the original text of this early author on Gypsies.
14. See, for example, R. Körber, *Volk und Staat* (1936), cited in Zülch (1982), p. 31: 'Der Jude und der Zigeuner sind heute weit von uns entfernt, weil ihre Asiatische Vorfahren völlig andersartig als unsere nordische Ahnen waren.'
15. In Willems (1997), a long chapter is devoted to Borrow's life and works.
16. The initial series of the *Journal of the Gypsy Lore Society* appeared

from 1888 to 1892 in Edinburgh; the second from 1907 to 1916; the third from 1922 to 1973; the fourth from 1974 to 1978; in 1991, a fifth began in the United States. The history of this influential society, which in 1994 still comprised a reflection of the themes dominating Gypsy studies, i.e. ethnology and linguistics, has not yet been written. In his study Mayall (1988), pp. 71–93, was very critical about their findings, whereas Fraser (1990), pp. 1–14, saluted their learning and enthusiasm.

17. See Willems (1997), chapter 5, on the life and works of Robert Ritter and his influence on the Nazi government policies.

18. In the last 15 years a good deal of literature on the academic roots of Nazi ideology and policies has been produced. Two interesting if detailed studies in this area are Weingart et al. (1988) and Weindling (1989). See further Noakes (1984), pp. 75–94; Ganssmüller (1987); Proctor (1988); Pross and Aly (1989); Bäumer (1990); and Becker (1990), pp. 500–620.

19. See Ritter (1940) and Ritter (1941), pp. 137–55.

20. Ritter (1941), p. 139.

21. Ritter (1940), p. 12.

22. See Ritter (1941), pp. 38–41; Ritter (1942b), pp. 117–19; Ritter (1942a), pp. 535–9; and Ritter (1944), pp. 33–60.

23. Ritter (1942b), p. 117.

24. See Ritter (1942a), pp. 536–7, and Ritter (1941), pp. 38–9.

25. On this topic, see for example Willems (1997), chapter 5.

26. For the relation between Ritter's research and the Nazi policies, see Willems (1997), chapter 5.

27. In Chapter 5 of this volume we elaborate on the police context and influences on Ritter's rubrications.

28. Said (1978).

29. See Mason (1990); Lemaire (1986); and Corbey (1989). Their approach, which is strongly cultural-philosophic, has little affinity, however, with ours.

CHAPTER 3   THE CHURCH OF KNOWLEDGE:
REPRESENTATION OF GYPSIES IN ENCYCLOPAEDIAS

1. This chapter is a modified version of Willems and Lucassen (1990b), pp. 31–50. Since then our findings for the Dutch situation were confirmed by research on German encyclopaedias by Rao and Casimir (1993), pp. 111–24 and by Willems (1997), chapter 1, who explored English, French and German encyclopaedias as well as their main sources.

2. The forerunners of the encyclopaedias, the so-called dictionaries, are included as well. Obviously, the most specialized encyclopaedias (technical, art, etc.) are left outside of consideration. The entries are: Bohemians, Egyptians, Gypsies, Heathens, Tsiganes and Zigeuners. Our selection is based upon the dictionaries and encyclopaedias which can be found at the Royal Library in The Hague. The central catalogue of this library was consulted in order to complete the research.

Although this catalogue is by no means complete, and although we were unable to study all the works listed in the Royal Library, we do consider the 60 Dutch encyclopaedias we have studied to be representative.

3. Considering the extensive work which has been done on this subject, we have limited ourselves to those sources which are cited most often in the encyclopaedias, and which can be found in the Dutch libraries.

4. Earlier works also describe the Gypsy's features; however, these descriptions do not amount to more than a crude sketch. It is only after the middle of the nineteenth century that the Gypsy is described in more detail. The descriptions are frequently based upon anthropometric research. See Liebich (1863), p. 20; Schwicker (1883), pp. 104–5, whose work is largely based on the former; and also Wlislocki (1890), p. 164.

5. See Mosse (1978), pp. 17–34; Poliakov (1979), pp. 156–84.

6. See Mosse (1978), pp. 42–4; Poliakov (1979), p. 209.

7. This characteristic is first mentioned in the *Winkler Prins* encyclopaedia of 1954, which seems strange when we realize that at the end of the eighteenth century, research had already been done in Germany on the shape of Gypsy skulls (Blumenbach, 1793, pp. 3–4), and that this research was continued intensively from the middle of the nineteenth century onwards. The results of this research were, as far as we know, first mentioned by Diefenbach (1877), p. 106. For an extensive survey, see Wlislocki (1890), p. 163, note 1.

8. Grellmann (1787), p. 40.

9. Swinburne (1779), p. 30.

10. Twiss (1776), pp. 204–5; Salmon (1733), p. 472.

11. Grellmann (1787), pp. 329–32, names, among others, two seventeenth-century Dutch travelling accounts.

12. See, for example, Mosse (1978), pp. 41–2.

13. Serboianu (1930), p. 25.

14. Grellmann (1787), p. 80.

15. Kogalnitchan (1840), p. 30.

16. Wlislocki (1890), p. 196.

17. For example, from Liebich (1863) and Schwicker (1883). See Ruch (1986), pp. 191–284, and Willems (1997), chapter 4, for an extensive critical analysis of Wlislocki's publications on Gypsies.

18. Kogalnitchan (1840), p. 33. See also Block (1936), p. 101, who takes over this view unquestioningly.

19. See, among others, Borrow (1841) Vol. I, pp. 45–50; Paspati (1870), p. 22; Liebich (1863), p. 3.

20. For example, for Grellmann (1787), p. 94, and Twiss (1776), pp. 204–5.

21. Borrow (1841), pp. 30, 331 ff.

22. Serboianu (1930), p. 74.

23. Block (1936), p. 171.

24. See, for example, Okely (1983), pp. 201 ff.; Liégeois (1983), p. 98.

25. *Encyclopedia of Nieuwhuis* (1856), Vol. H, p. 262; *Algemene Nederlandsche Encyclopedie* (1866), Vol. VII, p. 281; *Sijthof Encyclopedia* (1890), Vol. IV, p. 475.

26. For instance, the 1870 *Winkler Prins* encyclopaedia states: '... they

grovel before the powerful of the earth'. Liebich (1863), p. 18, on the other hand, claimed that Gypsies always hang on to their pride, something which supposedly distinguishes them from the Jews (who are considered obsequious). Wlislocki (1890), p. 10, repeated this word for word, but later on in his book, when the character of the Gypsies is mentioned ('keineswegs ein erfreulicher', p. 166), they suddenly appear to be marked by 'entwürdigende Kriecherei in Thun und Wesen'.

27. Borrow (1841), Vol. I, p. 355.
28. Bloch (1953), p. 39.
29. *Katholieke Encyclopedie* (1938), Vol. 245, p. 591; (1955), Vol. 25, p. 320, but also the *Christelijke Encyclopedie* (1961), Vol. VI, p. 679; (1977), Vol. VI, p. 697. The nineteenth century witnesses the spreading of the idea that the criminality of the Gypsies has increased particularly because they have intermixed with indigenous criminals and antisocial characters. This 'degeneration thesis' can already be found in Dirks (1850), pp. 152–3. Later, this thesis is worked out by such German scholars as Robert Ritter (1937 and 1938). Even after the Second World War, there are some who continue to be influenced by this racist idea; see, among others, the opinions of Arnold (1958 and 1965); van Kappen (1965), pp. 7, 139; and finally Küther (1976), p. 25.
30. Grellmann (1787), p. 190.
31. Borrow (1841), Vol. I, p. 19.
32. Schwicker (1883), p. 113.
33. Leland (1893), p. 124.
34. De Chalmot (1789), Vol. XI, pp. 2910–11; *Grote Spectrum Encyclopedie*, (1979), Vol. XX, p. 374.
35. Borrow (1841), Vol. I, pp. 102–4.
36. Grellmann (1787), pp. 50–1.
37. Block (1936), pp. 6, 66.
38. Grellmann (1787), pp. 48–59.
39. Borrow (1841), Vol. I, pp. 82–3; Serboianu (1930), p. 68.
40. Block (1936), pp. 64–5.
41. Avé-Lallemant (1858–62), Vol. II, p. 52, note 3. As far as we can tell at this moment, this author was one of the first to examine the Gypsies from a criminological point of view. They do not yet appear like this in Jageman (1854).
42. Ibid., p. 11.
43. Liebich (1863), pp. 95–7; Lombroso (1887), p. 317; (1894), pp. 138 ff; (1902), pp. 34 ff.
44. Gross (1904), Vol. I, pp. 318–45.
45. There is a general agreement on this subject as well, starting at the beginning of the eighteenth century: supposedly, Gypsies were heathens who lacked any kind of religious feeling; see, for example, Salmon (1733), p. 503, and Grellmann (1787), p. 141. The latter is well known for the following statement: 'Es fällt ihm eben so leicht, mit jedem neuem Dorfe seine Religion zu verändern, als andern Menschen, ein anderes Kleid anzuziehen.'
46. Van Kappen (1965), pp. 136–7.
47. Ibid., p. 272.

48. Kogalnitchan (1840), p. 27.
49. See, for example, Derlon (1981).
50. The representation of this subject is based largely on Grellm denke aber nicht, dass die Werkstätte des Schmiedes beständig vom pochenden Hammer wiederhalle, oder andere ihren andern Verrichtungen so fleissig obliegen' (1787, p. 112). And yet Grellmann praised the Gypsies highly for their craftmanship (p. 84). However, he undercuts these skills earlier in his work, claiming that the Gypsies only make small objects because heavy forging would take too much of an effort (p. 82). This opinion was adopted by, among others, Schwicker (1883), p. 118; Wlislocki (1890), p. 198; and Kuhinka (1957), pp. 80 ff.
51. Block (1936), p. 117.
52. Schwicker (1883), pp. 159–87; Liebich (1863), p. 97.
53. Wlislocki (1890), pp. 310 ff.
54. After Wlislocki, Aichele and Block (1926) in particular enriched the general knowledge about Gypsy fairy tales. This part of Gypsy culture in Europe was further explored by Kuhinka (1957), pp. 93–127, and recently the Uhlik and Radivic (1977).
55. See, among others, Acton (1974) and Okely (1983).

CHAPTER 4 ETERNAL VAGRANTS? STATE FORMATION, MIGRATION AND TRAVELLING GROUPS IN WESTERN EUROPE, 1350–1941

1. This chapter is a modified version of L. Lucassen (1997), pp. 227–53.
2. Geremek (1980), p. 71. See also Woolf (1986), pp. 17–18; and Sachße and Tennstedt (1980), p. 36.
3. Geremek (1991), p. 53.
4. Geremek (1980), p. 71. For the 1351 Act see also Miskimin (1975), pp. 45–6.
5. Geremek (1974), p. 349.
6. Lis and Soly (1979), p. 82.
7. De Vries (1976), pp. 184–7.
8. J. Lucassen (1987).
9. Beier (1985), p. 9.
10. Ibid., p. xix.
11. Lis and Soly (1979); Hufton (1974).
12. Moch (1992).
13. Fertig (1997), pp. 203–4.
14. Woolf (1986), pp. 17–20; Jütte (1994), pp. 100–2.
15. Clasen (1984), pp. 109–14.
16. Woolf (1986), p. 19.
17. Lis and Soly (1979); for a good overview of this and other motives see van Leeuwen (1994).
18. Sachße and Tennstedt (1980), p. 31.
19. Reith (1989), p. 2.
20. Mayall (1992), pp. 25–6.

21. Egmond (1993), p. 96.
22. Beier (1985); and Slack (1987).
23. L. Lucassen (1996), p. 56.
24. Tilly (1990), p. 79; Chandler (1976), p. 65.
25. Redlich (1964/65), pp. 173–4.
26. L. Lucassen (1996), chapter 2.
27. J. Lucassen (1994), p. 786.
28. Schubert (1983), p. 292; and Bog (1975), p. 1001.
29. Zysberg (1987). See also Schubert (1983), p. 292.
30. L. Lucassen (1996), chapter 2.
31. Vaux de Foletier (1961), pp. 152–60.
32. Liégeois (1986), pp. 95–7.
33. Zysberg (1987), pp. 65–7. In the period 1680–1715 only some 50 'Gypsies' were sent to Marseilles, against 137 in the following period 1716–48. Together with vagrants and beggars the numbers were respectively 698 (5.9 per cent) and 1,323 (13 per cent).
34. Egmond (1993).
35. Gatrell (1990), pp. 243–4.
36. Snell (1985), p. 107. See also Beier (1985), pp. 171–5.
37. Petit et al. (1991), pp. 75–6, and Perrot (1980), pp. 9–56.
38. Schwartz (1988), pp. 250–1. His conclusions at this point are somewhat weakened by Adams (1990), p. 119.
39. Schwartz (1988), p. 153.
40. Gutton (1973), pp. 180–1; Norberg (1985), pp. 223–4.
41. Schwartz (1988), p. 169; Finzsch (1990), pp. 2–23. See also Woolf (1986), p. 28.
42. Nitschke (1990), p. 183.
43. In England this process had started already around 1770 and was speeded up after 1810. See Snell (1985), pp. 73–80.
44. Moch (1992), chapter 4.
45. Chevalier (1978), and Stedman-Jones (1971/84).
46. Carson and Idzikowska (1989), p. 273; Davis (1991), p. 4; Jones (1982), pp. 178–209; Roberts (1988), p. 282; Storch (1989), pp. 218–19.
47. Emsley (1991), p. 49.
48. Steedman (1984), p. 57.
49. Mayall (1988), p. 147. A similar judgement is given by Jones (1982), p. 207: 'One of the most flexible, useful and criminal-making statutes of the century.'
50. Leigh (1979), p. 108.
51. Cottaar et al. (1992), p. 57.
52. Forstenzer (1981), p. 109.
53. Davis (1991), pp. 5–6; Perrot (1978), p. 220.
54. See Chapter 5 in this volume.
55. Lüdtke (1989), p. 82.
56. Jessen (1991), pp. 35–6; Haupt (1986), pp. 228–30; Becker (1992), p. 119; Wirsing (1992), p. 67.
57. Brubaker (1992), p. 63.
58. Noiriel (1988), p. 89.
59. Gatrell (1990), pp. 245–52.

60. Jones (1985), p. 83.
61. Jaumain (1985), pp. 314–18; Chatelain (1971), p. 375.
62. Leeuwen (1994), p. 589.
63. Becker (1992), p. 119.

CHAPTER 5 'HARMFUL TRAMPS': POLICE
PROFESSIONALIZATION AND GYPSIES IN GERMANY,
1700–1945

1. This chapter is an abridged version of Lucassen (1997) – and largely based on Lucassen (1996). The most important studies are mentioned throughout this chapter.
2. Notable exceptions are Fricke (1991) and (1996) (we received a copy of the latter after our manuscript was completed).
3. Exceptions are the work of Burleigh and Wippermann (1991) and Zimmermann (1996).
4. For example, Jessen (1991); Spencer (1992); Reinke (1993); and Lüdtke (1992).
5. An exception is Nitschke (1990).
6. Lüdtke (1982).
7. Spencer (1992), p. 62.
8. Jessen (1991), pp. 192–9.
9. For a critical overview see Lucassen (1996); Willems (1997); and Chapter 2 in this volume.
10. Nitschke (1990), pp. 190–3.
11. Bader (1962), p. 303.
12. Tilly (1990), p. 107.
13. Finzsch (1990), p. 450.
14. Lucassen (1996), p. 80.
15. Based on a sample from the first half year of 1852 in the *Allgemeiner Polizey Anzeiger*.
16. Blasius (1976).
17. Sachße and Tennstedt (1980), p. 196.
18. Lucassen (1996), p. 140.
19. Ibid., p. 142.
20. Willems (1997).
21. Jessen (1991), p. 63, and Spencer (1992), pp. 50, 52 and 166.
22. See Hehemann (1987), pp. 243–4.
23. See Lucassen and Willems (1995).
24. Hehemann (1987), pp. 245, 323 and 277.
25. Sample from the years 1866, 1870, 1875, 1880, 1885 and 1890. From the 39 descriptions of groups of Gypsies only six came from Austria, Hungary, Bohemia and Croatia.
26. Becker (1992), pp. 126–7.
27. Jessen (1994), p. 161.
28. Ibid., pp. 167–8, 178–9.
29. Strauss (1986), p. 44.
30. Lucassen (1996), pp. 255–6.

31. Ibid., Appendix 7B.
32. Strauss (1986), p. 68.
33. Among others the *Süddeutscher Verein reisender Schausteller und Handelsleute* from Nürnberg and the *Reichsverband ambulanter Gewerbetreibenden.* See Lucassen (1996), p. 193.
34. Their licence to perform an itinerant profession was amplified with a special *Schutzvermerk* (protective notice).
35. Karanikas, cited by Strauss (1986), p. 84.
36. We will not treat this period in full, but only select those developments which are of direct relevance for the main question in this chapter. For a more thorough overall analysis, see Zimmermann (1989 and 1996); Eiber (1993); Riechert (1995); and Willems (1997).
37. Eiber (1993), p. 51. From these 33,524, 18,138 were classified as 'Gypsies', 10,788 as 'people living like Gypsies' and 4,598 'other travellers'. Note that the 3,350 persons published by Dillmann also consisted of these categories.
38. In 1905 the 'people living like Gypsies' made up 28 per cent of Dillmann's 613 full descriptions. In 1938 this had risen to some 38 per cent and if we include the 'other travellers' as well in the equation its share increases to 43 per cent.
39. Zimmermann (1989), pp. 18–22.
40. Also known as the *Rassenhygienische und bevölkerungsbiologische Forschungsstelle.* See Zimmermann (1989), p. 33.
41. Willems (1997), Chapter 5.
42. In a letter of 17 October 1939 from the *Reichssicherheitshauptamt* to the *Staatliche Kriminalpolizei* the local police and gendarmerie were ordered to make lists of all the 'Gypsies' and mixed Gypsies in their resort. See Riechert (1995), p. 105.
43. Eiber (1993), pp. 99–111.
44. Zimmermann (1989), p. 36; (1996), p. 370.
45. L. Lucassen (1996), p. 208.
46. Siemann (1983), p. 76.
47. For these concepts see Tilly (1990), p. 107.

CHAPTER 6   A SILENT WAR: FOREIGN GYPSIES AND THE
DUTCH GOVERNMENT POLICY (1969–89)

1. This chapter is a modified version of Willems and Lucassen (1992).
2. See, for this migration, among others, Ficowski (1989); De Vaux de Foletier (1981), pp. 115–37; Mayall (1988), p. 91; Salo and Salo (1986), pp. 85–96; and Lucassen and Willems (1995).
3. This decision was meant as a gesture to other European countries. As is well known, there exists no policy at the international level towards stateless Gypsies, which results in the customary toing and froing of such groups at the borders. Only vague resolutions which can be interpreted freely have been taken, such as a recommendation to take measures against the discrimination of Gypsies and to promote their well-being, which was passed in the Assembly of the Council of Europe in 1969 at

the initiative of the Netherlands, and a similar resolution passed in 1975.
4. Willems and Lucassen (1990a).
5. See Chapter 3 of this volume.

CHAPTER 7 THE MAKING OF A MINORITY: THE CASE OF
DUTCH TRAVELLERS

1. This chapter has not been published as an article before. It contains some of the main findings of Cottaar (1996). Trans. by Don Bloch.
2. For an overview of how caravan-dwellers see themselves as a group in relation to how they look at Dutch society, see Cottaar and Willems (1992), pp. 67–80.
3. Penninx (1988), p. 48.
4. Ibid., p. 51.
5. Ibid., pp. 49–50.
6. For the most up-to-date data, see Overbekking (1994).
7. Cf. two other minority groups: in 1993 191,500 Turks and 148,000 Moroccans lived in the Netherlands. See *Maandstatistiek.*(1993), p. 29.
8. Penninx (1988), p. 55.
9. Ibid.
10. For a more elaborate analysis, see Chapter 10.
11. See Chapter 5 for the German equivalent, the *Heimatrecht.*
12. Cf. the Aliens Act (*Vreemdelingenwet*) of 1849 (for regulating the admission and exclusion of foreigners), Articles 1 and 11.
13. *Verslag der staatscommissie* (1913).
14. From 7 November 1944 until 2 July 1945 the Caravan Act of the Military Authorities obtained in the liberated zone. Any movement of a caravan was prohibited unless the military authorities extended explicit permission, which meant that the pre-liberation situation still remained in effect. See Sijes (1979), p. 137.
15. Cottaar (1996), p. 277.
16. See, too, Jeurgens (1987), pp. 22 ff.
17. Cottaar (1996), p. 278.
18. See Jeurgens (1987) for a review of Catholic involvement in government policies.
19. Cottaar (1996), p. 278.
20. To this end the Minister for Social Welfare set up the Caravan Council (*Beraad Woonwagenwerk*) whose members were representatives from the ministries and people from concerned church and private groups.
21. Dercksen and Verplanke (1987), p. 241.
22. Overbekking (1994), p. 66.
23. Lucassen (1996) has identified the same trend in Germany.
24. Initially known as *The United Kingdom Showmen's* and *Van-Dwellers' Protection Association.* See Mayall (1988), p. 142.
25. Ibid., pp. 138–40.
26. This is one of the reasons the Showmen's Guild managed to get the Liberty and Property Defence League on their side.
27. Acton (1974), pp. 121–3.

28. Sexton (1989), pp. 40–2.
29. See Jansen (1987), p. 125.
30. Ibid., pp. 150–2.
31. Ibid., pp. 119, 147–8, 174.
32. Ibid., pp. 139, 155, 223, 225.
33. Willems and Cottaar (1989), pp. 177–83, 194–203.

CHAPTER 8 A BLIND SPOT: MIGRATORY AND TRAVELLING GROUPS IN WESTERN EUROPEAN HISTORIOGRAPHY

1. This chapter is a modified version of L. Lucassen (1993b).
2. Kamen (1986), pp. 167–93.
3. Wehler (1987), pp. 174–6.
4. For the sake of variation, the term 'travellers' is also used.
5. For example by Stedman-Jones (1984) and Jones (1982).
6. The most important works of Arnold are: *Vaganten* (1958); *Die Zigeuner* (1965); and *Fahrendes Volk* (1980).
7. To be defined as the way of thinking that stresses the importance of biological and hereditary traits to explain negative social behaviour. This concerns not only so-called races, but also social groups such as casual workers or 'antisocials' whose behaviour is considered a product of hereditary traits.
8. On Ritter, see Chapter 2 of this volume.
9. Arnold (1958), p. 33.
10. Ibid., pp. 37–43.
11. Ibid., p. 47.
12. Küther (1976).
13. Küther (1983).
14. Küther (1976), p. 14.
15. Ibid., pp. 25–6.
16. Among others: Endres (1974–75); Ay (1979); Sachße and Tennstedt (1983); Reinicke (1983); Reif (1984); and Rohrbacher (1984).
17. Schubert (1983).
18. See in this respect also Schubert (1988).
19. In Arnold's most recent work of 1983 his interpretation of the socio-economic role of itinerant groups has become even more positive.
20. Finzsch (1990), p. 26. See also Danker (1988), p. 431, and Nitschke (1990), p. 41.
21. An elaborate list can be found in Beier (1985). A more recent evaluation of the anti-society idea is found in Jütte (1994), pp. 178–85.
22. Slack (1987).
23. Graus (1981).
24. Ibid., p. 398; see in this respect also Jütte (1988), pp. 28–34.
25. Gutton (1973), p. 21; Schwartz (1988).
26. Gutton (1971), p. 54.
27. Gutton (1973), pp. 180–1.
28. Ibid., p. 198. This is supported by the analysis of the relationship between marginality and migration in Moch (1992), pp. 88–93.

29. See Lis and Soly (1979), pp. 224–5 on the weakness of traditional (neo-Malthusian) explanations.
30. Ibid., pp. 79 and 188–90.
31. Many of them were not involved in wage-labour, at least not systematically, but were 'penny capitalists'. See for this concept Benson (1983).
32. Reif (1981) and Schubert (1988), pp. 128–9 and 138–43.
33. See, for example, Baulant (1979), p. 118.
34. J. Lucassen (1987).
35. Ibid., pp. 88–92. See also Fontaine (1996).
36. J. Lucassen and L. Lucassen (1997).
37. Among others Höher (1985); Demetz (1987); Zucchi (1992); Reininghaus (1993); Fontaine (1996); and Oberpenning (1996).
38. Demetz (1987).
39. Stieda (1898).
40. The same conclusions can be found in Benson (1983), p. 102, and in Alexander (1970), p. 63.
41. Among others Chatelain (1971) and De Vries (1976).
42. Chatelain (1971), p. 380, and De Vries (1976), pp. 146–7, are much more optimistic than, for example, Jaumain (1985), pp. 352–3, and Benson (1983), pp. 100–1.
43. Chatelain (1971), p. 371.
44. An exception is Egmond (1993).
45. Fricke (1991) and his latest book of 1996.
46. Mayall (1988).
47. For an overview see Gmelch (1986) and Rao (1986).
48. Cottaar (1996).
49. J. Lucassen (1987).
50. L. Lucassen (1990), pp. 162–8.
51. See Mayall (1988), pp. 13–70; Hehemann (1987), pp. 181, 203, 205, 238, 295, 328–9, 364–5; and Fricke (1991), pp. 76–85.
52. For an analysis of German police journals see L. Lucassen (1996) and Fricke (1996).
53. L. Lucassen (1990).
54. For the latter see Cottaar et al. (1995).
55. Zucchi (1992), pp. 10–13. Some information on the groups mentioned can also be found in L. Lucassen (1990), pp. 234–5 and 367–9.
56. Acton (1974); Okely (1983). For the Netherlands see Cottaar (1996).
57. J. Lucassen (1987), pp. 152 and 157.
58. Spufford (1984), pp. 14–31.
59. Marx divided the poor in *Das Kapital* (Vol. I, Chapter 23, sub. 4, p. 586) into four categories: (a) the vagrants, criminals and prostitutes (the real lumpenproletariat); (b) the unemployed, hit by temporary crisis; (c) orphans and abandoned children; and (d) the disabled and the old. See also Woolf (1986), p. 71, note 1.
60. Ibid., pp. 31–2.

CHAPTER 9   THE CLINK OF THE HAMMER WAS HEARD
FROM DAYBREAK TILL DAWN: GYPSY OCCUPATIONS IN
WESTERN EUROPE (NINETEENTH-TWENTIETH CENTURIES)

1. This chapter is a revised version of L. Lucassen (1993a). For the Dutch background see also Cottaar et al. (1995).
2. Gmelch (1986); Rao (1986); Cottaar et al. (1995).
3. Hoyland (1816), p. 169.
4. Mayall (1988), p. 49.
5. See, for example, the itinerant pottery pedlars from the Westerwald in the Netherlands around 1850, in Schrover (1996), p. 116.
6. Klein (1898), p. 371.
7. Demetz (1987), p. 54.
8. L. Lucassen (1993a), p. 80.
9. Ibid.
10. Keller (1898).
11. Gmelch (1986), p. 312.
12. Gmelch and Langan (1975), pp. 49–50.
13. Seebach (1990).
14. Cuttriss (1915), pp. 262–3.
15. L. Lucassen (1990), p. 144.
16. Mayall (1988), p. 53.
17. Günther (1985), pp. 31–2.
18. Höhne (1929), pp. 170–1; Strauss (1986), p. 112.
19. Bott-Bodenhausen (1988), p. 27; Hehemann (1987), pp. 203, 205, 364–5.
20. L. Lucassen (1990), pp. 137–46.
21. Mayall (1988), pp. 58–9.
22. For the following, see Lucassen (1990), pp. 64–7 and 74–81; see also De Vaux de Foletier (1981), pp. 115–37; idem (1983), pp. 134–6; Fraser (1992), pp. 226–35; and Lucassen and Willems (1995).
23. L. Lucassen (1990), p. 41.
24. Winstedt (1913), pp. 287–8.
25. L. Lucassen (1990), p. 78.
26. Simson (1865), pp. 354–5.
27. Gmelch and Langan (1975), p. 28.
28. L. Lucassen (1990), p. 81.
29. Burke (1978), pp. 94–6; Schubert (1995), pp. 226 ff.
30. Benson (1983), p. 68.
31. Zucchi (1992); van Tiggelen (1982–3); L. Lucassen (1990), pp. 367–75.
32. Lucassen and Willems (1995).
33. Vukanovic (1959); L. Lucassen (1990), pp. 87–91.
34. Hehemann (1987), pp. 209–11.
35. L. Lucassen (1990), p. 90.
36. De Vaux de Foletier (1981), pp. 134–8.
37. L. Lucassen (1993a), p. 88.
38. Benson (1983), p. 65.
39. Acton (1974), pp. 111, 116–23; De Vaux de Foletier (1981), pp. 31, 188; L. Lucassen (1990), pp. 203–4; Cottaar (1996), pp. 172–3.
40. Renner (1988), pp. 127–8; L. Lucassen (1990), p. 204; Cottaar et al. (1995), pp. 132–4.

41. Weltzel (1938), p. 37; and Dollé (1980), pp. 168 ff.
42. Beynon (1936), p. 363.
43. Fraser (1992), pp. 46–8.
44. Thomas (1984), pp. 282–91; de Blécourt (1992), pp. 357–61; Burke (1978), pp. 106–7.
45. Mayall (1988), pp. 51–2.
46. Cuttriss (1915), pp. 91–2.
47. L. Lucassen (1996), pp. 147–8.
48. Gmelch (1986), p. 307.
49. Levy (1953), p. 133.
50. Reyniers (1991), p. 22.
51. Cuttriss (1915), p. 68; Maccol and Seeger (1986), p. 13; Samuel (1976), p. 138.
52. Mayall (1988), pp. 63–4.
53. Strauss (1986), pp. 111, 118; see also L. Lucassen (1996), p. 179.
54. L. Lucassen (1996), pp. 192–6; Acton (1974), pp. 103–25; Cottaar et al. (1995), pp. 139–40.

CHAPTER 10 DUTCH TRAVELLERS: DWELLINGS, ORIGINS AND OCCUPATIONS

1. This chapter has not been published as an article before. It contains some of the findings of Cottaar (1996) and profited enormously from the richly illustrated work of Cottaar et al. (1995). Trans. by Don Bloch.
2. Heymowski (1969).
3. See Wernink (1959), pp. 33–62; Bruggemeijer (1980), pp. 27–54; and van Ooijen (1993), pp. 48–55.
4. L. Lucassen (1990), pp. 233–5.
5. Halters (1992), pp. 33–46. See also Lourens and Lucassen (1987), pp. 30–4, on brickmakers who slept in the *tichelkamer* (stove room) where cabinet-beds were built into the wall near the oven.
6. L. Lucassen (1990), pp. 69, 76–7.
7. Verheul (1990), p. 4.
8. Wernink (1959), pp. 53–4; and van der Baan (1986), p. 282.
9. *Uitkomsten volkstelling 1879*, published 1881.
10. Gemeentelijke Archiefdienst Amsterdam, *Keeten Register*, 1874–92, two volumes.
11. See the interviews with showmen in Jansen (1987), pp. 139, 164. We also found an occasional fair traveller who lived in a boat in the Amsterdam *Keeten Register*.
12. The source we draw on most significantly here is Horsten (1992).
13. Horsten (1992), pp. 128–9.
14. Ibid.
15. A pavement which consists of two layers of broken stone, rough and fine, on a foundation of paving stones laid down according to the recipe of the Scottish engineer McAdam.
16. Ward-Jackson and Harvey (1978), p. 29.
17. Van der Woud (1987), p. 169, concluded that first two conditions had to be met: (a) the extension of the prerogatives of municipalities and

provinces after 1850 and their having budgets of their own; (b) repair and improvement of waterways to facilitate the transport of materials (stones, gravel and such like) needed for upgrading country roads.

18. English, French and German sources yielded only sketchy information. The history of Belgian caravan-dwellers remains to be written.

19. Mayall (1988), p. 25; Ward-Jackson and Harvey (1978), pp. 28–39. From Mayall's statistics on p. 23 we can deduce that between 1861 and 1911 the number of people living in tents and caravans increased considerably, whereas those sleeping in sheds fell sharply. Mayall offers no conclusions, however, pertaining to the quantitative relation between tent- and caravan-dwellers.

20. To judge from the books of the English writer George Borrow, caravans were already driving around in England in the 1820s but we hesitate to cite this as a reliable source. The works concerned, *Lavengro* and *The Romany Rye*, are to be sure set in the 1820s but were only published in 1851 and 1857, respectively. In his book *Wild Wales* of 1852, Borrow described a 'wooden house on wheels drawn by two horses'. *The Old Curiosity Shop* by Charles Dickens, which contains a description of a caravan lived in by a showman, appeared in 1840. From Ward-Jackson and Harvey (1978), pp. 29–31.

21. Arnold (1983), p. 120. In his chapter on fair and circus travellers he reports on p. 279 a caravan from 1885.

22. In addition one used the names *Rollwagen* (1841) or *Korfwagen* (1854). See Lucassen (1996), chapter 4.

23. Vaux de Foletier (1981).

24. We can be confident that the dating of the drawings is fairly accurate and that in any event they are not from a later date because they were published in the same years in the periodical *L'Illustration*. The earliest images of inhabited covered wagons in the Netherlands date from around 1876. In that year the Teylers Museum in Haarlem purchased the painting 'Aan de Buitensingel' by H.J. Scholten in which a group of acrobats is depicted. See Cottaar et al. (1995), p. 28.

25. Stolz (1869). Only the sixth edition of 1886 is to be found in the Netherlands. In the 1869 volume of *L'Illustration* (p. 60) there are three renderings of wooden caravans as well.

26. Mayall (1988), pp. 36, 38. These are two plates from *The Illustrated News* of 29 November 1879 (p. 504) and 13 December 1879 (p. 545). In one George Smith of Coalville is shown who dedicated his life from the late 1870s on to the fate of the Gypsies. A few unique drawings of caravans are also reproduced in an article by this social reformer in *The Graphic*, 13 March 1880, pp. 275–6.

27. See Cottaar et al. (1995), pp. 28–9. The photo of the covered carts on p. 8 is, according to its owner, from 1883; if that is true, then this is the earliest pictorial representation of a caravan in the Netherlands.

28. Perhaps a decade before that in England if we may trust the information in note 20. In that event extremely small numbers were probably in use.

29. In Cottaar et al. (1995), pp. 26–7, there is a picture of a married couple of chair-bottomers with two dog carts exhibiting such a superstructure. Three dogs who presumably pulled the carts lie on the ground nearby.

Willem Netten from Schiedam told us that the pair were his parents, Martinus Netten and Johanna van Gulik, who in the photograph were repairing chair bottoms where they resided in Kaatsheuvel in about 1900.
30. See van Gendt's illustrations of wagons in Voorschoten (1902, pp. 536–7). The painting mentioned in note 24 dates from before 1876, true, but it is not certain the image shows a Dutch scene.
31. This was true, too, for the wagons, already mentioned, in the English and French drawings from 1869, 1872 and 1879.
32. See the photographs in Cottaar et al. (1995), pp. 8, 29.
33. Ibid., pp. 16–17, 32, 36.
34. In the province of Overijssel in the 1920s 21 per cent of the caravans on the road were less than four metres long, a percentage which in the 1930s dipped to 9 per cent, falling yet further in the early 1940s to 4 per cent. The most common length for a caravan in the period from 1920 to 1945 was 4.5 metres, with a width of 2.15 metres.
35. See Cottaar (1996), p. 33.
36. Ibid., p. 34.
37. The selected caravan-dwellers (generation 1) were traced back, where possible, four generations.
38. See, for example, Wernink (1959, pp. 56–9), who writes that he left these groups out of consideration because they were not 'real' caravan-dwellers or travellers. It remains an open question, however, whether in the past these occupations weren't current among caravan-dwellers. It is also unclear whether the public at large and policy-makers were always able to distinguish between various 'sorts' of caravan-dwellers.
39. Wage labourers include casual workers as well as those with jobs in a factory or on the land.
40. In his study of the situation in Helmond (1913–37) van der Baan arrived at respective percentages of 11 per cent artisans, 62 per cent tradesmen, 6 per cent showmen and 18 per cent labourers. Although his statistics may differ a bit, relations among the groups (and their size) agree fairly closely with our findings for The Hague and Overijssel.
41. Information on women's sales activities comes primarily from my own and published interviews, for in photographs and descriptions only men feature as such petty traders. The 'portrait' of 1938 showing Antje van der Ven (Cottaar et al., 1995, p. 109) with the inevitable basket of fancy goods for sale on her arm is an exception.
42. When men hawked such items, they usually sold them out of a chest which they carried on their back or belly, slung in place with a leather strap. Sometimes they went out selling with a trunk full of merchandise.
43. These figures are consistent with those presented by van der Baan (1986), p. 160, for Helmond (1913–37) and Wernink (1959), p. 116, for all of the Netherlands (late 1950s). For travelling artisans, they respectively report 11 per cent and 16 per cent.
44. Hooijman and Brent (1982), p. 25, cite a letter from 1653 in which the administrators of 's Gravenmoer describe the municipality of Loon op Zand as follows: 'The fiefdom and village of Loon is a very high, dry and salty place, consisting for the most part of extremely infertile, poor and worthless estates.'

Bibliography

Acton, Th., *Gypsy Politics and Social Change*. London and Boston: Routledge & Kegan Paul, 1974.

Adams, Th. McStay, *Bureaucrats and Beggars*. *French Social Policy in the Age of Enlightenment*. New York and Oxford, OUP, 1990.

Agulhon, M. (ed.), *Les marginaux et les autres*. Paris, Imago, 1990.

Aichele, W. and M. Block, *Zigeunermärchen*. Jena: Diederichs, 1926.

Alexander, D., *Retailing in England during the Industrial Revolution*. London, Athlone Press, 1970.

Arnold, H., *Vaganten, Komödianten, Fieranten und Briganten. Untersuchungen zum Vagantenproblem an vagierenden Bevölkerungsgruppen vorwiegend der Pfalz*. Stuttgart: Verlag Georg Thieme, 1958.

Arnold, H., *Die Zigeuner. Herkunft und Leben im deutschen Sprachgebiet*. Olten und Freiburg: Walter-Verlag, 1965.

Arnold, H., *Fahrendes Volk. Randgruppen des Zigeunervolkes*. Neustadt a.d. Weinstrasse, 1980; reprinted in 1983, Landau/Pfalz.

Avé-Lallemant, F.C.B., *Das deutsche Gaunerthum* (four volumes). Leipzig, 1858–62.

Ay, K.L., 'Unehrlichkeit, Vagantentum und Bettelwesen in der vorindustriellen Gesellschaft', in W. Grab (ed.), *Jahrbuch des Instituts für deutsche Geschichte*, Vol. VIII. Tel Aviv, 1979, pp. 13–38.

Baan, P.J. van der, '*Een eigenaardig slag volk.' Onderzoek naar de woonwagenen woonschepenbewoners in Helmond 1919–1937, en hun voorouders*. Utrecht University, MA thesis, 1986.

Bader, K.S., 'Kriminelles Vagantentum im Bodenseegebiet um 1800. Zu einer Jaunerliste des Reichenauer Obervogts Friedrich v. Hundbiss aus dem Jahre 1804', *Schweizerische Zeitschrift für Strafrecht*, Vol. 78 (1962), pp. 291–333.

Baulant, M., 'Groupes mobiles dans une société sédentaire: la société rurale autour de Meaux au XVIIe et XVIIIe siècles', in *Les marginaux et les exclus dans l'Histoire*. Paris: Cahiers Jussieu, 1979, pp. 78–154.

Bäumer, A., *NS-Biologie*. Stuttgart, Hirzel, 1990.

Becker, P., 'Vom "Haltlosen" zur "Bestie". Das polizeiliche Bild des "Verbrechers" im 19. Jahrhundert', in A. Lüdtke (ed.), '*Sicherheit' und 'Wohlfahrt'. Polizei, Gesellschaft und Herrschaft im 19. und 20. Jahrhundert*. Frankfurt am Main, Suhrkamp, 1992, pp. 97–132.

Becker, P.E., 'Die Protagonisten und ihre Wege ins Dritte Reich', in *Sozialdarwinismus, Rassismus, Antisemitismus und Völkerische Gedanke. Wege ins Dritte Reich*, Vol. II. Stuttgart and New York, G. Thieme, 1990, pp. 500–620.

Beier, A.L., 'Vagrants and the social order in Elizabethan England', *Past and Present*, Vol. 64 (August 1974), pp. 3–29.

Beier, A.L., *Masterless Men. The Vagrancy Problem in England 1560–1640*. London, Methuen, 1985.

Benson, J., *The Penny Capitalists. A Study of Nineteenth-Century Working-Class Entrepreneurs*. Dublin, Gill and Macmillan, 1983.

Beynon, E.D., 'The gypsy in a non-gypsy economy', *American Journal of Sociology*, No. 3 (1936), pp. 358–370.

Black, G.F., *A Gypsy Bibliography*. London: Folcroft, 1974 (first edition: Edinburgh, 1914).

Blasius, D., *Bürgerliche Gesellschaft und Kriminalität. Zur Sozialgeschichte Preußens im Vormärz*. Göttingen, Vanhoeck & Ruprecht, 1976.

Blécourt, W. de, 'Typen van toverij', in P. te Boekhorst, P. Burke and W. Frijhoff (eds), *Cultuur en maatschappij in Nederland 1500–1850*. Meppel and Amsterdam: Boom, 1992, pp. 319–63.

Bloch, J., *Les tsiganes*. Paris: Presses Universitaires de France ("Que sais-je?"), 1953.

Block, M., *Zigeuner. Ihr Leben und ihre Seele, dargestellt auf Grund eigener Reisen und Forschungen*. Leipzig: Bibliographisches Institut, 1936.

Blumenbach, J.F., *Decas altera collectionis suae craniorum gentium illustrata*. Gottingae, 1793.

Bog, I., 'Über Arme und Armenfürsorge in Oberdeutschland und in der Eidgenossenschaft im 15. und 16. Jahrhundert', *Zeitschrift für Fränkische Landesforschung*, Vols 34–5 (1975), pp. 983–1002.

Borrow, G., *The Zincali: Or, an Account of the Gypsies of Spain*. London: John Murray, 1841.

Borrow, G., *Lavengro; The Scholar – The Gypsy – The Priest*. London: John Murray, 1851.

Borrow, G., *The Romany Rye*. London: John Murray, 1857.

Bott-Bodenhausen, K. (ed.), *Erinnerungen an 'Zigeuner'. Menschen aus Ostwestfalen-Lippe erzählen von Sinti und Roma*. Düsseldorf, 1988.

Braudel, F., *La Méditerranée et le monde méditerranéen à l'époque de Philippe II*, 2 vols. Paris, Armand Colin, 1976.

Brubaker, R., *Citizenship and Nationhood in France and Germany*. Cambridge, Mass., Harvard UP, 1992.

Bruggemeijer, B.G.P.G., *Bewogen bestaan. Een historische analyse van de fysieke en sociale milieus van de Nederlandse woonwagenbevolking. Schets van een mogelijke benadering van de problematiek van de woonwagenbevolking in de Nederlandse samenleving*. 's-Gravenhage: VUGA-boekerij, 1980.

Burke, P., *Popular Culture in Early Modern Europe*. London, Temple Smith, 1978.

Burleigh, M. and W. Wippermann, *The Racial State. Germany 1933–1945*. Cambridge, Cambridge UP, 1991.

Carson, K. and H. Idzikowska, 'The social production of Scottish policing 1795–1900', in D. Hay and F. Snyder (eds), *Policing and Prosecuting in Britain 1750–1850*. Oxford, Clarendon Press, 1989, pp. 267–97.

Chalmot, J.A. de, *Algemeen Huishoudelyk, Natuur-, Zedekundig en Konstwoordenboek*. Campen/Amsterdam, 1789.

Chandler, D., *The Art of Warfare in the Age of Marlborough*. London, Hippocrene Books, 1976.

Chatelain, A., 'Lutte entre colporteurs et boutiquiers en France pendant la première moitié du XIXe siècle', *Revue d'Histoire Economique et Sociale*, Vol. XLIX (1971), pp. 359–84.

Chaunu, P. (ed.), *Marginalité, déviance, pauvreté en France XIVe–XIXe siècle.* Paris, Annales de Normandie, 1981.

Chevalier, L., *Classes laborieuses et classes dangereuses à Paris, pendant la première moitié du XIX siècle.* Paris, Librairie Général Française, 1978.

Clasen, C.P., 'Armenfürsorge in Augsburg vor dem Dreißigjährigen Kriege', *Zeitschrift des historischen Vereins für Schwaben*, Vol. 78 (1984), pp. 65–115.

Clébert, J.P., *De zigeuners.* Antwerpen-Zeist, 1964 (first edition: Paris, 1961).

Corbey, R., *Wildheid en beschaving.* Baarn, Ambo, 1989.

Cottaar, A., *Kooplui, kermisklanten en andere woonwagenbewoners. Groepsvorming en beleid, 1870–1945.* Amsterdam: Het Spinhuis, 1996.

Cottaar, A. and W. Willems, 'The image of Holland: caravan dwellers and other minorities in Dutch society', *Immigrants and Minorities*, Vol. 11, No. 1 (March 1992), pp. 67–80.

Cottaar, A., L. Lucassen and W. Willems, 'Justice or injustice? A survey of the policy towards Gypsies and caravan dwellers in Western Europe in the 19th and 20th centuries', *Immigrants and Minorities*, Vol. 11, No. 1 (March 1992), pp. 42–66.

Cottaar, A., L. Lucassen and W. Willems, *Mensen van de reis. Woonwagenbewoners en zigeuners in Nederland (1868–1995).* Zwolle: Waanders, 1995.

Cuttriss, F., *Romany Life. Experienced and Observed during Many Years of Friendly Intercourse with the Gypsies.* London, 1915.

Danker, U., *Räuberbanden im alten Reich um 1700. Ein Beitrag zur Geschichte von Herrschaft und Kriminalität in der frühen Neuzeit.* Frankfurt am Main, Suhrkamp, 1988.

Davis, J., 'Urban policing and its objects: comparative themes in England and France in the second half of the nineteenth century', in C. Emsley and B. Weinberger (eds), *Policing Western Europe.* New York, Greenwood, 1991, pp. 1–17.

Demetz, M., *Hausierhandel, Hausindustrie und Kunstgewerbe im Grödenthal. Vom 18. bis zum beginnenden 20. Jahrhundert.* Innsbruck, Wagner, 1987.

Dercksen, A. and L. Verplanke, *Geschiedenis van de onmaatschappelijkheidsbestrijding in Nederland 1868–1995.* Meppel: Boom, 1987.

Derlon, P., *Geheime geneeskunst van zigeuners.* Deventer: Ankh-Hermes, 1981 (first edition: Paris, 1978).

Diefenbach, L., *Die Völkerstämme in der Europäischen Turkei.* Frankfurt am Main: C. Winter, 1877.

Dirks, J., *Geschiedkundige onderzoekingen aangaande het verblijf der heidens of Egyptiërs in de Noordelijke Nederlanden.* Utrecht: C. van der Post, 1850.

Dollé, M.P., *Les tsiganes Manouches.* Sand, 1980.

Egmond, F., *Underworlds. Organized Crime in the Netherlands, 1650–1800.* Cambridge, Polity Press, 1993.

Eiber, L. (ed.), *'Ich wußte, es wird schlimm.' Die Verfolgung der Sinti und Roma in München 1933–1945.* München, Buchendorfer, 1993.

Emsley, C., *The English Police. A Political and Social History.* New York, St. Martin's Press, 1991.

Endres, R., 'Das Armenproblem im Zeitalter des Absolutismus', in *Jahrbuch für fränkische Landesforschung*, Vol. 34–5 (1974–5), pp. 1003–20.

Fertig, G., 'Transatlantic migration from the German-speaking parts of Central Europe, 1600–1800: proportions, structures, and explanations', in N. Canny (ed.), *Europeans on the Move. Studies on European Migration 1500–1800*. Oxford, Clarendon Press, 1994, pp. 192–235.

Fertig, G., 'Eighteenth century transatlantic migration and early German anti-migration ideology', in J. Lucassen and L. Lucassen (eds), *Migrations, Migration History, History: Old Paradigms and New Perspectives*. Bern, Peter Lang, 1997, pp. 271–89.

Ficowski, J., *The Gypsies in Poland. History and Customs*. s.l., 1989.

Finzsch, N., *Obrigkeit und Unterschichten. Zur Geschichte der rheinischen Unterschichten gegen Ende des 18. und zu Beginn des 19. Jahrhunderts*. Stuttgart, Steiner, 1990.

Fontaine, L., *History of Pedlars in Europe*. Durham, Polity Press, 1996.

Forstenzer, Th.R., *French Provincial Police and the Fall of the Second Republic*. Princeton, NJ, Princeton UP, 1981.

Fraser, A., 'A rum lot', in M.T. Salo (ed.), *100 years of Gypsy Studies*. Cheverly, Md., 1990, pp. 1–14.

Fraser, A., *The Gypsies*. Oxford, Blackwell, 1992.

Fricke, Th., *Zwischen Erziehung und Ausgrenzung. Zur Württembergischen Geschichte der Sinti und Roma im 19. Jahrhundert*. Frankfurt am Main, Peter Lang, 1991.

Fricke, Th., *Zigeuner im Zeitalter des Absolutismus. Bilanz einer einseitigen Überlieferung*. Pfaffenweiler, Centaurus, 1996.

Fritschius, A., *Diatribe historico-politica de zygenorum origine, vita ac moribus*. Jenae: Georg II Sengenwalds, 1660.

Ganssmüller, C., *Die Roma im Westungarisch-Burgenländischen Raum zwischen 1850 und 1938*. University of Vienna, MA thesis, 1988.

Gatrell, V.A.C., 'Crime, authority and the policeman-state', in F.M.L. Thompson (ed.), *The Cambridge Social History of Britain 1750–1950*. Cambridge, Cambridge UP, 1990, Vol. 3, pp. 243–310.

Gendt, E. van, 'Woon- of kermiswagens', *Eigen Haard* (23 August 1902), pp. 536–7.

Geremek, B., 'Criminalité, vagabondage, paupérisme: la marginalité à l'aube des temps modernes', *Revue d'histoire moderne et contemporaine*, Vol. XXI (July–September 1974), pp. 337–75.

Geremek, B., *Truands et misérables dans l'Europe moderne (1350–1600)*. Paris, Gallimard, 1980.

Geremek, B., *Les fils de Caïn. L'image des pauvres et des vagabonds dans la littérature européenne du XVe au XVIIe siècle*. Paris, Flammarion, 1991.

Gmelch, S., 'Groups that don't want in: gypsies and other artisan, trader and entertainer minorities', *Annual Review of Anthropology*, Vol. 15 (1986), pp. 307–30.

Gmelch, S. and P. Langan, *Tinkers and Travellers*. Dublin, O'Brien Press, 1975.

Goeje, M.J. de, 'Zigeunerwoorden in het Nederlandsch', in *Album Kern*. Leiden: Brill, 1903.

Goff, J. le, 'Les marginaux dans l'occident médiéval', in *Les marginaux et les exclus dans l'histoire*. Paris: Cahiers Jussieu, 1979, pp. 19–28.

Grant, A.P., 'Issues in the documentation of the European Romani lexicon, with special reference to plagiarism and lexical orphans', concept version, 1995.

Graus, F., 'Randgruppen der städtischen Gesellschaft im Spätmittelalter', *Zeitschrift für historische Forschung*, Vol. 8, No. 4 (1981), pp. 385–437.

Green, N.L., 'The modern Jewish diaspora: Eastern European Jews in New York, London, and Paris', in D. Hoerder and L. Moch (eds), *European Migrants: Global and Local Perspectives*. Boston, Northeastern UP 1996, pp. 263–81.

Grellmann, H.M.G., *Die Zigeuner. Ein historischer Versuch über die Lebensart und Verfassung, Sitten und Schicksale dieses Volks in Europa, nebst ihrem Ursprunge*. Dessau and Leipzig, 1783; second edition, Göttingen: Johann Christian Dieterich, 1787.

Gronemeyer, R., *Zigeuner im Spiegel früher Chroniken und Abhandlungen. Quellen vom 15. bis zum 18. Jahrhundert*. Giessen, Focus, 1987.

Gross, H., *Handbuch für Untersuchungsrichter als System der Kriminalistik*. München, Schweitzer, 1904.

Günther, W., *Die preussische Zigeunerpolitik seit 1871 im Widerspruch zwischen zentraler Planung und lokaler Durchführung*. Hannover, ANS Verlag, 1985.

Gutton, J.P., *La société et les pauvres. L'example de la géneralité de Lyon 1534–1789*. Lyon, Bibliothèque de la Faculté des Lettres de Lyon, 1971.

Gutton, J.P., *L'état et la mendicité dans la première moitié du XVIIIe siècle. Auvergne, Beaujolais, Forez, Lyonnais*. n.p., Centre d'Etudes Foreziennes, 1973.

Halters, J., 'Van wat verdween, deel VIII: Over scharenslijpers en schuurslapers', *Tijding. Kroniek van de heemkundekring het Zuiderkwartier*, Vol. 2 (1992), pp. 33–46.

Hancock, I., 'Gypsy history in Germany and neighboring lands: a chronology leading to the Holocaust and beyond', in D. Crowe and J. Kolsti (eds), *The Gypsies of Eastern Europe*. New York and London, Sharpe, 1991, pp. 11–30.

Haupt, H.G., 'Staatliche Bürokratie und Arbeiterbewegung', in J. Kocka (ed.), *Arbeiter und Bürger im 19. Jahrhundert. Varianten ihres Verhältnisses im europäischen Vergleich*. München, Oldenbourg, 1986, pp. 220–54.

Hehemann, R., *Die Bekämpfung des Zigeunerunwesens im Wilhelminischen Deutschland und in der Weimarer Republik, 1871–1933*. Frankfurt am Main, Haag & Herchen, 1987.

Heymowski, A., *Swedish 'Travellers' and Their Ancestry. A Social Isolate or an Ethnic Minority?* Uppsala: Almqvist & Wiksell, 1969.

Hobsbawm, E., *Bandits*. New York, Weidenfeld & Nicolson, 1969.

Höher, P., *Heimat und Fremde. Wanderhändler des oberen Sauerlandes*. Münster, Coppenrath Verlag, 1985.

Hohmann, J.S., *Zigeuner und Zigeunerwissenschaft*. Marburg and Lahn: Reihe Metro, 1980.

Hohmann, J.S., *Geschichte der Zigeunerverfolgung in Deutschland*. Frankfurt am Main and New York: Campus, 1981.

Höhne, W.K., *Die Vereinbarkeit der deutschen Zigeunergesetze und -verordnungen mit dem Reichsrecht, insbesondere der Reichsverfassung*. Heidelberg, 1929.

Hooijman, S. and A. Brent, *Het stroatje blijft het stroatje. Een onderzoek naar de ontwikkelingen in de beroepenstructuur van 'Het Stroatje'*. Utrecht University, History Department, BA thesis, 1982.

Horsten, F.H., *Historische wegenatlas van Nederland: 16e tot 19e eeuw*. Amsterdam: Universiteit van Amsterdam, 1992.

Hoyland, J., *A Historical Survey of the Customs, Habits & Present State of the Gypsies; designed to develope The Origin of this Singular People, and to promote the Amelioration of their Condition*. York, Wm. Alexander, 1816.

Hufton, O., 'Begging, vagrancy, vagabondage, and the law: an aspect of the problem of poverty in eighteenth century France', *European Studies Review*, Vol. 2, No. 2 (1972), pp. 97–123.

Hufton, O., *The Poor of Eighteenth-Century France 1750–1789*. Oxford, Clarendon Press, 1974.

Jagemann, L., *Criminallexicon*. Erlangen: Enke Verlag, 1854.

Jansen, G.H., *Een roes van vrijheid. Kermis in Nederland*. Meppel and Amsterdam: Boom, 1987.

Jaumain, S., 'Un métier oublié: le colporteur belge au XIXe siècle', *Revue Belge d'histoire contemporaine*, Vol. 16 (1985), pp. 361–408.

Jessen, R., 'Polizei, Wohlfahrt und die Anfänge des modernen Sozialstaats in Preußen während des Kaisserreichs', *Geschichte und Gesellschaft*, Vol. 20, No. 2 (1994), pp. 157–180.

Jessen, R., *Polizei im Industrierevier. Modernisierung und Herrschaftspraxis im Westfälischen Ruhrgebiet 1848–1914*. Göttingen, Vanhoeck & Ruprecht, 1991.

Jeurgens, C., *40 jaar (1946–1986) Landelijk Woonwagenwerk*. Tilburg: Gianotten, 1987.

Jones, D., *Crime, Protest, Community and Police in Nineteenth-Century Britain*. London, Routledge & Kegan Paul, 1982.

Jones, D., 'The Welsh and crime, 1801–1891', in C. Emsley and J. Walvin (eds), *Artisans, Peasants and Proletarians 1760–1860*. London, Croom Helm, 1985, pp. 81–103.

Jütte, R., *Abbild und soziale Wirklichkeit des Bettler- und Gaunertums zu Beginn der Neuzeit. Sozial-, mentalitäts- und sprachgeschichtliche Studien zum Liber Vagatorum (1510)*. Köln, Böhlau, 1988.

Jütte, R., *Poverty and Deviance in Early Modern Europe*. Cambridge, Cambridge UP, 1994.

Kamen, H., *European Society 1500–1700*. London, Hutchinson, 1986.

Kappen, O. van, *Geschiedenis der zigeuners in Nederland*. Assen: Van Gorcum, 1965.

Keller, E., 'Frammersbach und sein Hausierhandel', in W. Stieda (ed.), *Untersuchungen über die Lage des Hausiergewerbes in Deutschland*, Vol. I. Leipzig, 1898, pp. 349–58.

Kenrick, D. and G. Puxon, *The Destiny of Europe's Gypsies*. New York, Chatto, 1972.

Kersbergen, M.M., *Indische probleemgezinnen? Beleid en praktijk in de wooncentra, 1955–1960*. Rotterdam University, History Department, MA thesis, 1995.

Klein, K.H., 'Die Hausierdörfer des Bezirksamtes Frankenthal (Pfalz)', in

W. Stieda (ed.), *Untersuchungen über die Lage des Hausiergewerbes in Deutschland*, Vol. I. Leipzig, 1898, pp. 359–390.

Kogalnitchan, M. von, *Skizze einer Geschichte der Zigeuner*. Stuttgart: J.F. Cast'sche, 1840 (first French edition: Berlin, 1837).

Kuhinka, E.M.G., *Zigeuners, geschiedenis van een zwervend volk*. Rotterdam: Wyt, 1957.

Küther, C., *Räuber und Gauner in Deutschland*. Göttingen: Vanhoeck & Ruprecht, 1976.

Küther, C., *Menschen auf der Strasse*. Göttingen: Vanhoeck & Ruprecht, 1983.

Leeuwen, M. van, 'Logic of charity: poor relief in preindustrial Europe', *Journal of Interdisciplinary History*, Vol. XXIV, No. 4 (Spring 1994), pp. 589–613.

Leigh, L., 'Vagrancy and the criminal law', in T. Cook (ed.), *Vagrancy. Some New Perspectives*. London, Academic Press, 1979, pp. 95–118.

Leland, C.G., *Gypsy Sorcery and Fortunetelling*. New York: Dover, 1971 (first edition: London, 1891).

Leland, C.G., *The English Gipsies and Their Language*. London: Kegan, Paul, Trench, Trübner & Co., 1893 (first edition: 1873).

Lemaire, T., *De Indiaan in ons bewustzijn. De ontmoeting van de Oude met de Nieuwe wereld*. Baarn, Ambo, 1986.

Levy, B., *As Gypsies Wander*. London, 1953.

Liebich, R., *Die Zigeuner in ihrem Wesen und in ihrer Sprache*. Leipzig: F.A. Brockhaus, 1863.

Liégeois, J.P., *Tsiganes*. Paris: La Découverte/Maspero, 1983.

Liégeois, J.P., *Gypsies. An Illustrated History*. London, Al Saqi Books, 1986.

Lis, C. and H. Soly, *Poverty and capitalism in Pre-industrial Europe*. Sussex, 1979.

Lombroso, C., *Der Verbrecher in Anthropologischer, ärtzlicher und juristischer Beziehung*. Hamburg, 1887 (first Italian edition: 1876).

Lombroso, C., *Neue Fortschritte in den Verbrecherstudien*. Leipzig, Friedrich, 1894.

Lombroso, C., *Die Ursachen und Bekämpfung des Verbrechens*. Berlin, Bermühler, 1902.

Lourens, P. and J. Lucassen, *Lipsker op de Groninger tichelwerken: een geschiedenis van de Groningse steenindustrie met bijzondere nadruk op de Lipper trekarbeiders 1700–1900*. Groningen: Wolters-Noordhoff, 1987.

Lucassen, J., *Migrant Labour in Europe between 1600 and 1900. The Drift to the North Sea*. Beckenham, Croom Helm, 1987.

Lucassen, J., 'No golden age without migration? The case of the Dutch Republic in a comparative perspective', in S. Cavaciocchi (ed.), *Le migrazioni in Europa Secc. XIII–XVIII*. Prato, 1994, pp. 775–97.

Lucassen, J. and L. Lucassen, 'Introduction', in J. Lucassen and L. Lucassen (eds) *Migrations, Migration History, History: Old Paradigms and New Perspectives*. Bern, Peter Lang, 1997.

Lucassen, L., *En men noemde hen zigeuners. De geschiedenis van Kaldarasch, Ursari, Lowara en Sinti in Nederland, 1750–1945*. Amsterdam and Den Haag, Stichting Beheer IISG & SDU, 1990.

Lucassen, L., 'The power of definition. Stigmatisation, minoritisation and ethnicity illustrated by the history of gypsies in the Netherlands', *Netherlands' Journal of Social Sciences*, Vol. 27, No. 2 (October 1991), pp. 80–91.

Lucassen, L. 'Under the cloak of begging? Gypsy-occupations in Western-Europe in the 19th and 20th century', *Ethnologia Europaea*. *Journal of European Ethnology*, Vol. 23 (1993a), pp. 75–94.

Lucassen, L., 'A blind spot: migratory and travelling groups in Western European historiography', *International Review of Social History*, Vol. 2 (August 1993b), pp. 209–35.

Lucassen, L., '"Zigeuner" in Deutschland 1870–1945: ein kritischer historiographischer Ansatz', 1999. *Zeitschrift für Sozialgeschichte des 20. und 21. Jahrhunderts*, Vol. 10, No. 1 (1995a), pp. 82–100.

Lucassen, L., 'The domination of the national category. A review of some recent studies on (im)migration and nation-building', *Immigrants and Minorities*, No. 3 (November 1995b), pp. 319–31.

Lucassen, L., *Zigeuner. Die Geschichte eines polizeilichen Ordnungsbegriffes in Deutschland, 1700–1945*. Köln and Weimar: Böhlau-Verlag, 1996.

Lucassen, L., 'Eternal vagrants? State formation, migration and travelling groups in Western-Europe, 1350–1914', in J. Lucassen and L. Lucassen (eds), *Migrations, Migration History, History: Old Paradigms and New Perspectives*. Bern, Peter Lang, 1997, pp. 225–51.

Lucassen, L., '"Harmful tramps". Police professionalisation and gypsies in Germany, 1700–1945', *Crime, History and Societies*, Vol. 1, No. 1 (1997).

Lucassen, L. and W. Willems, 'Wanderers or migrants? The movements of gypsies from Eastern to Western Europe (1860–1940)', in R. Cohen (ed.), *The Cambridge Survey of World Migration*. Cambridge, Cambridge UP, 1995, pp. 136–41.

Lüdtke, A., '*Gemeinwohl', Polizei und 'Festungspraxis'. Staatliche Gewaltsamkeit und innere Verwaltung in Preußen, 1815–1850*. Göttingen, Vanhoeck & Ruprecht, 1982.

Lüdtke, A., *Police and State in Prussia 1815–1850*. Cambridge, Cambridge UP, 1989.

Lüdtke, A., (ed.), *'Sicherheit' und 'Wohlfahrt'. Polizei, Gesellschaft und Herrschaft im 19. und 20. Jahrhundert*. Frankfurt am Main, Suhrkamp, 1992.

Maandstatistiek van de bevolking, Vol. 41 (1993).

Maccol, E. and P. Seeger, *Till Doomsday in the Afternoon. The Folklore of a Family of Scots Travellers, the Stewarts of Blairgowrie*. Manchester, 1986.

Martins-Heuss, K., *Zur mythischen Figur des Zigeuners in der deutschen Zigeunerforschung*. Frankfurt am Main, Haag & Herchen, 1983.

Marx, K., *Das Kapital*. Hamburg, 1872; reprinted Berlin, Dietz, 1987, Marx-Engels Gesamtausgabe.

Mason, P., *The Deconstruction of America*. Utrecht, Routledge, 1990.

Mayall, D., *Gypsy-Travellers in Nineteenth-Century Society*. Cambridge: Cambridge University Press, 1988.

Mayall, D., 'The making of British Gypsy indentities c. 1500–1980', *Immigrants and Minorities*, Vol. 11, No. 1 (March 1992), pp. 21–41.

Miklosich, F., *Über die Mundarten und die Wanderungen der Zigeuner Europa's*. Wien: Kaiserliche Akademie der Wissenschaften, 1872–81.

Miles, R., *Racism*. London, Routledge, 1989.

Miskimin, H.A., *The Economy of Early Renaissance Europe, 1300–1460*. Cambridge, Cambridge UP, 1975.

Moch, L. Page, *Moving Europeans. Migration in Western Europe since 1650*. Bloomington, Ind., Indiana UP, 1992.

Mode, H. and J. Wölffling, *Zigeuner: der Weg eines Volkes in Deutschland*. Leipzig, 1968.

Moore, R.I., *The Formation of a Persecuting Society: Power and Deviance in Western Europe 950–1250*, Oxford, Blackwell, 1987.

Moormann, J.G.M., *De geheimtalen*. Nijmegen, Thieme, 1932.

Mosse, G.L., *Toward the Final Solution. A History of European Racism*. New York, Dent, 1978.

Münster, S., *Cosmographia universalis* (Book VI). Basilaea: Henrichus Petri, 1550.

Nitschke, P., *Verbrechensbekämpfung und Verwaltung. Die Entstehung der Polizei in der Grafschaft Lippe, 1700–1814*. Münster, Waxmann, 1990.

Noakes, J., 'Nazism and eugenics: the background to the Nazi Sterilisation Law of 14 July 1933', in B.J. Bullen et al. (eds), *Ideas into Politics*. London, Croom Helm, 1984, pp. 75–94.

Noiriel, G., *Le creuset français. Histoire de l'immigration XIXe–XXe siècles*. Paris, Editions du Seuil, 1988.

Noiriel, G., *La tyrannie du national. Le droit d'asile en Europe 1793–1993*. Paris, Calmann-Levy, 1991.

Norberg, K., *Rich and Poor in Grenoble 1600–1814*. Berkeley and London, UCLA, 1985.

Oberpenning, H., *Migration und Fernhandel im 'Tödden-System'*. Osnabrück, Rasch, 1996.

Okely, J., *The Traveller-Gypsies*. Cambridge: Cambridge University Press, 1983.

Ooijen, D.A.Th. van, *Je moet weg, hier komen mensen wonen. Woonwagenbeleid in Nederland 1890–1900*. 's-Gravenhage: SDU, 1993.

Overbekking, J., *Woonwagenbeleid, 20 jaar later halverwege. Een evaluatie van het sinds 1975 gevoerde beleid*. Rijswijk: Ministerie van WVC, 1994.

Paspati, A.G., *Etudes sur les Tchinghianés ou Bohémiens de l'Empire Ottoman*. Constantinople: A. Koroméla, 1870.

Penninx, R., *Minderheidsvorming en emancipatie. Balans en kennisverwerving ten aanzien van immigranten en woonwagenbewoners*. Alphen aan den Rijn: Samsom, 1988.

Perrot, M., 'Delinquency and the penitentiary system in nineteenth-century France', in R. Forster and O. Ranum (eds), *Deviants and the Abandoned in French Society*. Baltimore, Md., Johns Hopkins UP, 1978, pp. 213–45.

Perrot, M., *L'impossible prison. Recherches sur le système pénitentiaire au XIXe siècle*. Paris, Éditions du Seuil, 1980.

Petit, J.G. et al., *Histoire des galères, bagnes et prisons XIIIe–XXe siècles*. Toulouse, 1991.

Peyssonnel, C.C. de, *Observations historiques et géographiques sur les peuples barbares, qui ont habité les bords du Danube Pont-Euxine*. Paris: Tillard, 1765.

Poliakov, L., *De arische mythe*. Amsterdam, Arbeiderspers, 1979.

Proctor, R., *Racial Hygiene. Medicine under the Nazis*. Cambridge, Mass., Harvard UP, 1988.

Pross, C. and G. Aly (eds), *Der Wert des Menschen. Medizin in Deutschland 1918-1945*. Berlin, Ed. Hentrich, 1989.

Rao, A. (ed.), *The Other Nomads. Peripatetic Minorities in Cross-Cultural Perspective*. Köln, Böhlau, 1986.

Rao, A. and M.J. Casimir, 'A stereotyped minority. "Zigeuner" in two centuries of German reference literature', *Ethnologia Europaea* Vol. 23 (1993) pp. 111–24.

Redlich, F., *The German Military Enterpriser and His Work Force. A Study in European Economic and Social History*. Wiesbaden, Steiner, 1964–5, 2 vols.

Refish, F. (ed.), *Gypsies, Tinkers and Other Travellers*. London, 1975.

Reif, H., 'Vagierende Unterschichten, Vagabunden und Bandenkriminalität im Ancien Régime', *Beiträge zur Historische Sozialkunde* (1981), pp. 27–37.

Reif, H., (ed.), *Räuber, Volk und Obrigkeit. Studien zur Geschichte der Kriminalität in Deutschland seit dem 18. Jahrhundert*. Frankfurt am Main, Suhrkamp, 1984.

Reinicke, H., *Gaunerwirtschaft. Die erstaunlichen Abenteuer hebräischer Spitzbuben in Deutschland*. Berlin, 1983.

Reininghaus, W. (ed.), *Wanderhandel in Europa*. Dortmund, 1993.

Reinke, H. (ed.), '... *nur für die Sicherheit da...?' Zur Geschichte der Polizei im 19. und 20. Jahrhundert*. Frankfurt am Main, Campus Verlag, 1993.

Reith, R., 'Arbeitsmigration und Gruppenkultur deutscher Handwerksgesellen im 18. und frühen 19. Jahrhundert', *Scripta Mercaturae*, Vol. 23, No. 1–2 (1989), pp. 1–35.

Renner, E. (ed.), *Zigeunerleben. Der Lebensbericht des Sinti-Musikers und Geigenbauers Adolf Boko Winterstein*. Frankfurt am Main, 1988.

Reyniers, A., 'Pérégrinations des Jénis en France au XIXe siècle', *Etudes tsiganes*, No. 2 (1991), pp. 19–25.

Riechert, H., *Im Schatten von Auschwitz. Die nationalsozialistische Sterilisationspolitik gegenüber Sinti und Roma*. Münster and New York, Waxmann, 1995.

Ritter, R., *Ein Menschenschlag*. Leipzig: Georg Thieme, 1937.

Ritter, R., 'Zur Frage der Rassenbiologie und Rassenpsychologie der Zigeuner in Deutschland', *Reichsgesundheitsblatt*, No. 22 (1938), pp. 425–6.

Ritter, R., 'Das Asozialenproblem und die Möglichkeiten seiner Lösung', unpublished article, 1940. Copies in *State Archives Koblenz, ZSG* 142/22 (Sammlung Arnold).

Ritter, R., 'Die Asozialen, ihre Vorfahren und ihre Nachkommen', *Fortschritte der Erbpathologie, Rassenhygiene und ihrer Grenzgebiete*, Vol. V, No. 4 (1941), pp. 137–55.

Ritter, R., 'Erbärtzliche Verbrechensverhütung', *Deutsche medizinische Wochenschrift*, Vol. V, No. 21 (22 May 1942a), pp. 535–9.

Ritter, R., 'Das Kriminalbiologische Institut der Sicherheitspolizei', *Kriminalistik. Monatshefte für die gesamte kriminalistische Wissenschaft und Praxis*, Vol. 16, No. 11 (November 1942b), pp. 117–19.

Ritter, R., 'Die Artung jugendlicher Rechtsbrecher', *Deutsches Jugendrecht. Beiträge für die Praxis und Neugestattung des Jugendrechts*, No. 4 (1944), pp. 33–60.

Roberts, M.J.D., 'Public and private in early nineteenth-century London: the Vagrant Act of 1822 and its enforcement', *Social History*, Vol. 13, No. 3 (October 1988), pp. 273–94.

Rohrbacher, S., 'Räuberbanden, Gaunertum und Bettelwesen', in J. Bohnke-Kollwitz et al. (eds), *Köln und das rheinische Judentum*. Köln, Bachem, 1984, pp. 117–24.

Ruch, M., *Zur Wissenschaftsgeschichte der deutschsprachigen 'Zigeunerforschung' von den Anfängen bis 1900*. University of Freiburg, PhD thesis, 1986.

Rüdiger, J.C.C., *Neuester Zuwachs der teutschen, fremden und allgemeinen Sprachkunde in eigenen Aufsätzen, Bücheranzeigen und Nachrichten*. Leipzig und Halle, 1782–93.

Sachße, C. and F. Tennstedt, *Geschichte der Armenfürsorge in Deutschland vom Spätmittelalter bis zum 2. Weltkrieg*. Stuttgart, Kohlhammer, 1980.

Sachße, C. and F. Tennstedt, *Bettler, Gauner und Proleten. Armut und Armenfürsorge in der deutschen Geschichte. Ein Bild-Lesebuch*. Hamburg, Rowohlt, 1983.

Said, E., *Orientalism*. New York, Routledge & Kegan Paul, 1978.

Salmon, T., *Hedendaagsche historie of tegenwoordige staat van alle volken (deel V, Turksche ryk in Asia en Afrika)*. Amsterdam, Isaak Tirion, 1733.

Salo, M.T., 'Gypsy ethnicity. Implications of native categories and interaction for ethnic classification', *Ethnicity. An interdisciplinary journal of the studies of ethnic relations*, Vol. 6 (1979), pp. 73–96.

Salo, M.T. and S. Salo, 'Gypsy immigration to the United States', in *Papers from the sixth and seventh annual meetings of the Gypsy Lore Society, North American Chapter*. New York, 1986, pp. 85–96.

Samuel, R., 'Comers and goers', in H.J. Dyos and M. Wolff (eds), *The Victorian City. Images and Realities*. London, Routledge & Kegan Paul, 1976, pp. 123–60.

Schrover, M., 'Omlopers in Keulse potten en pottentrienen uit het Westerwald', in M. 't Hart et al. (eds), *Nieuwe Nederlanders. Vestiging van migranten door de eeuwen heen*. Amsterdam, Stichting Beheer IISG 1996, pp. 101–20.

Schubert, E., *Arme Leute. Bettler und Gauner im Franken des 18. Jahrhunderts*. Neustadt a.d. Aisch, Degener, 1983.

Schubert, E., 'Mobilität ohne Chancen: die Ausgrenzung des fahrenden Volkes', in W. Schulze (ed.), *Ständische Gesellschaft und soziale Mobilität*. München, Oldenbourg, 1988, pp. 113–64.

Schubert, E., *Fahrendes Volk im Mittelalter*. Bielefeld, Verlag für Regionalgeschichte, 1995.

Schwartz, R.M., *Policing the Poor in Eighteenth-Century France*. Chapel Hill, NC, University of North Carolina Press, and London, 1988.

Schwicker, J.H., *Die zigeuner in Ungarn und Siebenbürgen*. Wien und Teschen: K. Prochaska, 1883.

Seebach, H., *Altes Handwerk und Gewerbe in der Pfalz. Wandergewerbe. Fahrende Handwerker, Wanderarbeiter und Hausierhändler in der Pfalz*. Annweiler-Queichhambach, 1990.

Serboianu, P.C.J., *Les tsiganes*. Paris: Payot, 1930.

Sexton, R.D., *Travelling People in the United Kingdom*. University of Southampton, 1989.

Siemann, W., 'Polizei in Deutschland im 19. Jahrhundert. Institutionen. Operationsebenen, Wirkungsmöglichkeiten. Mit neuen Dokumenten', in J. Schönert (ed.), *Literatur und Kriminalität. Die gesellschaftliche Erfahrung von Verbrechen und Strafverfolgung als Gegenstand des Erzählens. Deutschland, England und Frankreich 1850–1880*. Tübingen, Niemeyer, 1983, pp. 68–95.

Sijes, B.A., *Vervolging van zigeuners in Nederland 1940–1945*. 's-Gravenhage: Martinus Nijhoff, 1979.

Simson, W., *A History of the Gypsies*. London, Sampson Law & Marston, 1865.

Slack, P.A., 'Vagrants and vagrancy in England 1598–1664', in P. Clark and D. Souden (eds), *Migration and Society in Early Modern England*. London, Hutchinson, 1987, pp. 49–76.

Smart, B.C. and H.T. Crofton, *The Dialect of the English Gypsies*. London: Ascher & Co., 1875.

Snell, K.D.M., *Annals of the Labouring Poor. Social Change and Agrarian England, 1660–1900*. Cambridge, CUP, 1985.

Spencer, E.G., *Police and the Social Order in German Cities. The Düsseldorf District, 1848–1914*. Dekalb, Northeastern Illinois UP, 1992.

Spufford, M., *The Great Reclothing of Rural England. Petty Chapmen and Their Wares in the Seventeenth Century*. London, Hambledon Press, 1984.

Stedman-Jones, G., *Outcast London. A Study in the Relationship between Classes in Victorian Society*. London, 1971, reprinted Harmondsworth, 1984.

Steedman, C., *Policing the Victorian Community. The Formation of English Provincial Police Forces 1856–1880*. London, Routledge & Kegan Paul, 1984.

Stieda, W., (ed.), *Untersuchungen über die Lage des Hausiergewerbes in Deutschland*. Leipzig, 1898.

Stolz, Mme de, *La maison roulante*. Paris: Hachette, 1886.

Storch, R.D., 'Policing rural southern England before the police – opinion and practice, 1830–1856', in D. Hay and F. Snyder (eds), *Policing and Prosecuting in Britain 1750–1850*. Oxford, Clarendon Press, 1989, pp. 212–66.

Strauss, E., *Die Zigeunerverfolgung in Bayern 1885–1926*. Ludwig-Maximilians University, Munich, MA thesis 1986.

Sway, M., *Familiar Strangers. Gypsy Life in America*. Urbana and Chicago, University of Illinois Press, 1988.

Swinburne, H., *Travels through Spain in the Years 1775 and 1776*. London, 1779.

Tawney, R.H., *The Agrarian Problem in the Sixteenth Century*. London, Harper & Row, 1967.

Thomas, K., *Religion and the Decline of Magic. Studies in Popular Belief in Sixteenth and Seventeenth Century England*. Harmondsworth, Penguin, 1984.

Thomasius, J., *Gründliche historische Nachricht von denen Ziegeunern*. Frankfurt and Leipzig, 1748 (first edition: Lipsiae, 1671).

Tiggelen, Ph.J. van, 'Musiciens ambulants et joueurs d'orgue au XIXe siècle. Approche socio-historique du phénomène de la musique de colportage dans la région bruxelloise', *Special issue of the 'The Brussels Museum of Musical Instruments, Bulletin'*, Vols XII–XIII (1982–3).

Tilly, C., *Coercion, Capital, and European States A.D. 990–1990*. Oxford, Blackwell, 1990.

Twiss, R., *Voyage en Portugal et en Espagne fait en 1772 & 1773*. Berne, 1776 (first English edition: London, 1775).

Uhlik, R. and B. Radivic, *Zigeunerlieder*. Leipzig, 1977.

Urbancová, V., *Samuel Augustini ab Hortis: Cigáni v Uhorsku/Zigeuner in Ungarn (1775)*. Bratislava, 1994.

Vaux de Foletier, F. de, *Les tsiganes dans l'ancienne France*. Paris, Connaissance du Monde, 1961.

Vaux de Foletier, F. de, *Mille ans d'histoire des tsiganes*. Paris: Fayard, 1970.

Vaux de Foletier, F. de, *Les bohémiens en France au 19e siècle*. Paris: J.C. Lattès, 1981.

Vaux de Foletier, F. de, *Le monde des tsiganes*. Paris, 1983.

Verheul, M., *Wie woont er nu op het water?!* Utrecht University, MA thesis, 1990.

Verslag der Staatscommissie, ingesteld bij Koninklijk Besluit van 22 september 1903, no. 51. 's-Gravenhage: Algemeene Landsdrukkerij, 1913.

Vossen, R., *Zigeuner*. Frankfurt am Main, Berlin, Wien: Ullstein, 1983.

Vries, B.W. de, *From Pedlars to Textile Barons. The Economic Development of a Jewish Minority Group in the Netherlands*. Amsterdam, KNAW, 1989.

Vries, J. de, *The Economy of Europe in an Age of Crisis, 1600–1750*. Cambridge, 1976.

Vukanovic, T.P., 'Gypsy bear-leaders in the Balkan Peninsula', *Journal of the Gypsy Lore Society*, Vol. 38 (1959), pp. 106–27.

Wagenseil, J.C., *De civitate Noribergensi commentatio*. Altdorf, 1697, pp. 435–50.

Walter, K., 'Herder und Heinze. Aus der Geschichte des weimarischen Gymnasiums', in J. Illberg and B. Gerth (eds), *Neue Jahrbücher für das klassische Altertum, Geschichte und Deutsche Literatur und für Pädagogik*, Vol. 11, Part 22 (1908), pp. 36–59.

Ward-Jackson, C.H. and D.E. Harvey, *The English Gypsy Caravan. Its Origins, Builders, Technology and Conservation*. Newton Abbot: David & Charles, 1978.

Wehler, H.U., *Deutsche Gesellschaftsgeschichte. Vom Feudalismus des Alten Reiches bis zur defensiven Modernisierung der Reformära 1700–1815*. München, Beck, 1987.

Weindling, P., *Health, Race and German Politics between National Unification and Nazism, 1870–1945*. Cambridge, Cambridge UP, 1989.

Weingart, P., J. Kroll and K. Bayertz, *Rasse, Blut und Gene. Geschichte der Eugenik und Rassenhygiene in Deutschland*. Frankfurt am Main, Suhrkamp, 1988.

Weltzel, H., 'The Gypsies of Central Germany', *Journal of the Gypsy Lore Society*, Vol. 17 (1938), pp. 9–23, 30–8, 73–80, 104–10.

Wernink, J.H.A., *Woonwagenbewoners. Sociologisch onderzoek van een marginale groep*. Assen: Van Gorcum, 1959.

Willems, W., *Op zoek naar de ware zigeuner. Zigeuners als studieobject tijdens de Verlichting, de Romantiek en het Nazisme*. Utrecht: Uitgeverij Jan van Arkel, 1995.
Willems, W., *In Search of the True Gypsy. From Enlightenment to Final Solution*. London: Frank Cass, 1997.
Willems, W. and A. Cottaar, *Het beeld van Nederland. Hoe zien Molukkers, Chinezen, woonwagenbewoners en Turken de Nederlanders en zichzelf?* Baarn: AMBO, 1989.
Willems, W. and L. Lucassen, 'A silent war. Foreign gypsies and the Dutch government policy: 1969–1989', *Immigrants and Minorities*, Vol. 11, No. 1 (March 1992), pp. 81–101.
Willems, W. and L. Lucassen, *Ongewenste vreemdelingen. Buitenlandse zigeuners en de Nederlandse overheid: 1969–1989*. Den Haag, SDU, 1990a.
Willems, W. and L. Lucassen, 'The church of knowledge. The gypsy in Dutch encyclopedias and their sources', in M.T. Salo (ed.), *100 years of Gypsy Studies*. Cheverly, Md., 1990b, pp. 31–50.
Winstedt, E.O., 'The gypsie coppersmiths' invasion of 1911–1913', *Journal of the Gypsy Lore Society*, Vol. 6 (1913), pp. 244–303.
Wirsking, B., ' "Gleichsam mit Soldatenstrenge": Neue Polizei in süddeutschen Städten. Zu Polizeiverhalten und Bürgerwidersetzlichkeit im Vormärz', in A. Lüdtke (ed.), *'Sicherheit' und 'Wohlfahrt'. Polizei. Gesellschaft und Herrschaft im 19. und 20. Jahrhundert*. Frankfurt am Main, Suhrkamp, 1992, pp. 65–94.
Wlislocki, H. von, *Vom wandernden Zigeunervolke. Bilder aus dem Leben der siebenbürger Zigeuner*. Hamburg: Act.Gesellschaft, 1890.
Wlislocki, H. von, *Volksglaube und religiöser Brauch der Zigeuner*. Münster: Aschendorff, 1891.
Woolf, Stuart, *The Poor in Western Europe in the Eighteenth and Nineteenth Centuries*. London, Methuen, 1986.
Woolner, A.C., 'The Indian origin of the Gypsies in Europe', *Journal of the Panjab Historical Society*, Vol. 2 (1914), pp. 118–37.
Woud, A. van der, *Het lege land. De ruimtelijke orde van Nederland*. Amsterdam: Meulenhoff Informatief, 1987.
Wright, G., *Between the Guillotine and Liberty. Two Centuries of the Crime Problem in France*. New York and Oxford, 1983.
Yoors, J., *Wij zigeuners*. Brussels and Den Haag: A. Manteau, 1967 (first English edition: New York and London, 1967).
Zimmermann, M., *Verfolgt, vertrieben, vernichtet. Die nationalsozialistische Vernichtungspolitik gegen Sinti und Roma*. Essen, Klartext Verlag, 1989.
Zimmermann, M., *Rassenutopie und Genozid. Die nationalsozialistische 'Lösung der Zigeunerfrage'*. Hamburg, Christians, 1996.
Zucchi, J.E., *The Little Slaves of the Harp. Italian Child Street Musicians in Nineteenth-Century Paris, London and New York*. Montreal, McGill-Queens UP, 1992.

Index

	DATE DUE		
DEC 0 6 2000			